Christianity and the
Postmodern Turn

Six Views

Edited by Myron B. Penner

BrazosPress
Grand Rapids, Michigan

© 2005 by Myron B. Penner

Published by Brazos Press
a division of Baker Publishing Group
P.O. Box 6287, Grand Rapids, MI 49516-6287
www.brazospress.com

Second printing, December 2006

Printed in the United States of America

Library of Congress Cataloging-in-Publication Data
Christianity and the postmodern turn : six views / edited by Myron B. Penner.
        p.   cm.
    Includes bibliographical references.
    ISBN 10:1-58743-108-4 (pbk.)
    ISBN 978-1-58743-108-1 (pbk.)
    1. Postmodernism—Religious aspects—Christianity. I. Penner, Myron B.,
    1968– . Title
    BR115.P74C47 2005
    230′.09′05—dc22   2005000260

To

C. Scott Baker

Contents

Acknowledgments

I am very fortunate to work with such fine colleagues in this book, and I am indebted to each of the contributors for his willingness to participate and see it through to such a good result. It goes without saying that this project would not have been possible without their generosity and charitable spirits. John R. Franke, Kevin J. Vanhoozer, and R. Douglas Geivett, in particular, offered much additional support in terms of advice and encouragement.

I also wish to express my deep appreciation to Stanley J. Grenz, whose friendship and advocacy for this project were vital to its inception and development. Scott Baker, Oz Lorentzen, and James Enns graciously offered additional and invaluable perspectives on parts of the manuscript, and Steven Martz provided friendship and a discriminating ear throughout its development. I also owe a special debt of gratitude to Karyn Ironside for lending her superlative editorial expertise to the preparation of parts of the final manuscript, more than making up for my vast inadequacies in that regard. Finally, my wife, Jodi, is a constant companion indeed, and a true partner. This book would not be possible without the innumerable forms her love and dedication take. Thank you, Jodi.

The bulk of the material in this volume is previously unpublished. However, two chapters in Part I of the book are revised versions of articles previously published in academic journals. The permission and cooperation of those journals is appreciatively acknowledged.

An earlier version of chapter 5 originally appeared in James K. A. Smith, "A Little Story about Metanarratives: Lyotard, Religion, and Postmodernism Revisited," *Faith and Philosophy* 18: 3 (July 2001): 353–68.

Chapter 6 was originally published in Merold Westphal, "Perspectivism, Onto-Theology, and the Gospel," *Perspectives* (April 2000), 6–10.

Contributors

John R. Franke
Associate Professor of Theology, Biblical Theological Seminary

R. Douglas Geivett
Professor of Philosophy, Talbot Department of Philosophy, Biola University

Myron B. Penner
Associate Professor of Philosophy and Theology, Prairie College

James K. A. Smith
Associate Professor of Philosophy and Director of the Seminars in Christian Scholarship, Calvin College

R. Scott Smith
Associate Professor of Ethics, Biola University

Kevin J. Vanhoozer
Research Professor of Systematic Theology, Trinity Evangelical Divinity School

Merold Westphal
Distinguished Professor of Philosophy, Fordham University

Introduction

Christianity and the Postmodern Turn: Some Preliminary Considerations

Myron B. Penner

Instead of asking, what is postmodern?, we should ask, where, how and why does the discourse flourish?, what is at stake in its debates?, who do they address and how?

Steven Connor[1]

Christianity and the Postmodern Turn is inspired by three sets of concerns. First, while the terminology of postmodernity[2] has entered the Christian lexicon and is frequently employed in many quarters, the form it takes in these conversations demonstrates that it is rarely well understood. My suspicion is that the majority of us agree with the indubitable words of Moe, the surly owner and bartender of "Moe's Tavern" in the TV cartoon *The Simpsons,* when he explains to Homer that postmodernism means "weird for the sake of weird." The diversity of images, definitions, and expressions of postmodernism can bewilder the casual observer; in fact, producing confusion may seem the whole point of the postmodern turn in philosophy.[3] Unfortunately, much of what has been written about postmodernism—including the literature of those tagged with the "postmodernist" label—often does little to render it more intelligible, so that "proper" interpretations of the postmodern turn seem not only oxymoronic but impossible to achieve. This book aspires to provide

Christians a clear introduction to the issues of concern precipitated by the postmodern turn in philosophy and, hopefully, to remove some of the confusion surrounding these concerns.

Second, and more importantly, however, this book was initiated by a specific occasion. In the autumn of 2002 I attended the Evangelical Theological Society annual meetings in Toronto and sat in on some sessions that focused on postmodernism and Christianity. It was largely as a result of the exchanges that took place at this conference that I became convinced of the need for a book such as this. Two things became apparent in these meetings. First, the topic of postmodernism is one that can easily divide Christians. Generally we have two polar opposite positions emerging in the Christian intellectual community in response to the postmodern turn—those who are *for* the postmodern turn and see its value in articulating the gospel (these constitute, somewhat ironically, a minority among their peers); and those who are *against* the postmodern turn and view it as a clear and present danger to the integrity of the faith and Christian community (and these make up a much larger group). The first group of Christian scholars, who favor postmodernism, tend to believe that the postmodern naysayers just do not "get it," that they are too blinded by their modern prejudice and categories to engage with postmodernity meaningfully. Meanwhile, the tendency of the Christian critics of postmodernity is to believe that the first group is slipping into heresy by merely mentioning the possible value of the insights of the postmodern turn. Second, I also noticed that the two sides often are like the proverbial ships passing in the night—they do not always seem to refer to one and the same concept by the name *postmodernism*. If a worldview or concept is to be disputed or rejected, it is always good practice to be sure one understands that worldview or concept from the inside—that is, that one understands the concept(s) involved in the same way as one's opponent does—lest one risk refuting what is not at issue. I discovered that what often is rejected as "postmodern" is not at all what those described as postmodern subscribe to. Conversely, not all defenders of modernity recognize as their own what is rejected by those who make the postmodern turn. It occurred to me that it might be helpful to have a forum in which the two sides may speak *with* and *to* each other, rather than talking *past* each other. It is in this spirit that I present this collection of essays.

The third factor motivating this project concerns the scope or forum that discussion of Christianity and postmodernism tends to take. As indicated above, the range of Christian responses is often presented as a dichotomy: either one is for it or one is against it. The actual fact of the matter is more complex than that. Not only is the Christian community beginning to realize that the postmodern turn is varied and complex, but it is also learning that responses to it may be varied. For example, an important question concerns whether the two alternatives described above are really the only options for Christian response to the postmodern turn. Might not there be other options? Perhaps the current debate regarding the postmodern turn is more complex than the categories of a simple binary opposition allow?

With these concerns in mind I assembled a panel of Christian thinkers to respond to the question: "What perils and/or promises does the postmodern turn hold for the tasks of Christian thinkers?" I had two important aims in selecting contributors. First, I wanted the essays to reflect a range of interpretations of and responses to the postmodern turn so that a genuine dialogue could be pursued throughout the book—and beyond it—as to what postmodernism is, what is at stake in its discourse, and how the postmodern turn should be considered by Christians. I therefore sought out Christian scholars who hold perspectives on postmodernism that traverse a spectrum that ranges from a fundamental rejection to a general acceptance. Second, I wanted to elicit responses to this question from both the disciplines of philosophy and theology. Not only does the postmodern turn in philosophy have serious ramifications for the substance and method of theological reflection, but, somewhat ironically, it is in theology that the impact of the postmodern turn initially has been felt the strongest within the Christian community. In any case, reflection on the scope and content of the Christian faith, or the contours of the Christian mind, if you will, lies in the interstices between the disciplines of Christian philosophy and theology. The fortunes of Christian thought rest with neither discipline exclusively. Ever since St. Paul was authorized as an apostle of Jesus Christ in the first century, the Christian church has had its intellectuals and scholars—its theologians and philosophers. Though the tasks of Christian thinkers have been variously conceived over the centuries, the central vocation of the Christian intellectual has been to elucidate and articulate the content of the Christian faith in ways that are intelligible within their particular cultural context. This is not to say that the only, or even primary, goal of Christian thought is apologetic; rather, I wish merely to highlight the historical situatedness of Christian thought. To put it simply, the task of the Christian intellectual and scholar is to make sense of "the old, old story of Jesus and his love" for those in its social, cultural, and linguistic milieu. Thus, the life of reason has always been a central element in Christian reflection, whether philosophical or theological, despite sharp disagreements as to how exactly faith and reason stand in relation to each other. This vision of the Christian intellectual entails that the Christian philosopher and theologian have complementary tasks. Subsequently, a further interest of this book is to facilitate cross-disciplinary conversation between philosophers and theologians.

On (Not) Defining the Postmodern Turn

How does one begin a conversation about a contentious issue such as Christianity and the postmodern turn? The difficulty is compounded in our case because of the controversial nature of postmodernism in Christian intellectual circles. The dilemma facing an introduction of this sort is to broach the issue of the postmodern turn without transgressing its categories; that is, to say what postmodernism *is* so that the question regarding the nature of postmodernism remains a permanent feature of the discourse about postmodernism. The very definition of postmodernism is rightly a contested thing, and the differences between perspectives regarding its nature, let alone its value, are intractable. There is thus a fundamental irony in a discussion with a dialogical aim, such as this, because it must negotiate the tension between a refusal to put an end to the discussion and a mode of discourse that seeks to provide a conclusion. In the end we must live somewhere in between and try to cope with provisional definitions. It is precisely for this reason that I generally prefer to use "the postmodern turn" rather than "postmodernism" to refer to the philosophical situation that materializes in postmodernity. With this in mind, I shall leave it to the subsequent essays to discuss various interpretations of postmodernism in more detail as they present their versions of the postmodern turn. Instead, my objective in this chapter is to orient the reader to the postmodern turn more descriptively, to locate it on a conceptual map, so to speak, and to display some of the central concerns it presents to Christian thought.

Following the lead of certain authors, I want to suggest that the postmodern turn is best understood when one resists the temptation to define it categorically, as either a field of beliefs or a set of philosophical theses—except in a most general way.[4] One may, of course, speak in a very general way of the sort of beliefs postmodern philosophers share, or certain philosophical moves or vantage points that are common to them; but ultimately there are too many deep and intractable differences along philosophical lines for this approach to define the postmodern turn comprehensively. For example, at bottom, Jacques Derrida's deconstructive program is quite different from Richard Rorty's neopragmatism or Gadamer's hermeneutics, and Michel Foucault would find little to agree with in Jean-Luc Marion's talk of God beyond metaphysics, or Emmanuel Levinas's emphasis on the face of the other. To complicate matters further, those who are most often thought to embody the term regularly deny they are postmodernists.[5] There is little hope of unifying the various postmodern expressions under a single slogan.

For this reason Calvin Schrag's suggestion that rather than attempt to identify the postmodern according to its philosophical content, we should understand it "more like an assemblage of attitudes and discursive

practices,"[6] seems to hold some promise. The main idea is that postmodernism is best approached from the standpoint of trying to understand
what each of the postmodernists is trying to accomplish, how each
attempts to achieve this, and why each wishes to do it. Taken this way,
occupying the postmodern vantage point is akin to undergoing a paradigm shift, or a conversion, if you will. The idea is that the postmodern
turn signals a fundamental change in the way the world is perceived
and its problems posed. Postmodernism is not simply the conclusion of
a philosophical debate, nor is it just about a shift in the locus of "first
philosophy." In the end, postmodernism is an *ethos*. It is an intellectual
attitude or frame of mind that shapes the style and substance of thought
and provides one with a starting point for reflection. Postmodernism
is a *Zeitgeist,* or a worldview; it is a total cognitive interpretation and
affects one's general outlook. In some respects postmodernism is more
descriptive of a personal and social reality than a philosophy—although
it quite obviously entails certain philosophical theses.[7] What is of importance, then, in thinking about postmodernism, is to ask why such
conversions take place, and what their value is. One may decide that the
postmodern turn ultimately is disadvantageous and holds little promise
as a worldview, but one will have neglected to address the substance of
its character if its character as an ethos is overlooked. Correspondingly,
when one uncritically embraces the postmodern ethos or attitude, as a
Christian, one foregoes the opportunity to interrogate certain elements
of its worldview that many in the Christian fold find troubling.

  In addition to accounting for the complexity and variety of postmodern positions, understanding the postmodern turn as a discursive
event enables one to avoid one of the most frequent sources of confusion surrounding the term, which stems from conflating the essence
of the postmodern turn with the philosophical positions of those who
have made it. For example, the fact that some of the more recognizable
"founding fathers" of postmodernism are atheists has led many Christian
thinkers to conclude that postmodernism, in its essence, is atheistic as
well.[8] Not only is such a conclusion descriptively false, for there really
are those who claim to do postmodern theology, it begs the more fundamental question of what it means to make the postmodern turn. A
further benefit of focusing on the discursive nature of postmodernity is
that this practice avoids misrepresenting postmodernism as merely an
abstract philosophical position, which may appear inordinately esoteric.
Postmodernism becomes much more intelligible when it is narrated
within a stream of philosophical practices and developments. The discursive practices of postmodernity, in other words, demand an account
of how these practices emerged and what their goals are.[9] In particular,
this approach to postmodernism entails that we situate it historically,
stressing the postmodern turn as a concrete phenomenon.

"Where" Is the Postmodern?

The term *postmodernism* itself suggests that it is indexed by the term *modern*. What is not obvious, though, is the sort of relation the modern has with the postmodern. Basically, there are three options from which to choose when addressing this issue. First, one may place postmodernism conceptually *beyond* modernism, as that which comes after or is on the far side of modernity, as a movement that transcends and moves beyond modernism. Here the mind-set of postmodernity stems from a profound disillusionment with modernity and, as a result, attempts to move beyond the assumptions and goals of modernity. Thomas Oden's remarks offer a case in point:

> The postmodern person has been through the best and the worst that modernity has to offer. The postmodern person is looking for something beyond modernity, some source of meaning and value that transcends the assumptions of modernity. Neck deep in the quicksands of modernity, the postmodern mind is now struggling to set itself free.[10]

From this standpoint the postmodern is an attempt to break with modernity and supersede its categories. This first option, then, treats the postmodern turn as a movement that is largely discontinuous with modernity and shares little with it, except a rejection of its basic assumptions.

The second alternative locates the postmodern turn as a moment *within* the modern, as a kind of hypermodernity, in which the logical ends of modernity's assumptions come home to roost. For example, Richard Middleton and Brian Walsh stress the postmodern celebration of virtual reality as a continuation of modernity's emphasis on self-conscious social construction. Middleton and Walsh contend that "in a fundamental sense, then, the postmodern is a continuance and *intensification* of (one aspect of) the modern. . . . We could say that it is *hyper*modern or *ultra*modern."[11] Perspectives of this kind accentuate the continuity between modernism and postmodernism, and the manner in which modernity paved the way, philosophically and culturally, for the postmodern turn. Here the postmodern is located within the modern, but at its frontier as an extreme form of it. The postmodern turn is interpreted as extending the modern stress on human autonomy, especially with regard to rational explanation, only in an obverse way. Viewed like this, postmodernity is more like a cynical (or perhaps honest) version of modernity. It is modernity come of age.

Our third option is to follow Jean-François Lyotard and place postmodernism conceptually *before* modernism, as an incipient form of modernity. Lyotard informs us that the postmodern is "undoubtedly part of the modern," and that "a work can become modern only if it is first postmodern. Postmodernism thus understood is not modernism at its end but in the nascent state, and this state is constant."[12] This cryptic remark is not easily deciphered, but it will help to bear in mind that for Lyotard the postmodern turn is a condition marked by a set of attitudes, chief of which is a deep-seated suspicion about universal explanations—particularly those of modern science.[13] In the condition of postmodernity we are sensitive to differences, willing to tolerate incommensurability, and engaged in a "war on totality."[14] Lyotard's point could be that the very circumstances celebrated by postmodernity constitute the exact set of problems modernity wishes to solve. In this way, modernity is the attempt to overcome postmodernity. Lyotard therefore places postmodernity logically prior to, and ever-present with, modernity as the source of modern anxiety and its central problematic. Doubtless, Lyotard is confounding the temporal issue purposefully, here, in order to situate himself *within* the postmodern event, so that he may both perpetuate and observe it.[15] Whatever the case may be, it is doubtful that he means that postmodernism predates modernism in the linear sense of modern historiography. In other words, Lyotard's modernist perceives the exigencies of the postmodern condition—i.e., incommensurability, plurality, diversity, etc.—as an eminent threat, which the entire modern program is designed to alleviate.

Regardless which of these three strategies one opts for, the common theme among them is that postmodernity becomes intelligible through its relation to modernity. Subsequently, my attempt to treat the postmodern turn discursively will take the form of a brief sketch of Western philosophy that involves a series of turns, starting with premodernism ("before" modernity), modernism, and postmodernism ("after" modernity). I do not offer the categories of premodern, modern, and postmodern as referring strictly to historical epochs, because, to my mind, it is hopeless to attach dates to them. While it is true that there are general historical eras that correspond approximately to each of these categories, their value lies not so much in their ability to demarcate strict historical periods as in their ability to highlight general philosophical attitudes and trends. They are heuristic tools and perhaps could be viewed like the ladder of Wittgenstein's tractarian propositions, which must be climbed and then thrown away once understood.[16]

"When" Is the Postmodern Turn?

The concept of rationality has played a central role in the history of Western thought. One may even venture so far as to argue that rational explanation is the focal point of reflection for the Western philosophical tradition.[17] Western philosophy,[18] in fact, can be recounted as a narrative of rational inquiry into the scope, limits, sources, and content of human knowledge. The assumption has been that rational explanation is the goal of any inquiry and that cultivation of the life of reason is the goal of a human life. Subsequently, philosophy has placed a premium on the interconnecting values of truth, knowledge, and reality. Likewise, Christianity shares with the Western philosophical tradition the fundamental notion that human being is rational being and that rational prehension of the universe is both possible and important. In keeping with this, one may relate the discursive moves of the postmodern turn against the background of the nature and role of rational explanation in philosophy. In this section I briefly outline the narrative of the postmodern turn against the backdrop of the premodern metaphysical turn, in which the primary goal of philosophical reflection is the theory of reality, and the modern epistemological turn, which focuses on the theory of knowledge.[19] Of course, not only are other versions of this narrative possible, they are *necessary* if we are to describe the contours of the postmodern turn adequately.

Our story begins in ancient Greece—Ionia, to be precise—with Thales and his naturalist friends, who first turned their backs on *mythos* in favor of *logos*. The central concern for these early philosophers was the way in which the world is to be explained. The Greek term *logos* enjoyed a broad range of meanings, including "account," "story," "word," or "speech"; but the Presocratic philosophers capitalized upon the meaning of *logos* that signifies "reason," both in its sense of the human rational capacity and in the sense of "explanation." The history of philosophy—and by all rights the history of Western culture—begins with a profound dissatisfaction with mythological interpretations of the world (*mythos*), in favor of rational explanations (*logos*). What was at issue for the first philosophers was the chaotic, and even capricious, portrait of the universe painted by the Greek myths. It was an enchanted world in which not only were the gods innumerable but they acted whimsically. It would be a mistake, however, to portray the mythological worldview prior to the Presocratic philosophers as entirely irrational or unsystematic in its account of the cosmos.[20] The Greek mythological interpretation of the world accounted for cause and effect, as well as for the nature of reality. What happens in the premodern shift from *mythos* to *logos*, however, is the self-conscious attempt to explain the universe in a lawlike (rational) way.

Premodern philosophy may thus be described as making *the metaphysical turn*. The Presocratic philosophers turn away from mythological explanations of the cosmos, and rational inquiry into the nature of the universe becomes the sine qua non of Western thought. The primary question of premodern philosophy concerns the limits and scope of human rational access to the world as it *really* is. The ancient Greeks spell this out in terms of a *logos*-doctrine, according to which the human mind is structured in a manner sufficiently similar to the world such that the human mind is able to grasp (in its thoughts) reality as it is. For Aristotle, and the philosophical tradition that followed, human being is *rational* being, the "living being with *logos*" (*zōon logos echon*),[21] and what distinguishes humans from the other animals is the exercise of *nous* (mind or understanding).[22] Human beings are rational because they have a faculty that allows them to participate in the rational structure of the universe. The philosophical program of premodernity, therefore, is focused on providing a metaphysical account of the universe through a relatively direct inquiry into the nature of things.

I cannot exhaustively spell out the implications of the metaphysical turn here, but there are several features I wish to highlight. Most importantly for the tale I am telling is the notion that reason (*logos*) is embedded in the structure of the universe. In other words, the premodern concept of rationality is what may be called an ontological conception of rationality. Reason is not a property of human consciousness but of the universe itself. Humans are rational insofar as they participate in the rationality—the *logos*—that inheres in the cosmos. Subsequently, in premodernity reason and reason giving are *teleological,* or purpose-oriented. The universe is created according to an intelligent design, and one rationally explains it according to the reasons with which it is imbued.

This ontological rationality underscores three other significant characteristics of the premodern turn. First, in premodernity rational thought begins with an attitude of wonder, and the basic orientation for philosophical reflection is characterized as an attempt to explain the perplexities of the universe (which cause one to wonder).[23] The significance of this is subtle, but it consists in the fact that philosophical reflection begins with what is apparent to the mind. In other words, the existence of the cosmos is a "given" that constitutes the fodder for rational reflection. The source and ground of a human being's rational thought lies beyond oneself, and one is, in a sense, beholden to someone or something else in one's acts of rationality—a being or thing before which one can only wonder. There is a sense of awe and mystery, and even gratitude, that accompanies premodern philosophical reflection. Second, there is no intrinsic antithesis between faith and reason. In premodernity, the life of faith and the life of reason are entirely consonant. The premoderns' attempt to explain the purposeful universe naturally led them to metaphysical theology, which posited God as a First Cause or Uncaused Cause who is the source of all other causes. Thus, premodern philosophy naturally and peacefully coexists with religion. Third, the life of reason is a communal event. Philosophical reflection takes place within a like-minded community. The ontology of human being—that is, the sort of creature a human is—matters a great deal to the way in which reason is characterized. For the premodern philosopher, a human life achieved its unity in its harmonious relations within a community. A human being, Aristotle observes, is a "political animal,"[24] and the good at which a human aims is achieved in society with other humans. The premodern mind, therefore, has a natural acceptance of civic, religious, and intellectual authorities. Furthermore, the life of reason in premodernity is not one of unfettered self-sufficiency, but is very much bound to the predetermined nature of the universe (of which humans are a part) and grounded in the particular community in which a human being lives.[25] A rational human agent is an embodied creature with a definite place in society and, indeed, the universe. This picture of the nature of rationality remains essentially the same for St. Augustine, St. Anselm, and St. Thomas Aquinas as it is for Plato and Aristotle.[26]

The modern, Enlightenment picture of reason is very different.[27] The modern program shares the Greek assumption that rational explanation, or knowledge [*episteme*], is self-evidently superior to opinion [*doxa*], and it assumes this as its point of departure for rational reflection. However, in modernity the premodern metaphysical turn is radicalized, and the question of *whether* the world can be known occupies the center of philosophical analysis. Modern philosophers take issue with the simple mind/world connection assumed in the premodern *logos*-doctrine, including the ontological dimensions of reason and all it entails.[28] The trouble for modernity concerns the premodern naïveté regarding the process of justifying beliefs, especially beliefs about the nature of the world.[29] Modernism, then, may be said to make *the epistemological turn*. The primary objective of rational explanation in modernity is to establish a set of infallible beliefs that can provide the epistemological foundations for an absolutely certain body of knowledge. It is not that the metaphysical concern has dropped out of view, for metaphysics is very much alive in modernity (as epistemology is in premodernity); it is rather that modern metaphysics is at the mercy of theories about what knowledge is and how it is acquired. That is, modern theories of reality are bounded by the limits that modern theories of knowledge place on the scope and substance of human knowledge. In the end, the shift is quite dramatic. Reason (*logos*) acquires certain metaphysical rights, so to speak, in a way that premoderns did not designate. The ontological assumption of reason is intensified to the point where reason becomes its own ground. The boundaries of what may be rationally thought are determined by the nature of human rational faculties, not the extra-human rational structure of them both.

The stark contrast between the modern and premodern views of human reason stems from the modern detachment of human reason from its premodern ontological moorings and its relocation within human consciousness. The premodern *logos*-doctrine entails that human rationality is an external event that comes to one, as it were, from the outside, as the human mind participates in the discourse of the cosmos. Premodern philosophers think of knowledge as an act by which the human soul encounters the world, so that their task, as Jack Caputo aptly notes, is "not to break out of an internal prison into the external world but to clarify the vague and unclarified contact with the world in which we are all along immersed."[30] Modernity, however, grounds philosophy and philosophical reflection in a rational, self-conscious, and self-possessed human agent. Whether it is René Descartes's self-knowing-self, or Immanuel Kant's transcendental subject who is able to unify the manifold field of empirical experience, modern versions of the paradigmatic rational human being are those who ultimately are detached from empirical reality. The isolation from the *kinesis,* or motion, of the material world is what enables the modern human subject to make universal pronouncements, to be the final arbiter of truth, and to operate as an atemporal epistemological pivot capable of establishing absolute foundations for infallible knowledge.

Without its grounding in a shared structure between mind and cosmos, there is a further shift from the premodern *logos* to a procedural and formal view, in which reason becomes technical and methodological ("scientific" in the modern sense). Modernism is not only the Age of Reason; it is also the Age of Science. Modern science, however, is not the natural science of premodernity, but is *empirical* science—a science that, following Francis Bacon, purports to beg no questions about the theoretical status of its object (the universe) and proceeds in a purely inductive fashion, using only the five senses. A split therefore opens in the modern consciousness between the world, conceived along the metaphor of a machine, and the human person, who is the disembodied, conscious, and free center of rational thought. The embodied *logos* of premodernity is transformed into an abstract *logic* or algorithm in modernity. In the end, the modern concept of rationality is in paradox with the material universe, separated off from it; and it becomes the task of reason to measure, categorize, and intellectually master and control an otherwise irrational and brute universe.[31] Rational explanation, therefore, becomes increasingly formalized in scientific and mathematical terms in an effort to unify what Kant articulated as the three culture-spheres of science, morality, and art under a single body of knowledge.[32]

Finally, in modernity the life of reason becomes a solitary task performed by an individual person. It is up to each human being to be rational for and by himself or herself. Modernism develops "the Enlightenment doctrine of prejudice" formulated by Kant in his "What is Enlightenment?" which, as Hans-Georg Gadamer sums up, was: "Have the courage to make use of your *own* understanding."[33] This emphasis on rational autonomy, of course, becomes possible because of the modern notion of the autonomous rational agent just described. Modern rational autonomy, in turn, places a responsibility on the modern individual to exercise rational autonomy to ferret out all one's false beliefs and establish, for oneself, a body of beliefs that are grounded upon infallible epistemic foundations.[34] Gadamer further describes the essence of the modern ethos as "the prejudice against prejudice itself, which denies tradition its power."[35] Another way of stating Gadamer's insight is to describe the Enlightenment as instituting a tradition that prides itself on not being a tradition. The form of rational inquiry inherited from the premoderns becomes, in modernity, inherently suspect. The rational individual exercises one's rational capacities to think for oneself, and does not accept what is passed down from other sources. Thus, doubt, not wonder, is the fundamentally rational posture, for doubt is the only means for a modern self to guarantee that he or she is not deceived.[36] In modernity, indubitability becomes both the goal and criterion of rational thought, and methodological doubt is the means of substituting genuine proof and observation for the scholastic (i.e., premodern) reliance upon authority and tradition (i.e., the church) as reliable guides to truth.[37] Rational explanation is therefore freed from the shackles of both tradition and religion, as they require implicit faith and trust—each susceptible targets of modern doubt.

Christianity and Some Varieties of the Postmodern Turn

Postmodernism is what happens when modernity is given up, or forgotten, or no longer valued. Postmodernism is the material result of a series of ruptures in the modern philosophical project. The philosophical trajectory I have charted thus far through premodernity to modernity has moved from engaging the world directly (premodern metaphysics) to engaging the self that knows the world (modern epistemology). With the postmodern turn, no longer knowledge or metaphysics but language becomes the focal point of rational explanation. What is now philosophically engaged is the language that constitutes the self that knows itself and the world. Postmoderns call into question both the ontological and technical versions of reason in the premodern and modern eras. That is why we may think of postmoderns as making *the linguistic turn*.[38] In the postmodern turn language, knowledge, and reality become co-implicated, and it is difficult to speak or think of any of these spheres in isolation from the others. But the hyperconsciousness of language (the linguistic turn) in postmodernity, I would argue, does not treat language under modernist categories as forming a new epistemological *grundlage* ("ground-layer" or substratum) for metaphysics to build a new description of the world as it really (truly) is. Instead, the linguistic nature of the postmodern turn signals a shift in the basic framework for theoretical thought, or the starting point for rational reflection, after one has given up on the modern project. And this point of departure for thought begins with a denial of the metaphysically construed rationality of Kant and Descartes. Postmodern perspectives do not claim to describe the way things have to be, nor do they circumscribe the boundaries of what is rationally possible for thought, so much as they are the attempt to think (or theorize, or self-interrogate) after absolute certainty is given up.

So, what are we to make of the postmodern turn, and, in particular, its implications for Christian thought? Does the postmodern turn leave any room for rational explanation? What happens to the philosophical values of truth, knowledge, and reality after the postmodern turn? Is there a concept of reason left after modernity has been jettisoned, or transcended, or staunchly resisted?

For the most part, these issues define the nucleus of the problems addressed in the Part I essays of this book. The goal of the essays in Part I is to outline each contributor's understanding of the postmodern turn and its relation to Christian faith. Our first two essays, both by philosophers, are critical of the postmodern turn and are skeptical about its ability to provide promise for Christian thought. Douglas Geivett's essay addresses some epistemological issues in postmodernity and defends the thesis that a version of fallibilist or moderate foundationalist epistemology is necessary for Christian theology. The focus of his essay is on the postmodern *narrative turn* away from foundationalism, which he finds in the recent theologies of Nancey Murphy, Stanley Grenz and John Franke, and Kevin Vanhoozer. As Geivett explains, the postmodern view refuses to speak in "metanarratives," which purport to capture reality objectively and completely, in favor of "local, micronarratives," which count as only some groups' story of reality and make no claims to universality. His concern is that the narrative turn fails to ground these micro-narratives in an objective and intelligible account of the universe. If adopted by Christian theologians, the narrative turn reduces the Christian doctrine to mere fictional stories and jeopardizes Christian orthodoxy.

In the second Part I essay, ethicist Scott Smith worries that the linguistic nature of the postmodern turn is unable to avoid idolatry. In particular, he argues that the linguistic turn made by Stanley Grenz, John Franke, Stanley Hauerwas, and Brad Kallenberg lacks the conceptual resources to provide a coherent account of the language-world relation. In the end, Scott argues, the linguistic turn of these thinkers presupposes what it explicitly denies—that they have epistemic access to the world as it really is outside of language. The problem, Scott argues, is that they each conceive of the language-world relation as *internal* to a given community's system of reference. On this view, as Scott sees it, communities *construct* reality, which is an unacceptable position for Christian thinkers to hold. If we cannot get outside of our language and linguistic communities, then Christians must be constructing their conception of God too. But this is idolatry, is it not?

Not necessarily. Kevin Vanhoozer is quick to point out the demonic desire for knowledge that is characteristic of modernity. Vanhoozer is not quite a postmodernist, though. He does not exactly renounce the postmodern turn, but he does not entirely accept it either. As a Christian theologian, Vanhoozer prefers to "dispute" with postmodernity. However, he is clear that there is no going back to modernity. Vanhoozer analyzes postmodernism as a version of the "bulverist turn," a metaphor borrowed from C. S. Lewis. Postmodern bulverism makes a philosophical position out of the ad hominem fallacy—it believes that "arguments need not be refuted, only situated." This essay locates postmodernity through a wide range of "postmodern" philosophers, more specifically Heidegger, Derrida, Rorty, Wittgenstein, Nietzsche, Gadamer, Ricoeur, and Marion. Through these eyes, Vanhoozer sees the postmodern turn as a radicalization of modern subjectivity to the point where the human self is emancipated from false consciousness. The trouble is that there is not much left of the human subject on which to ground any normative discourse on truth, goodness, and beauty. Vanhoozer wishes instead to steer a course between modernity and postmodernity by rehabilitating C. S. Lewis's antimodern notions of *mythos* and the imagination as vehicles of reason and truth—ideas he finds antithetical to postmodernism. Vanhoozer's Christian way of going forward from modernism without being postmodern is to situate Christian reason within what he refers to as "the mythopoetic framework of scripture."

The last three Part I essays are, each in their own way, appreciative of the postmodern turn, seeing its value to Christian thought. John Franke comes to our question as another theologian; but rather than disputing with postmodernity, he wishes to engage it. By and large, Franke sees postmodernism as a basic fact and a cultural reality. He finds this situation is not nearly so bleak as modernity proved for Christian theology, and, in fact, believes it presents Christian theology with an opportunity. Franke is interested in the nonfoundationalist turn of postmodern discourse. The heart of this turn, for Franke, is the concept of a "chastened rationality" that has given up on the modern quest for absolute certainty and indubitable foundations for knowledge. The nonfoundationalist turn occasions the genuine possibility for a theology modeled on a dialogical concept of conversation. This theology enjoys the theological advantage of taking the Holy Spirit's revelatory and illuminating role as the source of theological understanding seriously, as the Spirit speaks to Christians in local settings through the interplay of scripture, culture, and tradition. Despite denying modernist claims of universal rationality or infallibility, such a theology is global, Franke argues, in its faithfulness to ecumenical orthodoxy.

Perhaps the first question that comes to mind, especially after reading our first two essays, concerns the putative anti-Christian nature of the postmodern turn. How does one be a Christian *and* a postmodernist? Jamie Smith, another philosopher, returns to the narrative turn in his essay and seeks to correct a common misunderstanding about the post-modernist, namely Lyotard's discussion of metanarratives. Jamie's thesis is that the (mis)perception that the postmodern turn as anti-Christian rests on a misunderstanding of postmodern conception of metanarratives; and that once this misconception is corrected, it becomes possible to see the Christian potential of postmodernism. Metanarratives, as Lyotard means them, are not just megastories that make sense of all reality, as the biblical narrative does. That is just what all narratives do, plain and simple. Instead, the metanarratives postmodernists mistrust are special types of narratives that seek to legitimate their own discourse by claiming universality and a God's-eye-view. Jamie argues that the essence of the postmodern turn is the thesis that "all knowledge is rooted in *some* narrative or myth." What becomes clear in postmodernity, then, are the faith-commitments inherent in *all* knowledge-claims (including, or especially, those of "science"), not just religious ones. Such a brand of postmodernist discourse, instead of closing off faith commitments, provides Christian thinkers with a philosophical context for a truly Christian philosophy that does not have to begin by denying that it is Christian.

What sort of faith would one have, though, in postmodernity? The common perception is that postmodernism is deeply committed to epistemological relativism, where truth becomes whatever one may get away with saying; and subsequently it is very difficult to see how a postmodern faith could have any real teeth to it. Merold Westphal uses his training and expertise as a philosopher to address the issue of relativism in postmodern theory. Quite remarkably, Westphal ends up defending some of the usual postmodern suspects—his "Gang of Six": Nietzsche, Heidegger, Derrida, Foucault, Lyotard, and Rorty—from the charge of relativism. Rather than relativistic nihilism, the seminal point Westphal takes from Nietzsche's perspectivism, Heidegger's hermeneutical circle, Derrida's deconstruction, Foucault's genealogical analysis of knowledge as power, and Rorty's idea that our vocabularies are not dictated by reality but are optional, is that we are not God. The bulk of his essay consists in putting Heidegger's critique of onto-theology and Lyotard's incredulity toward metanarratives in service of Christian theology. The former is often misunderstood as a protest against God, or theology, but Heidegger does not describe it that way. Instead, onto-theology occurs for Heidegger when God is brought into philosophical discourse on *its* terms and in service of *its* project. Heidegger's analysis is not even aimed at God or Christian theology, but at philosophical systems such as Aristotle's and Hegel's. Likewise, Lyotard's suspicion of metanarratives does not have Christianity as its target, nor is it the sort of narrative he criticizes. Westphal turns all this into a flat-out argument for a Christian perspectivism that is relative only in the sense that it is fallibilist and does not claim to ground its own truth-claims, and that its truth-claims are true only from the standpoint from which they are made. This is the sort of faith Westphal finds in St. Paul, who emphasized the relationship between sin and our inability to know truth (Rom. 1:18), the chasm between God's thoughts and ours (Rom. 3:4), and an eschatological transformation of our present knowledge (1 Cor. 13:12–13).

On Refuting Postmodernism

In Part II our contributors delve more deeply into what they believe is at stake for Christians in the postmodern turn. After reading the other Part I essays, each contributor offers a second chapter interacting with the different points of view expressed in the other Part I chapters and extending their own arguments in light of them. These essays are collected in Part II and reflect the sort of disagreement that typifies the wider Christian community regarding the perils and promises of the postmodern turn and reveal some of the substantive issues at stake in the postmodern turn for the Christian community.

As Kevin Vanhoozer remarks in his Part II essay, if the work in this volume is a reflection of the broader Christian community, we still have a long way to go until we are no longer speaking past each other on the issue of the postmodern turn and its value to Christian thought. Key concepts such as foundationalism, perspectivism, antirealism (or constructivism), and cognitive idolatry are employed equivocally throughout the discourse, which contributes to breakdowns in the conversation. For example, Scott takes the constructivism or antirealism of the narrative turn to constitute the claim that linguistic communities literally construct how the world really is, whereas Westphal argues that all that antirealism or constructivism means is that a community's *perception* of reality is constructed. Likewise, Geivett and Scott define foundationalism as a minimalist theory about how beliefs are justified and argue that this concept enjoys wide acceptance among contemporary epistemologists and is rarely, if ever, addressed by "postfoundationalist" rejections of modernity. Franke, however, argues that his "postfoundationalist" theology aims at *classical* foundationalism, which is associated with the Enlightenment visions of infallible foundations for knowledge, not the "soft" or "modest" form of foundationalism popular among contemporary analytic epistemologists. Careful attention to these and many other details is required if the dialogue begun here is to advance any further.

Despite leaving much room for further conversation, the essays collected here also point us toward significant points of agreement and directions for further conversation. It would not be helpful at this juncture to review the substance of the arguments in the Part II essays. The types of disagreements may be predicted quite easily through a careful reading of Part I, and they range from the status of our knowledge of the external world to theological method and the status of theological discourse. The exchanges in Part II are trenchant, passionate, revealing, and at times surprising; but most of all they ably display and reinforce the logic of the contributors' divergent perspectives on the postmodern turn in a way that will resonate with, and be of use to, those in the wider Christian community. At very least, the controversy and dialogue generated by the postmodern turn in this volume will, I trust, lead thoughtful Christians to reflect more substantively on the relationship between one's social, cultural, and linguistic milieu and one's theology (doctrine, theological propositions). Regardless of our orientation coming to the issue of postmodernism, we need carefully to ask and answer the question: How does my language, my culture, and my social environment affect the (Christian) categories I use to understand God, the world, and others? A theology that does not significantly address this question hardly seems fit for the twenty-first century—at the very least it will not deal well with the postmodern turn and those who make it.

As I see it, at the crux of the debate over Christianity and the postmodern turn is the concept of truth, and whether Christianity can be said to be true in any meaningful way after making the postmodern turn. My judgment is that, on one hand, most of the critiques of the postmodern turn fail to understand a dominant feature of the sort of postmodern discourse preferred by some of our contributors, in which a postmodern Christianity purportedly retains a concept of truth. What needs showing, if criticisms are to be successful, is how these Christian appropriations fail to accomplish what Christian theologies are supposed to accomplish (i.e., explain the world Christianly) *according to their own criteria;* or one must painstakingly demonstrate that there is no promise in adopting the postmodernist point of view, and do so in a way that addresses and alleviates whatever is legitimate in the postmodern concerns about modernity.

Too much "refuting" of postmodernism takes the form of pointing out that a certain postmodern thinker or position fails to address a particular set of modernist concerns, or violates modernist categories.

By way of illustration, when Foucault declares, "I am fully aware that I have never written anything other than fictions,"[39] one simply will not understand what Foucault means by interpreting him according to categories alien to his thought. It will be a colossal error to construe Foucault's statement to assert what an epistemic realist would mean if *she* were to say something like that (which of course she never would, for it is so obviously a violation of her most basic categories). All one achieves by this is to identify that Foucault is not a realist about knowledge—a point with which everyone, including Foucault, agrees already. Foucault is perfectly aware that his statement is self-referentially incoherent, and repeating the point does not illuminate the situation.[40] The question to ask is: Why would Foucault make a statement like that, and what does he mean by it? The critic's concern should be to demonstrate that Foucault's program cannot complete itself—that it fails according to its own criteria and that his genealogical program cannot carry out the function he wishes and in the manner he intends.[41] In this way the critic will have been careful to understand Foucault and will have taken his critique of modernity seriously; at the same time the critic will have provided a way to move forward past his objections.

On the other hand, I am concerned that Christians who accept the postmodern turn be careful not to become complicitous with certain forms of the postmodern turn that make a reactionary move toward subjectivity, which empties it of the possibility of asserting anything as true. The dual challenge for Christian thought after the postmodern turn is, first, to avoid allowing a false and un-Christian philosophical paradigm to dictate how Christians believe and think, and, second, to establish a coherent concept of normativity that affords Christians the resources for grounding Christian identity and a legitimate basis for Christian proclamation.

The lesson to be learned from the dialogue on Christianity and the postmodern turn, I believe, is that the way forward for Christians is to proceed with caution—but proceed we must. We are, right now, culturally and philosophically, situated in the throes of postmodernity. What it will be, or what we will be, we do not yet know; but responsible and thoughtful Christians must come to terms with and work *through*[42] the postmodern turn and its implications for faith, not ignore or retreat from it. Above all, Christians must persevere in our faith through hope and love.

Ultimately I offer this book to you, the reader, trusting that whatever your conclusions regarding the postmodern turn and its significance for Christian thought, you will be edified by the essays offered here.

Notes

1. Steven Connor, *Postmodernist Culture: An Introduction to the Theories of the Contemporary* (Oxford: Basil Blackwell, 1989), 10.

2. Throughout this chapter I will not, as some authors have, distinguish between "the postmodern turn," "postmodernism," "the postmodern," or "postmodernity." I use them all to refer to the same philosophical subcategory.

3. This may also be the estimation of the more informed observer. Note Christian philosopher Alvin Plantinga's comment in *Warrant: The Current Debate* (Oxford: Oxford University Press, 1993), 52: "There may also be those who (perhaps like some French philosophers) believe it is their duty to try to spread as much darkness and confusion as possible."

4. Connor, *Postmodernist Culture*, 10; and Ingeborg Hoesterey, "Introduction: Postmodernism as a Discursive Event," in *Zeitgeist in Babel: The Postmodernist Controversy*, ed. Ingeborg Hoesterey, ix ff.

5. In an address to the 2003 fourth bi-annual Villanova colloquium on religion and postmodernism, John D. Caputo, well-known interpreter of Jacques Derrida's deconstructive philosophy and postmodern approaches to religion, remarked on this phenomenon, noting that Derrida regularly refuses the label of "postmodernist." Caputo then humorously remarked that he himself uses the term *postmodernism* only when he wants money.

6. Calvin O. Schrag, *The Resources of Rationality: A Response to the Postmodern Challenge* (Bloomington: Indiana University Press, 1992), 14.

7. Notice my break with certain conceptions of worldviews in which they are characterized as philosophical systems in their own right. While worldviews certainly have implications for such systems and orient us to philosophical questions in definite and important ways, I see them as always operative prior to our formalizing them into such systems; and, as such, the assumptions and beliefs they engender are importantly different from those we hold as the conclusions of a process of philosophical dialectic.

8. For just one example of this approach, Brian D. Ingraffia, in his thoroughly researched *Postmodern Theory and Biblical Theology: Vanquishing God's Shadow* (Cambridge: Cambridge University Press, 1995), argues that postmodern theory is fundamentally contrary to Christian biblical faith because it "not only continues the modern opposition to Christian theology, but also goes on to criticize the secularization of Christian theology in modern ontotheology" (6). Ingraffia's method of defining postmodernism is to identify and analyze the basic tenets of those identified with postmodernity and then impute these to all those who would be postmodern. In particular, he focuses on the postmodern triumvirate of Friedrich Nietzsche, Martin Heidegger, and Jacques Derrida. As none of the postmodern thinkers he studies are Christians, he concludes that postmodern theory is just an extension of modern atheism. Interestingly, Ingraffia makes numerous references to Søren Kierkegaard and (fewer to) Paul Ricoeur, both of whom are self-consciously Christian thinkers and justifiably can be regarded as having made the postmodern turn, but he never considers them as postmodern thinkers in their own right. To be sure, Ingraffia's claim is that postmodernity is antithetical to *biblical* theology, but it seems rather heavy-handed to preclude Kierkegaard and Ricoeur from biblical Christianity.

9. I realize that this way of putting things begs a crucial question to which some postmoderns, especially those with a Nietzschean bent, such as Michel Foucault, will object, on the grounds that it illicitly imports a notion of teleology. My point here is merely to note that at minimum an accounting of our present

position needs to be given, or at least *can* be given, even if such an account does not enjoy universal validity. I take this point to be conceded by the Nietzschean and Foucaultian emphases on genealogy.

10. Thomas C. Oden, *After Modernity . . . What? An Agenda for Theology* (Grand Rapids: Zondervan, 1990), 60.

11. For example, see J. Richard Middleton and Brian J. Walsh, *Truth Is Stranger Than It Used to Be: Biblical Faith in a Postmodern Age* (Downers Grove, IL: InterVarsity Press, 1995), especially 41–42; see also 109, 111, 146, 152, and 153.

12. Jean-François Lyotard, *The Postmodern Condition: A Report on Knowledge*, trans. Geoff Bennington and Brian Massumi (Minneapolis: University of Minnesota, 1984), 79.

13. See Lyotard's oft-cited definition of postmodernism in *The Postmodern Condition*, xxiv: "To simplify in the extreme, I define *postmodernism* as an incredulity toward metanarratives [*grands récits*]." Jamie Smith and Merold Westphal develop Lyotard's definition in much more detail in chapters 4 and 5. I do not wish to preempt their immensely valuable discussions. At this juncture, I merely wish to point out how Lyotard locates the postmodern vis-à-vis the modern.

14. Lyotard, *Postmodern Condition*, xxv, 82.

15. I am grateful to Scott Baker for helping me see this.

16. Ludwig Wittgenstein, *Tractatus Logico-Philosophicus*, trans. D. F. Pears and B. F. McGuinness (New York: Routledge, 1961), 74: "My propositions serve as elucidations in the following way: anyone who understands me eventually recognizes them as nonsensical, when he has used—as steps—to climb up beyond them. (He must, so to speak, throw away the ladder after he has climbed up it.)"

17. Cf. Schrag's comment, in *Resources of Rationality*, 1: "The history of Western philosophy is pretty much a history of the conflicting interpretations on the understanding and use of reason."

18. Throughout the remainder of this chapter I will simply use "philosophy" to refer to "Western philosophy" and "Western thought."

19. I want to be clear that this is my reading of the postmodern turn, and that this interpretation is not necessarily shared by the other contributors.

20. Robin Waterfield, "Introduction," in *The First Philosophers: The Presocratics and Sophists*, trans. Robin Waterfield (Oxford: Oxford University Press, 2000), xx–xxiv.

21. For different accounts of this, see Barry Allen, *Truth in Philosophy* (Cambridge: Harvard University Press, 1993), 19–20; and Schrag, *Resources of Rationality*, 1, 17–18.

22. W. K. C. Guthrie elaborates on this in *The Greek Philosophers: From Thales to Aristotle* (New York: Harper Torchbooks, 1950), 158 ff.

23. See Aristotle's comment in *Metaphysics*, Book I, 982B: "It is through wonder that men now begin and originally began to philosophize; wondering in the first place at obvious perplexities, and then by gradual progression raising questions about the greater matters too." Aristotle, "Metaphysics," in *Greek Philosophy: Thales to Aristotle*, 2nd ed., ed. Reginald E. Allen, trans. Hugh Tredennick (New York: Free Press, 1985), 310.

24. Aristotle, *Politics*, trans. C. D. C. Reeve (Indianapolis: Hackett, 1998), 4 ff. and *passim*. Note that this signals for Aristotle, and premodern thought, that while human being is rational being, it is never simply or reductively rational. Human being is more than just rational being.

25. A premodern community often thinks of itself as the *true* community, and in that way has a sort of claim to universality about it—whether that be a

national, philosophical, or religious community—but premodern communities are exclusionary and emphasize a kind of rivalry between ways of being human embodied in the different cultures and philosophies. In premodernity there are no inklings of the global village, human equality, or a universal human dignity that all people naturally enjoy—the provisions for the alien in the Judaic law, perhaps, notwithstanding.

26. I am, of course, using the premodern to cover an extremely broad range of thinkers, including those from ancient Greece through Hellenistic to medieval philosophy. My contention is not that there is a philosophical unanimity across these periods, rather that they share a basic philosophical orientation in which reason is embedded in the structure of the universe and the goal of philosophical reflection is to draw those reasons out of nature.

27. I will treat *modern* and *Enlightenment* as synonyms, as the Enlightenment is the zenith of modernity.

28. Nonetheless, Jacques Derrida applies his concept of logocentrism to both modern and premodern philosophy to indicate that both assume the possibility of the pure presence of an essence in the mind. This contention is present throughout his literature; but I point the reader to Derrida's seminal *Of Grammatology* (Baltimore: Johns Hopkins University Press, 1974), whose central theme is the logocentric nature of Western thought expressed through a bias against writing in favor of the voice. I am not here disputing this claim of Derrida's—that premodern and modern philosophy each presume a pure mental presence. My point instead is that this presence is imagined differently in modernity compared with premodernity.

29. This is reflected in the major difference between epistemological theories and modern ones. Ancient and medieval epistemologies generally accept what is evident to the senses as constituting a belief that needs no further justification, whereas modern epistemologies do not. Alvin Plantinga makes a similar argument in "Reason and Belief in God," in *Faith and Rationality: Reason and Belief in God,* ed. Alvin Plantinga and Nicholas Wolterstorff (Notre Dame, IN: University of Notre Dame Press, 1983), 44–59, especially 58–59.

30. John D. Caputo, *On Religion* (New York: Routledge, 2001), 45.

31. This shift is masterfully chronicled in Edmund Husserl, "Philosophy and the Crisis of European Man," in *Phenomenology and the Crisis of Philosophy,* trans. Quentin Lauer (New York: Harper Torchbooks, 1965), 149–192, especially 178–191.

32. These are the subject matter of Immanuel Kant's famous three critiques: *Critique of Pure Reason,* trans. Norman Kemp Smith (London: Macmillan, 1950); *Critique of Practical Reason,* trans. Lewis White Beck (Indianapolis: Bobbs-Merrill, 1956); and *Critique of Judgment,* vol. 5, 165–485, trans. James Creed Meredith (Oxford: Clarendon Press, 1952). One may add a fourth culture-sphere, religion, if one counts Kant's *Religion within the Limits Alone,* trans., Theodore M. Greene and Hoyt H. Hudson (New York: Harper Torchbooks, 1960), as a fourth critique.

33. Hans-Georg Gadamer, *Truth and Method,* 2nd rev. ed., trans. and rev. by Joel Weinsheimer and Donald G. Marshall (New York: Continuum, 1999), 271; his italics.

34. The modern sense of epistemic responsibility is nowhere better captured than by William K. Clifford, the nineteenth-century British philosopher and mathematician who, in "The Ethics of Belief" (in *The Rationality of Belief in God,* ed. George I. Mavrodes [Englewood Cliffs, NJ: Prentice-Hall, 1970], 159),

imperiously declared: "To sum up: it is wrong always, everywhere, and for anyone, to believe anything upon insufficient evidence."

35. Gadamer, *Truth and Method*, 270.

36. This aspect of modernity is chronicled in René Descartes, *Meditations on First Philosophy: In Which the Existence of God and the Distinction of the Soul from the Body Are Demonstrated*, 3rd ed., trans. Donald A. Cress (Indianapolis: Hackett, 1993), which is a kind of manifesto for modernist philosophical method. See especially his comment, "But reason now persuades me that I should withhold my assent no less carefully from opinions that are not completely certain and indubitable than I would from those that are patently false. For this reason, it will suffice for the rejection of all of these opinions, if I find in each of them some reason for doubt" (17).

37. To be sure, there is a critical engagement with tradition in premodernity and a constant process of revision and reform, so that the goal of philosophical inquiry was truth or the Good, not just simply a rephrasing of inherited tradition. Such inquiry, however, took place within a stream of inherited wisdom—which may be disagreed with, but only carefully and with respect—and the goal of inquiry (truth or the Good) was realized *within* these intellectual communities.

38. This in no way clarifies the relationship of postmodernism to modernism. It is entirely possible to view the history of analytic philosophy, which is usually understood as a modernist movement, to begin with a new sensitivity to language.

39. Michel Foucault, "Interview with Lucette Finas," in *Michel Foucault: Power, Truth, Strategy*, eds. Meaghan Morris and Paul Patton (Sydney: Feral Publications, 1979), 75. Quoted in Hubert L. Dreyfus and Paul Rabinow, *Michel Foucault: Beyond Structuralism and Hermeneutics*, 2nd ed. (Chicago: University of Chicago Press, 1983), 204.

40. Gadamer, in *Truth and Method*, 344–45, compares the crass charge of self-referential incoherence against a postmodern "skeptic" or "relativist" (perhaps like Foucault) to the kind of "inner hollowness" of the arguments of the Sophists in ancient Greece, and he argues that it poses a bigger problem for the modernist who makes it than for the postmodernist. Gadamer, in effect, asks for whom this is a bigger problem. Why is the self-referential feature of postmodern claims to have the truth a dilemma for the postmodernist, whose thesis entails that such absurdities are unavoidable, and not for the modernist, who demands that our language about truth must be free from formal contradiction? The charge of self-contradiction, Gadamer contends, is damned by its own success when used against a postmodernist. Truth is a concept that operates logically independent from formal justification. Therefore, it makes just as much (logical) sense to see the successful charge of self-reference against the postmodern "relativist" as vacating formal argument of its philosophical cogency and its ability to tell the truth, as to construe it as a blight against the skeptical-relativist thesis.

41. Alasdair MacIntyre performs this kind of critique of Foucault's thought in *Three Rival Versions of Moral Inquiry: Encyclopaedia, Genealogy, and Tradition* (Notre Dame, IN: University of Notre Dame Press, 1990), 32–57, 196–215.

42. I refer the reader to Gary Madison's illuminating deployment of this phrase in his "Introduction," in *Working through Derrida*, ed. Gary B. Madison (Evanston, IL: Northwestern University Press, 1993), 3–4.

Part I

Christianity and the Postmodern Turn

1

Is God a Story?
Postmodernity and the Task of Theology

R. Douglas Geivett

> Is God a story? Can we, each of us examining our faith—I mean
> its pure center, not its consolations, not its habits, not its ritual
> sacraments—can we believe anymore in the heart of our faith that
> God is our story of Him?
>
> E. L. Doctorow[1]

I'm not a theologian. I'm not even the son of a theologian. And yet,
I'm about to advise theologians about how to do theology. What could
explain such bluster?

A direct question deserving a straight answer: there is no uniquely
authoritative theological perspective on how to do theology. Please note:
this is not a concession to perspectivalism; I'm not commending an
anything-goes wave of the hand. It is, rather, a verdict about the limitations of theology. In any sphere of inquiry the highway of methodology
is paved with epistemological commitments.[2] In theology, as in all the
disciplines, method is controlled by assumptions about the aims of
inquiry, the possibility of knowledge, the conditions for its attainment,
and so forth. Sooner or later—and the sooner the better—responsible
theologians must test their dexterity on the tangle of epistemological

alternatives advertising their respective virtues. Working the tangles is something some philosophers do for a living. They are called "epistemologists." My contribution—the advice I offer as an epistemologist—is intended as a service to theology.

At any rate, theologians have a way of keeping philosophers in business. Although philosophy has its own subject matter, it is also a second-order discipline. And in its second-order activity the motto might be: "They propose; we depose." Deposition is a kind of cross-examination conducted in the interests of understanding better what is being proposed and moving from an improved understanding to an intelligent assessment of what is being proposed. Christian philosophers stand ready—all too ready, some must think—to assist in clarifying and evaluating the proposals of theologians within their community.

My own work along these lines has focused primarily on innovations that lately and prominently have been proposed within soteriology and theology proper. And so, for example, I've described the misgivings I have about the spirited promulgation of something called "evangelical Inclusivism" and about the alleged explanatory power of open theism, especially in relation to the problem of evil.[3]

My present concern is with a growing shift in theological method—toward a new way of doing theology that threatens to bring in its train many more substantive innovations in theology and thus promises to keep Christian philosophers in business for the foreseeable future. In particular, I focus on one aspect of the "narrative turn" in postmodern theology: its retreat from the project of epistemic justification in the practice of theology.

The Shift from Accounts to Narratives

To theologize is to engage in a human activity. The result of this activity, a particular theology, is an account of *theos*—of God and God's ways. If you really want to be fashionable, you might call this account a story or a narrative. Caution is needed, though, since the words *story* and *narrative* are now ensconced in theological (and general academic) parlance as terms of art. They are loaded with technical import and used in order to nuance. The nuance of these terms is lost on anyone who lacks exposure to a certain world of discourse—the world of postmodernity.

Consider a fairly traditional way to characterize the relationship between an *account* and a *narrative*. An account may be likened to an explanation, in the sense of "making intelligible" some state of affairs. The force of an account depends on its compliance with criteria for rational belief. An account is compelling if it represents *the world,* or some part of the world, in a way that invites conviction about how things actually are. An account purports to assist us in getting our bearings within the world. We seek an account when we desire to find our place in the world by taking its measure, adopting accurate beliefs about it, and acting in accordance with those beliefs—often on the supposition that our flourishing is at stake.

A narrative, on the other hand, is associated with the idea of story. The power of a particular story or narrative may depend on our capacity to suspend belief (or disbelief). A narrative is compelling if it represents *a world*, or part of a world, in a way that supports imaginative entrance into that world, irrespective of how things actually are. This effect of story may require the suspension of conviction about how things stand within the actual world. We become denizens of a world of make-believe. And making believe is not the same as believing. We *make* believe when we play a role *as if* we believed. Thus, the world of make-believe must at least be believe-*able*.

The craft of a narrative requires imagination. But imagination can contribute to the development of an account as well. With narrative, imagination has more or less free reign. If it's an account one seeks, then imagination subserves the interests of getting an accurate representation of reality. A great work of literature may create a fantastic world of make-believe and at the same time offer a window to the actual world. Generalities that hold in the actual world may be expressed with eye-opening poignancy in the particularities of a world of make-believe. This effect of literature will depend upon an affinity between the world of make-believe that the reader comes to inhabit imaginatively and the real world of which he or she is an actual part. The world of make-believe, then, provides an avenue for insight into the pathways of the actual world. And, of course, a story need not be fictional, even if it is partial.

Characterized in the way just described, accounts and narratives differ in important respects. But these differences do not preclude harmonious coexistence. The single most important thing they have in common is propositional structure. The chief difference between an account and a narrative is that an account beckons the subject to make a doxastic commitment, whereas a narrative invites imaginative participation in a story.[4]

The above description is approximately how I view the relationship between an account and a narrative. While it countenances the concept of story, even when doing theology, it would be a mistake to confuse this with sympathy for postmodernism, whose method makes much of the concept of narrative.

Postmodernity is opposed to my conception of accounts, and of narratives in the service of accounts. On the postmodern view, accounts (or explanatory pictures) are hypernarratives or metanarratives that presume to capture reality in objective and intelligible terms. But for the postmodern, there is no such thing as a metanarrative. There are only local micronarratives that masquerade as metanarratives (or accounts). A micronarrative functions in much the same way as narrative does in the above description, except that now narrative-craft is all there is to inquiry. It does not subserve the aim of providing an intelligible account of reality. This aim is abandoned.

Strictly speaking, a narrative in the postmodern sense makes no claims upon our doxastic lives. While each narrative has a propositional structure, that structure is doxastically idle. It does little more than provide a storyline for the lives of individuals. Indeed, individuals are free to sample a repertoire of narratives to fit the exigencies of their lives in a purely ad hoc manner. There is no doxastic price to be paid for adopting this or that storyline for one's life.

Postmodernity has spread to every discipline within the academy; but it is particularly pervasive within the humanities, where it has been carefully incubated and nurtured. And theologians who feel the greatest affinity for the humanities, especially the field of literature, are among postmodernity's most enthusiastic supporters. Theologians with postmodern sympathies favor a new method in doing theology, one that I believe threatens to subvert the enterprise of theology. For any method governed by the sensibilities of postmodernity will be hostile to the traditional aims of inquiry.

To appreciate this claim, it will be necessary in the next section to reprise the aims of epistemology. There I will also sketch an approach that I believe will be more fruitful for doing theology.

An Excursus on Epistemology

Epistemology—most English-users have never seen this word before, or heard it pronounced. 'Tis a pity. Weighing in at twelve letters and six syllables, its heft suggests that something large is at stake. Offspring of the union of two Greek words—*episteme* (meaning "knowledge") and *logos* (meaning "the study or theory of")—*epistemology* is the name of a major branch of philosophy. Its subject matter lives up to the exalted expectations induced by the daunting word itself. Not for the faint of heart, this field of study is endlessly fascinating. The issues are deep; the puzzles are complex. And yet, the phenomena investigated are among the things with which we are most intimately acquainted. As in so many areas of philosophy, epistemology is an expression of the wonder that results when items in routine experience are singled out for close examination.

In this case, the items singled out are instances of belief. And what could be more mundane than a belief? Beliefs are all around us or, rather, "in" us. It would be an extraordinary (and seriously underdeveloped) person, indeed, who didn't have beliefs, and lots of them. We can readily say what we believe about almost any matter. Our beliefs range from the trivial ("My car is parked in Lot C at John Wayne Airport") to the truly momentous ("God loves me and has a wonderful plan for my life"), and yet they are all entities of the same kind.

Doxastic Attitudes

So what is a belief as such? A belief is a mental state that has as its content some state of affairs that may or may not be actual. The state of affairs that provides the content of a belief is the object that the belief is of or about.

A mental state may be thought of as a kind of attitude. And the content of a belief, being of or about a state of affairs, is some proposition or other. Thus, a belief is sometimes called a "propositional attitude."[5] It is the attitude that this or that proposition is true. This is the attitude of *affirming* the proposition in question. To believe the proposition is to adopt the attitude that the proposition has the *value* of being true: the belief matches that portion or feature of the world that the belief is of or about. This is what makes it good or desirable to believe the proposition: its being true. Its seeming to be true is what makes the proposition worth believing to the believer. Thus, "true" is the *truth-value* of the proposition, from the perspective of the one who believes the proposition. Of course, one may affirm a proposition that is actually false. In that case, one is mistaken about the truth-value of the proposition. It does not have the value that one ascribes to it in the act of believing it.

Beliefs form only one class of propositional attitudes. There are other types of propositional attitudes. Another large class of propositional attitudes is the class of desires that a person has. There is also *the thought that P* (where *P* is some proposition or other). One may have the thought that *P* without having the belief that *P*. When a propositional attitude takes the form of a belief, it is called a doxastic attitude or doxastic state. *Doxastic* comes from the Greek word *doxa*, meaning "belief." A doxastic state is a mental state that is picked out by the presence or absence of belief—by the presence or absence of affirming the proposition that specifies the content of the belief.

Propositions are the sort of things about which a subject can take a doxastic attitude. For any proposition whatever, there is the possibility of believing that proposition or not. Believing just those propositions that are true is good, epistemically speaking. As D. W. Hamlyn has said, "belief is the appropriate state of mind to have toward what is true."[6] To adopt a positive doxastic attitude toward a proposition is to take it that the proposition is true. If one believes the proposition, then one would be prepared to assert the proposition.

Could one adopt a different doxastic attitude than the attitude of affirming? Yes. One could "disbelieve" the proposition in question. What is involved in disbelieving? This gets tricky. Strictly speaking, to disbelieve a proposition is to "not believe" that proposition. "Not believing" is clumsy language. Worse than that, it's not very precise, for there is more than one way to "not believe" a proposition.

First, one may hold that the proposition in question is false. This is the attitude of *denying* the proposition. To deny a proposition is an alternative to believing the proposition. But since it is only one of two important alternatives, it's best not to think of denying a proposition as the *opposite* of believing a proposition. To deny a proposition is to adopt the attitude that the proposition has the negative value of being false: the proposition fails to match that portion or feature of the world that the proposition is of or about. Its being false makes it desirable to deny the proposition. From the perspective of one who denies the proposition, "false" is the truth-value of that proposition. Now, if a proposition is false, then its contradiction is true (and if a proposition is true, then its contradiction is false). So, to deny a proposition is to affirm its contradiction. (For example, to deny the proposition "God exists" is to affirm the proposition "It is not the case that God exists," which is equivalent to "God does not exist.") To put it another way, denying a proposition is equivalent to affirming the negation of that proposition. To deny the proposition that God exists is to affirm the proposition that God does not exist.

The other alternative to believing a proposition is to "not believe" the proposition and at the same "not believe" its contradiction. This, too, is a doxastic attitude, since it is an attitude one might adopt about the truth-value of the proposition. This attitude is called "withholding." In withholding, one neither believes nor denies the proposition. Thus, the resulting doxastic state is peculiar in that it is marked out by the absence of belief that the proposition is true together with the absence of belief that the proposition is false. With respect to the proposition that God exists, to withhold is to be agnostic about the existence of God. But one may be agnostic about a great many things.

There are two additional things to note about withholding. First, this attitude is not to be confused with holding that a particular proposition does not, or may not, *have* a truth-value. A proposition has some truth-value or other, regardless of what one believes. For every proposition, there are exactly two possibilities: either the proposition is true or it is false. There is nothing in between true and false that could be the actual truth-value of a proposition. But between the attitude of believing a proposition and the attitude of denying a proposition there is a third possibility, the possibility of withholding.

The one who withholds acknowledges that the proposition in question is either true or false, but he does not choose between these two possible truth-values. Certainly, he's not forced to choose between them. When it comes to doxastic attitudes regarding any proposition that one considers, however, one has no alternative but to adopt one of these three possible attitudes.

Second, the possibility of adopting this or that doxastic attitude may not arise (for example, if one does not so much as consider a proposition). This too will be a state of nonbelief, but it will not be the result of reflection on the proposition in question. It is best to distinguish this from the more or less explicit attitude of withholding.

So, with respect to any proposition that one considers, there are exactly three doxastic attitudes that one might adopt. One must either affirm, deny, or withhold. To withhold is to adopt the attitude that although the proposition is either true or false, the truth-value of the proposition is in some sense indeterminate from the point of view of the one considering the proposition.

Why Do We Have Beliefs?

Why do we have beliefs, and why do we have the beliefs we do? There is an important difference between these two questions. Part of the answer to the first is that we cannot help having beliefs. If I consider some state-of-affairs X, I may not be able to resist having some belief or other about X. Beliefs happen. In fact, beliefs, like breathing, can happen without our conscious awareness. We may not know what we believe about a matter until we stop to consider. In that case, finding out what we believe is a kind of discovery. Discovery is often accompanied by an element of surprise. Sometimes the discovery of what we believe is accompanied by merely faint surprise. At other times, what we discover may be something of a shock to us, arresting our attention in an unexpected way. This can be disconcerting. (What would it be like for a person who thought he believed that God exists to discover that he really does not believe this after all?)

Of course, not all belief awaits discovery. We can be quite aware of what we believe precisely when we come to believe it. This happens, for example, when we are trying to decide what to believe. But if every belief had to pass through the filter of overt consciousness for individual inspection before it could be firmly instantiated in our system of beliefs, belief formation would be a very inefficient process. We would have precious little time and energy for anything else. So it is, in general, a good thing that we acquire beliefs with the comparative ease of inhaling and exhaling.

On the other hand, it would not be a good thing if we could not on occasion call up our beliefs for special inspection. It is to our great advantage to be able to do this on a case-by-case basis, as needed. A fresh act of terrorism may lead the federal government to impose, perhaps temporarily, new and exacting standards of inspection of passengers at airport terminals. Something like this happens in the realm of belief as well. Some circumstance may lead us to examine our beliefs about something or other, as when we meet well-informed people of good will who have radically different beliefs than our own about matters of great human significance. Also, belief plays an important role in our lives. It is action-guiding and a conditioner of our moods and dispositions. So it isn't as if it doesn't matter to us what we believe.

It's been said that we live in a "post-Christian world," which is to say that we live at a time when Christian belief is no longer socially sanctioned or reinforced in the pervasive ways that it once was. The diffidence of Western society about Christian belief encourages many would-be believers to give careful consideration to the grounds of belief prior to assent. This brings us to the other question.

Why Do We Have the Beliefs We Do?

Part of the answer to the second question is that we can help having at least some of the beliefs we do. While we may not be able to resist having some belief or other about state-of-affairs X, what we believe about X may be this (P_1), or that (P_2), or another thing (P_3). This raises the possibility that while we cannot help having beliefs, we may be able to help having the beliefs that we do, about some things at least. And thus we may be able to do something about what we believe.

Now we stand at the threshold of traditional epistemology's central motivation. The unifying concern of epistemology is the status of propositional knowledge. Propositional knowledge is a belief that enjoys a certain status. The status of a belief may be measured or described in different ways. The *psychological* status of a belief refers to the fact that something is believed and perhaps to the degree to which it is believed. Belief is a mental state without which knowledge would not be possible. Nothing is known if it is not believed. The *alethic* status of a belief refers to its standing in relation to the world. If a belief stands in the right relation to the world, then the belief is true. To count as knowledge, the proposition that is believed must be true. The psychological status of a belief refers to the relation of the proposition and the believer; the alethic status of a belief refers to the relation between the proposition and what the proposition is about (or what it pertains to).[7] Finally, the *epistemic* status of a belief refers to the adequacy of the grounds of the belief.

These three notions figure as components in the concept of propositional knowledge. One has propositional knowledge only if there is something one believes, what one believes is true, and this true belief that one has is adequately grounded. Of these three conditions for knowledge, two refer to properties of a belief. These are the normative conditions that a belief must satisfy if the belief is to count as an instance of knowledge. Knowledge is a belief that enjoys the dual status of being true and being adequately grounded or justified. To be an instance of knowledge, a belief has to be good in both ways. Thus, at the very least, knowledge is adequately grounded true belief.

There is an abundance of clear cases of knowledge that are readily identifiable even before we can say precisely what knowledge is. I know, for example, that there is an orange tree in my backyard and that the brightly colored orbs dangling from its branches are oranges. I know also that this tree was there before we moved into our home. I know that it is the only orange tree in our garden, and that if there was one other orange tree in our garden, the two would have to differ in some way or else there would not be two but one. I know that if the orange tree is taller than the peach tree and the palm tree is taller than the orange tree, then the palm tree is taller than the peach tree. I know that my in-laws, who live in Spokane, have a wonderful garden, but they do not have any orange trees or peach trees or palm trees. On the other hand, they do have evergreens, and pine needles—lots of them—and raspberries. And I know that pine needles taste different than oranges, though I confess that I've never knowingly eaten a pine needle.

These are just a few of the things I know. They include beliefs produced in standard ways: by means of sensory perception, testimony, rational inference, and so forth. In general, I feel confident that any argument that purported to demonstrate that I don't really know such things would rest upon premises that are more dubious than the knowledge claims they challenge.

So far, the examples I've given are mundane cases of knowledge. Naturally, we desire to have adequately grounded true belief about more substantial matters. Does God exist? If God exists, what is God like? What makes a morally right action right and a morally wrong action wrong? How are we to determine what is morally right and what is morally wrong? Is the human soul immortal? Do humans have souls? What is the nature of evil? Why is there evil in the world? Beliefs about such things have a peculiar existential traction for us that beliefs about oranges and orange trees generally do not (although my relatives do tend to marvel at the sight of a real orange tree or a real palm tree when they come to visit). One reason for this is that our beliefs about such things have a larger orienting effect on our conduct in the world. Again, it is difficult to remain indifferent about the status of our beliefs.

Belief Policies

It is a universal feature of the human condition to desire to have true beliefs rather than false beliefs. True belief is important to making our way in the world. If our beliefs are predominantly false, sooner or later we'll run into trouble. For our beliefs to be false is for them to fail to match the way the world is. Mistaking a jalapeño for an orange may have unwelcome consequences. Mistaking a busy interstate highway for a pastoral path in the wilderness can be devastating.

Since beliefs are action-guiding, we want our beliefs to be true so that our action is responsible and effective. For example, if we desire to cross safely to the other side of a busy street, we want to have the true belief that the traffic has died down enough to proceed safely across the street. But having the true belief that it is safe to cross is not enough to guide our action reliably and confidently. We need to have some way to tell whether or not the proposition that it's safe to cross is true or most likely true. We want some *indication* that the proposition is true. The sort of indication we desire is called "evidence." In the absence of adequate evidence that the proposition is true, we will not be able to act with conviction, even if it happens that the proposition is true and we believe it—assuming that we realize that our evidence is inadequate.

The possibility of action leads us to consider what is true about this or that state of affairs. If we desire to cross a busy street, we generally know what to do to determine whether the proposition "It is now safe to cross the street" is true or false. We simply look. Of course, we have to look in the right way, paying attention to the relevant features of objects in our visual field. And we may benefit from having background knowledge of a certain kind. For example, it will help to know approximately how long a car, traveling at the legal speed limit, will take to reach a certain point from such-and-such a distance (roughly estimated). (Actually, to be precise, we would most likely allow that we do not know even the approximate speed of the car, its approximate distance from a specified point, and the approximate time it will take for the car to get from point A to point B. What we actually have is a rough idea that if we step off the curb now and walk at a normal or comfortably brisk pace, there will be plenty of time to reach the other side safely, given how fast it seems the car is moving and how far away it is.)

The bottom line is that if we are to act responsibly in the world we want and need beliefs that are "justified." For a belief to be justified for some particular person is for the truth of the belief to be indicated with a satisfactory degree of probability by the evidence that person has. This evidence may indicate the likelihood that the proposition is true. If so, belief that the proposition is true is epistemically justified. But the evidence that indicates that it's likely that a proposition is true may not be strong enough to guarantee that the proposition is true. In fact, this is often the case. So it is possible to be justified in believing a false proposition.

For this reason, we are fallible about most of the things we believe. The evidence we have is "defeasible." There is a measure of risk in most of our doxastic practices. There may be a great many things that we know without knowing them. And there may be things we think we know that we do not actually know, either because we are mistaken about the adequacy of the evidence we have or because what we think we know is not actually true, regardless of the strength of our evidence.

So what counts as evidence? To be sure, some things I believe are justified in virtue of their relations to other things I believe, but only if these other things are themselves justified. And many of the things I believe seem to be justified in a more direct way. I don't make an inference from other things I believe when I see, and hence believe, that there is an orange tree in my back yard. The mode of direct acquaintance may be either experience or reason, depending on the content of belief. An astonishing variety of objects falls within the purview of direct acquaintance: physical objects, numbers, logical relations, persons, and so forth. This diversity accounts for much of the richness of my system of beliefs. Beliefs that are generated by direct acquaintance with the states they are of or about are characteristically justified.

Come to think of it, unless there are beliefs that are justified in this direct way, there won't be any justified beliefs at all. Beliefs that are not so directly justified will be justified only if they are appropriately related to such directly justified beliefs. So my justified beliefs will be justified through direct acquaintance with what they are of or about, or they will be inferentially grounded in beliefs of this more basic sort.

The point of believing, then, is to adopt the attitude that some proposition or set of propositions is true. And, as Michael Williams says, "where there is genuine belief, justification is always in the offing."[8] For any proposition we might ask: Which of the three possible doxastic attitudes does it make the most sense for me to adopt? What is more likely to be true, given my evidence? My answer to these questions will constitute my belief policy with regard to whatever proposition I consider for doxastic purposes.

Why Epistemology Is Important to Theology

The picture I have just drawn is foundationalist. Beliefs are either justified in the basic way through direct acquaintance, or they are inferentially grounded in beliefs that are formed in the more basic way. Although this picture has a long and prestigious history, it has come under vigorous attack.

Unfortunately, there is a good bit of confusion about the foundationalist picture of justification, especially among theologians well known for their sympathy with postmodernity. Routine caricatures of foundationalism inexplicably associate foundationalism as such with a commitment to absolutely certain foundations. Strictly speaking, foundationally justified beliefs are simply noninferentially justified beliefs. They need not be certain, they need not be self-justifying, and they need not be justificationally isolated from surrounding beliefs within the same noetic structure. A belief is foundationally justified if its justification is not exclusively grounded in its relations to other elements within a belief system, if something other than its relations to other beliefs confers justification upon the belief.

Since justification comes in degrees, a belief may be more or less justified. Justification must reach a particular threshold if a subject is to be justified in holding the belief. And there is a threshold of justification that is minimally necessary for knowledge. The bar of justification is most elevated for that species of knowledge called "certainty." But there are many degrees of positive epistemic standing short of this exalted form of knowledge, some of which are themselves species of knowledge. And, of course, one may have a justified belief that does not meet even the minimal requirements for knowledge.

A typical postmodern response to foundationalist epistemology is to mock the pretensions associated with it. Since we are here concerned with the bearing of epistemology on the practice of theology, my examples of this tendency all come from Christian theologians.

First, Nancey Murphy misrepresents foundationalism when she says that foundational beliefs "are self-supporting—that is, obviously true and therefore not in need of justification of any sort."[9] For Murphy, a foundational belief is a self-supporting belief, and a self-supporting belief is one that is not in need of justification. This is a confusion. Whatever one makes of the concept of a "self-supporting" belief, the foundationalist typically eschews the idea that foundational beliefs have no need of being justified. On the contrary, foundationalism is a theory about how beliefs may be directly justified. And to say that they are directly justified is a far cry from saying they are not justified. Furthermore, foundational beliefs need not be self-justified in order to be directly justified. They must simply be properly related to the objects that provide their content and that are available for direct inspection.[10]

A belief that is justified in the basic way is justified by something or other; it just won't be justified (exclusively) through its relation to other beliefs. Coherentism, the main alternative theory of justification, suffers fatally from the isolation problem. As an account of empirically justified beliefs, the theory implies that what the beliefs are of or about has no bearing whatsoever on their justification. As long as the beliefs themselves cohere with each other, they are justified, regardless of how the world is. Since coherence is only a necessary condition for a system of true beliefs, and not a sufficient condition, it is not clear how justification could be considered a truth-conducive theory of justification. And this is enough to cast doubt on its claim to be a theory of justification. For it is a desideratum of any theory of justification that it capture the truth-conducive character of justification. (It isn't only that we suppose justification to be truth-conducive, but we require that it is in order to have some chance at responsibly believing what's true.)

Two other theologians, Stanley Grenz and John Franke, remark as follows: "At the heart of the foundationalist agenda is the desire to over-come the uncertainty generated by our human liability to error and the inevitable disagreements and controversies that follow. Foundationalists are convinced that the only way to solve this problem is to find some means of grounding the entire edifice of human knowledge on invincible certainty."[11] Alas, this is simply another caricature of foundationalism. The foundationalist is not, as such, committed to "invincible certainty" as a goal or possibility. Grenz and Franke confuse "the quest for a means by which we can justify our claims to knowledge" with "the quest for epistemological certainty."[12] The foundationalist approach I have outlined certainly does reflect an interest in justified claims to knowledge. What would Grenz and Franke offer instead? No claims to knowledge? No *justified* claims to knowledge? How can a Christian theologian fulfill his calling without making knowledge claims and setting forth the grounds for his claims? What are Grenz and Franke up to in their book if they are not making claims and offering reasons in support of them?

In his book *Is There a Meaning in This Text?* Kevin Vanhoozer avows that "the [biblical] text can be a source of evidence and a means of knowledge."[13] But he reckons that "redeeming the text as a source of knowledge and interpretation as a means of knowledge,"[14] within the present postmodern climate, one must acknowledge the failure of foun-dationalist epistemology to provide "absolute evidential foundations."[15] He is unequivocal in his repudiation of foundationalist epistemology, even though the "Reformed epistemology" that he favors can be con-strued as foundationalist. His distrust of foundationalism seems to be tied, again, to the peculiar tendency of so many theologians to associate foundationalism with certainty regarding foundational beliefs. He asserts that "we do not have absolute knowledge, only human knowledge."[16] Apart from the idiosyncratic reference to "human knowledge," which needs further exposition before I can be confident that I understand what Vanhoozer means, one has to wonder why the denial of "absolute knowledge" requires an alternative to foundationalist epistemology.

These are but three examples of unfortunate lapses among theologians who decry the value of foundationalist epistemology.[17] They are all, to one degree or another, lured away from foundationalism by the blandishments of postmodernism. In this I think I detect a needless and risky trade-off.

Christian theism is a system of belief with its own knowledge tradition. Certainly, there is more to being a Christian than accepting the propositions constitutive of Christian theism. In fact, one may fail to believe any number of propositions constitutive of Christian theism and still be a Christian. This is true even if one must affirm at least some of the propositions of Christian theism in order to be a Christian.

At any rate, Christian theism has a propositional structure. From the postmodernist perspective, that may be enough to qualify it as a narrative. But from the perspective of postmodernism, all narratives are local. And so it would be an egregious mistake for any postmodernist to allow that Christian theism is a metanarrative, the correct account of the world or part of the world. It is, at best, a *story* of God and his ways. True, this story has a propositional structure. And yes, this structure might have an orienting effect in the life of anyone who enters imaginatively into "the Christian story." But as with any narrative, it would be possible to enter imaginatively into the narrative of Christianity without actually believing the propositions that are constitutive of that narrative. (Even to believe those propositions is to mistake the mininarrative of Christianity for a metanarrative.)

To my mind, theology's task cannot be reduced to the articulation of a narrative and the mapping of that narrative onto life. It is the business of Christian theology to specify as fully as possible the propositional content of the Christian story, together with the rational basis for responsible belief of that propositional content, and to relate the resulting theological account to the conditions of contemporary human existence so that Christian action in the world will be responsible and effectual. To eliminate the aspect of rational assessment by appropriate standards is to reduce theology to a purely pragmatic enterprise. The new pragmatists in theology have allowed ortho-praxis to supplant ortho-doxy, supposing that behaving Christianly can happen just fine without thinking Christianly. If thinking Christianly includes believing the propositions constitutive of the Christian story, then thinking Christianly must also be concerned with responsible belief. That is, Christians, and especially theologians working on behalf of the church, must seek to exhibit the epistemic standing of belief that is a *sine qua non* of personal engagement in the Christian story.

What the postmodernist offers is not an alternative theory of justification, but a substitute for any theory of justification. For a theory of justification is inherently concerned with specifying the conditions that indicate the likely truth of a belief. For the postmodernist, this is a hopeless task. Inquiry is not about fixing our beliefs in accordance with truth-conducive grounds. Arguably, it's not about fixing belief at all. For there is no concern about what to believe without concern for truth. And there is little point to being concerned about believing what's true if there's nothing one can do to improve one's stock of beliefs or one's chances of acquiring true beliefs. No wonder narrative has replaced explanatory account as the focus of postmodern reflection. The propositional ordering of our lives is inescapable. Narratives at least provide a framework for such ordering. But for the postmodernist, such ordering is doxastically vacuous.

God may figure prominently within the narrative framework of our lives. But faithfulness to our own humanity, to the theological enterprise, and to Christianity itself, requires that we ask: Can we believe that God *is* our story of him . . . and that Jesus is the sort of God God is?[18] Our theologians must have an answer that will bear the full weight of conviction. I know of no better way to do this than in terms of some foundationalist epistemology, appropriately modest about the degree of justification that is purchased, but still hopeful that it will yield reasonable belief in the truth.

Notes

1. From the novel *City of God*, by E. L. Doctorow (New York: Plume, 2000), 14.
2. Some theologians may be willing to purchase autonomy from philosophy by denying that their discipline is a mode of inquiry.
3. See, for example, R. Douglas Geivett, with W. Gary Phillips, "Christian Particularism: An Evidentialist Approach," in *Four Views on Salvation in a Pluralistic World*, ed. Dennis L. Okholm and Timothy R. Phillips (Grand Rapids: Zondervan, 1995); Geivett, "Some Misgivings about Evangelical Inclusivism," in *Who Will Be Saved?* ed. Paul R. House and Gregory A. Thornbury (Wheaton: Crossway Books, 2000); and Geivett, "Divine Providence and the Openness of God: A Response to Hasker," *Philosophia Christi* 4 (2002): 377–96.
4. I clarify the term *doxastic* later in this chapter.
5. Bertrand Russell coined the term *propositional attitude*.
6. D. W. Hamlyn, *The Theory of Knowledge* (London: Macmillan, 1970), 87.
7. There isn't space here to develop the correspondence theory of truth that is suggested here. It is the most long-standing and still most popular conception of truth among contemporary analytic philosophers. Some who deny this

conception do so on the grounds that truth of this sort is not epistemically accessible. But even if this were true, it would not follow that there is no such thing as truth in the sense of correspondence with reality. Others oppose the theory on the grounds that it cannot be made to jibe with conditional propositions for which there appears to be no corresponding facts or way the world is (for example, such counterfactual conditionals as "If I were a gastroenterologist, I wouldn't be teaching epistemology"). But true statements of this sort may only be anomalies for the view, and difficult to account for on any plausible alternative to a correspondence theory. Finally, the correspondence theory is challenged on the grounds that the specific relation of correspondence is at best vague and at worst incoherent. But on this point I doubt that the correspondence theorist is obliged to offer anything more than a fairly natural characterization of the relation.

8. Michael Williams, *Problems of Knowledge: A Critical Introduction to Epistemology* (Oxford: Oxford University Press, 2001), 20.

9. Nancey C. Murphy, *Reasoning and Rhetoric in Religion* (Valley Forge, PA: Trinity, 1994), 200.

10. See the helpful essays by Richard Fumerton and Laurence BonJour in *Resurrecting Old-Fashioned Foundationalism,* ed. Michael R. DePaul (Lanham, MD: Rowman & Littlefield, 2001). DePaul, a philosopher, contradicts a host of theologians when he observes that "foundationalism is alive and well; indeed, at least within Anglo-American analytic philosophy, I think it is safe to say that it remains the dominant position" (ibid., vii).

11. Stanley J. Grenz and John R. Franke, *Beyond Foundationalism: Shaping Theology in a Postmodern Context* (Louisville: Westminster/John Knox, 2001), 30.

12. Ibid., 31.

13. Kevin J. Vanhoozer, *Is There A Meaning in This Text? The Bible, the Reader, and the Morality of Literary Knowledge* (Grand Rapids: Zondervan, 1998), 282.

14. Ibid.

15. Ibid., 301.

16. Ibid., 300.

17. Other voices include William C. Placher, *Unapologetic Theology: A Christian Voice in a Pluralistic Conversation* (Louisville: Westminster/John Knox, 1989); Richard Lints, *The Fabric of Theology: A Prolegomenon to Evangelical Theology* (Grand Rapids: Eerdmans, 1993); John E. Thiel, *NonFoundationalism* (Minneapolis, MN: Fortress, 1994); and Eric O. Springstead, *The Act of Faith: Christian Faith and the Moral Self* (Grand Rapids: Eerdmans, 2002).

18. Whether we can believe that God is our story of him is E. L. Doctorow's question quoted in the epigraph to this chapter; see note 1 above. Ironically enough, Doctorow is often identified as a paradigmatic postmodern fictionalist. For the wonderful expression "Jesus is the sort of God God is," see James W. Sire, *Discipleship of the Mind* (Downers Grove, IL: InterVarsity Press, 1990), 18.

2

Christian Postmodernism and the Linguistic Turn

R. Scott Smith

While postmodernism is a multifaceted family of views, there are many aspects that bear a strong resemblance. For instance, many who are influenced by postmodern thought would stress the importance of local communities, as opposed to the autonomous individual, which was characteristic of the Enlightenment. Furthermore, they would tend to focus on the particularity of these communities' ways of living, their languages, and their truth claims, while they would have, as Lyotard says, incredulity toward metanarratives, as well as distrust toward the modern concept of universal human reason and related claims to know objective truth.

What is it that is driving these ideas? For those who give reasons why people ought to conceive the "world" along such lines, there is a core presupposition that something stands between us and a real "world," such that we cannot know it in itself as it "really" is. While this ought to remind us of Kant's view that we cannot know things in themselves (the noumena), but only as they appear to us (the phenomena), on a postmodern understanding we are not behind our experiences. Instead, it is language that stands between us and a "real" world. Since we cannot know language-in-itself, we may know only the various discrete languages. And since we cannot know a supposedly objective world as it would be apart from language, we *make* our own worlds by how we use our language. So language and world are internally related.

This emphasis upon language is characteristic of what has become known as the "linguistic turn" in philosophy. In this chapter, I will focus on this particular trait of postmodernism and the view that language and world are internally related. I will look at how four particular Christians make use of this idea, in order that we may see the broader lessons we may learn from this kind of approach. The four examples I have chosen are the theologians Stanley Grenz and John Franke; the theological ethicist Stanley Hauerwas; and a new defender of Hauerwas, the philosophical theologian Brad J. Kallenberg. We will see a strong constructive element in each author's thought, such that language use makes the world for the Christian community. Furthermore, they argue that this is how Christians ought to understand their faith. Even so, I will argue that they presuppose what they deny—an epistemic access to an extralinguistic, unconstructed world in order to get their own views off the ground. We may learn at least two important lessons from their particular views, and, by extension, we may apply those to others who also hold to the internal relation of language and world. First, their efforts to reconceive the Christian faith along linguistic lines will fail to meet their own criteria. They too will presuppose a way outside of language in order to deny such access. While that result is devastating to their views, a second result is even more important: their linguistic approach will undermine at least one essential doctrine of the faith.

The Internal Relation of Language and the World

Let us begin with Kallenberg, since he is quite clear and explicit in his writing. According to him, the later Wittgenstein repudiates the craving in philosophy for theoretical explanations, which he saw mainly in metaphysics. For Kallenberg, theorizing bifurcates language and world, since it depends upon an explanation of the world that is expressed in language and supposedly is different than that world. But this is a mistake, for as he puts it, "since all explanations are framed in language, we have no extra-linguistic means for explaining, validating, or justifying the way we use language."[1]

The bifurcation of language and world causes the philosophical confusion that Kallenberg's Wittgenstein seeks to clear up. Theorizing is a disease from which we need to be cured. It is the attempt to satisfy philosophical cravings for achieving general claims of how things really are, and so we invent essences. Wittgenstein expresses this idea in regard to language:

Here we come up against the great question that lies behind all these considerations.—For someone might object against me: "You take the easy way out! You talk about all sorts of language-games, but nowhere have said what the essence of a language-game, and hence of language, is: what is common to all these activities, and what makes them into language or parts of language . . ." And this is true.—Instead of producing something common to all that we call language, I am saying that these phenomena have no one thing in common which makes us use the same word for all,—but that they are related to one another in many different ways. And it is because of this relationship, or relationships, that we call them all "language."[2]

On Kallenberg's use of Wittgenstein, metaphysical theories cause confusion by offering a "totalizing," theoretical explanation. Instead, he proposes a method that replaces explanation with description.[3] This metaphysical theorizing deceives us into thinking we can know things as they really are. Consider how Wittgenstein discusses scientific claims about a gaseous medium:

There must not be anything hypothetical in our considerations. We must do away with all *explanation,* and description alone must take its place. And this description gets its light, that is to say its purpose, from the philosophical problems. These are, of course, not empirical problems; they are solved, rather, by looking into the workings of our language, and that in such a way as to make us recognize those workings: *in despite of* an urge to misunderstand them. The problems are solved, not by giving new information, but by arranging what we have always known. Philosophy is a battle against the bewitchment of our intelligence by means of language.[4]

We need to be cured from this disease of endless speculations that ceaselessly search for essences, according to Kallenberg's use of Wittgenstein. But how does this take place? It does not take place by not finding some theoretically independent standpoint from which we can discover objective, language-independent truths. Instead, we are cured when we realize that the problem is found in how we use language. This craving for such truths manifests itself in the attempt to find foundations for knowledge, but that also ignores the particularity of knowing subjects, who always know things from a certain standpoint. But once we realize that the never-ending "solutions" posed by the various kinds of metaphysical theories are actually problems created by how they are framed in language, then the solution is to shift our attention to how language actually is used.

Furthermore, Kallenberg's Wittgenstein also rejects representational-ism, which according to him is the view that somehow language can match up with, or correspond to, reality. But, for Kallenberg, this view is problematic since

> [t]here is no way to talk about what language gets compared with without *talking* about it; there is no criterion for knowing I've got the right "this" (this effect, this referent, this object, this sensa-tion, this word) unless language is already in place. Therefore, the "meaning" of a word can only be determined by its place in the linguistic system.[5]

Without such an ability to transcend language and match up words with their objects, the correspondence theory seems to become useless. For Kallenberg's Wittgenstein, meaning takes place *within* a language-game, and "it gives the wrong idea if you say that the connection between name and object is a psychological one."[6] As Wittgenstein puts it, "the con-nection between 'language and reality' is made by definition of words, and these belong to grammar, so that language remains self-contained and autonomous."[7]

If we cannot get outside language, and know an extralinguistic world as it really is, then our only contact with that world is by our language use. Hence, "it is in language that it is all done."[8] On Kallenberg's inter-pretation of Wittgenstein, we cannot know reality apart from language, including any "essence" of language. Attempts to find such an essence would be to return to the same diseased kind of metaphysics that craves after generalizations. Instead, we need to see that a language is *internally* related to a world. Kallenberg puts it quite clearly: "language does not represent reality, it *constitutes* reality."[9] There are only many languages, and thus there are as many worlds as there are languages.

Hauerwas's views also closely resemble this understanding of the later Wittgenstein. Like Kallenberg's Wittgenstein, Hauerwas wants to perform therapy upon his readers, but his emphasis is upon an ethical, as opposed to a conceptual, kind. He wants to perform ethical therapy by changing his readers' characters, and not by developing theory.[10] He tries to effect this character change by cultivating practical, moral skill in their lives, but this transformation is tied to a way of life, which for him is the Christian community.

According to Hauerwas, the Christian life mainly is one of vision and not just decision making. A moral vision enables Christians to perceive accurately moral truths, values, ourselves, along with the nature of the world and the meaningfulness of words and actions. Stories are neces-sary for having a moral vision, and they are ways of knowing that enable us to make connections between what we know about ourselves and the unknown of the world.[11] But more significantly, one must know a language to have a moral vision:

> The moral life is . . . not just the life of decision but the life of vision—that is, it involves how we see the world. Such "seeing" does not come from just perceiving "facts," but rather we must learn how the world is to be properly "seen" or better known. Such learning takes place by learning the language that intends the world and our behavior as it ought to be that the good might be achieved.[12]

We cannot just perceive "facts," for, as Hauerwas explains, "we never simply know facts, but that we know them for some reason."[13] On his view, facts are not somehow independent of our descriptions. Thus, facts are not brute givens that we simply can read off the world as they are apart from language use. Yes, some features (e.g., of tables) may exist in the world; but how we organize and group them by our language use makes them what they are.

The moral realm works in a similar fashion. Certain actions are moral ones due to how the community has established its grammatical rules. That is, we use our terms to group and organize actions as moral ones. But not just any usage counts; meaningful term usage requires the following of a language's rules. Consider Hauerwas's account of an act of lying:

> But to say that lying is an object of reason is to say that in our ability to use moral notions we have the ability to establish reasons why similar sets of factors should be understood as lying. To accept such reasons is the same thing as forming certain rules for the proper use of such notions. Therefore our moral notions are possible in so far as we are rule-following rational beings.[14]

Following rules is necessary for the possibility of forming and using moral concepts in discourse. Proper term usage is integrally related to developing a moral vision because "we do not come to know the world by perceiving it, but we come to know the world as we learn to use our language."[15] Having a moral vision requires being formed by a language, so that we can see the world rightly, and thereby act rightly.[16]

Now, these language users are members of a way of life and its particular language. Hauerwas repudiates the idea that as individuals we can create our own descriptions for actions, or intentions, as would be the case if a private language were possible. Quite to the contrary, Hauerwas maintains that the uses of descriptive and evaluative terms require that we "follow interpersonal rules in a public language."[17] Accordingly, "the beliefs and convictions we use to form and explain our behavior are not of our own making. To be a moral self is to be an inheritor of a language of a people."[18]

Apparently, a person must be in a way of life and be formed by its language to even exist as a moral self. He also claims that "the self that gives rise to agency is fundamentally a social self, not separable from its social and cultural environment . . . we are selves only because another self was first present to us."[19] Furthermore, Hauerwas informs us that "action and agency by their very nature are socially dependent."[20] But the meaningfulness of these and other terms is not intelligible apart from a way of life and its related language, which, in the case of the Christian community, is the gospel.

Now, members may perform moral actions verbally or nonverbally, depending on the grammar of the community, and so moral actions have a public and social dimension. The meaningfulness of an action requires that it "fall under some description which is socially recognizable as the description of an action."[21] But qua individuals, members may not use just any description for their actions; on the contrary, "the descriptions are public property because our language is public property."[22] So Hauerwas clearly wants to eliminate any place for a private language user.

How, therefore, do we know reality? In keeping with his views of the internal relation of language and world, Hauerwas does not believe we can know reality from some extralinguistic standpoint. But that does not mean we cannot know reality at all; instead, knowing "reality truthfully requires the ability to discriminate between true (good) and false (bad) stories."[23] Though we cannot know reality from some supposedly ahistorical vantage point, since there is none, nor can we know some overarching story of stories, truth still can be realized, and this requires being formed by a truthful narrative. For Christians, the story of Jesus enables them to see themselves, their situations, and the world as they truly are.[24]

Now at this point we should observe that for Christians, the meaning of *truth* and *truthfulness* come from the language of the church. They do not have to do with matching up with an extralinguistic reality. Kallenberg's explanation is helpful, in that "Hauerwas does not think that truthfulness has to do with a condition of correspondence that putatively exists between sentences and 'reality.' Rather, 'truthful' names the community that is able to shape a people who, in Wittgenstein's words, can 'see the world rightly.'"[25] Likewise, the same conclusion follows for the meaningfulness of behaviors that show the truthfulness of the gospel. Even the gospel is not a "story of stories" that transcends all particularity and gives meaning to these concepts and behaviors.

We may now see that Stanley Grenz's and John Franke's central presuppositions bear a close family resemblance to those of Kallenberg

and Hauerwas. In *Beyond Foundationalism*, Grenz and Franke aim to
spell out the contours of appropriate theological methodology, given our
living in a postmodern context. For them, there are no neutral starting
points, definitions, or methodologies from which we may begin to do
theology.[26] Rather, "experiences are always filtered by an interpretive
framework."[27] This interpretive grid is primarily linguistic, for language
"provides the conceptual tools through which we construct the world
we inhabit."[28] The main task of theology therefore becomes the explora-
tion of "the world-constructing, knowledge-forming, identity-forming
'language' of the Christian community."[29]

Grenz and Franke hold to a tight relationship of language and the
world. For instance, they explain forcefully that

> It is simply not possible to step back from the influence of tradi-
> tion in the act of interpretation or in the ascription of meaning.
> Interpretive communities that deny the reality of this situation and
> seek an interpretation unencumbered by the "distorting" influence
> of fallible "human" traditions are in fact enslaved by interpretive
> patterns that are allowed to function uncritically precisely because
> they are unacknowledged.[30]

While they are careful to qualify these comments with terms such as the
"distorting influence" of traditions, they state their views more clearly
elsewhere. For example, after surveying and appropriating insights from
sociology into their study of the church as community, they quickly
warn that these insights must not be allowed to "deteriorate into a new
foundationalism."[31] Why might this be a problem? Their terse reply is
instructive:

> Such degeneration occurs when speech about the church as com-
> munity begins with some generic reality called "community," which
> can *supposedly be discovered through objective observation* of the
> world, and then proceeds to fit the church into this *purportedly*
> universal phenomenon as if the community of Christ were a par-
> ticular exemplar of some more general reality.[32]

For them, foundationalism is the culprit that has bewitched us into
thinking we can have objective observations and know universally valid,
linguistically independent realities.

Furthermore, as we each live in some socially, linguistically constructed world, it likely will take on the semblance of objective existence,
"for it seems to be external to our personal consciousness."[33] Nevertheless, they confidently assert that just "as the demise of naïve realism
has led scholars from a variety of disciplines to conclude, we do not
live in a universe that is simply a given, external reality."[34] So it seems

clear that despite their qualifications that tradition and our cultural contexts do influence theologizing, they hold to a tight relationship of language and the world.

But does this mean that they give up on objectivity altogether? Not in the least; there are two senses in which they argue that we can speak of an objectivity of the world. The first sense is that construction of the world cannot extend to all of creation. Quite wisely, they admit that there is "a certain undeniable givenness to the universe apart from the human linguistic-constructive task,"[35] especially since the universe predates the existence of human beings. But while they have given up on the idea that we can know the world-in-itself, nonetheless they firmly believe that Christians can know the world in a second, eschatological sense—*as God wills it to be in the future.* This is what they mean by *eschatological realism,* which is the biblical narrative's vision of what kind of world (and new community) God is creating, which will be realized in the future. It is from this perspective, they claim, that the world gains its most fundamental sense of actuality, or objectivity.

This world-building enterprise is not, however, just the work of Christians by their language use. For Christians, that which governs proper linguistic use is scripture, and it is through this medium that the Holy Spirit speaks today to Christian communities and thereby builds the new community, the church. So while Christians are on the inside of language, God has broken through and given authoritative revelation in the written word of God, which is used by the Spirit, along with Christians, to construct that eschatological community.

Their appeal to the Spirit serves not only to break through human language and give revelation, but also to unite the otherwise discrete Christian communities. Grenz and Franke insist upon the local and particular character of all theological reflection, and therefore they emphasize the historical and cultural context within which the Spirit speaks to a localized community of Christians.[36] But by itself, this emphasis still seems to lead to the discreteness of all such "Christian" communities. Now, if we draw upon Alasdair MacIntyre's view, which indeed seems applicable to Grenz and Franke's own position, there cannot be such a thing as *Christian* language-as-such; there is only a multiplicity of discrete, local communities whose languages and practices bear a family resemblance to each other and may be called "Christian."[37] And this is what they claim: while all theology is specific and local, these various theologies still may bear a family resemblance in at least three respects, and, if so, they are indeed Christian.[38] But most of all, what unites these diverse Christian communities is that the Holy Spirit works with each community in its own context:

The Spirit continually speaks through the biblical text, illuminating subsequent generations to understand their present in light of the grand, *telic* narrative of God and guiding them in the task of living out in their own contexts the vocation all Christians share, namely, that of being the community of Christ in the contemporary world.[39]

We have seen that Grenz, Franke, Kallenberg, and Hauerwas share several views in common. For one, they all write explicitly as being members of the church and focus their reflections on the Christian community. Second, they share the view that there is no way outside of language, and the language use of a community makes the world in which that community lives. Third, since there is no essence to language, there are only languages, and the Gospels are the "grammar" that governs how Christians should use their language. Fourth, and importantly, they all hold to the view that the Christian story is the true story, although, as Hauerwas puts it, there is no way within history to prove it as such. With this common methodology in mind, let us now turn to see if these views will withstand scrutiny.

The Presupposition of Epistemic Access

If language has world-making power, and each social world is made by the members' linguistic use within local forms of life, then how do Hauerwas, Kallenberg, and Grenz and Franke arrive at the conclusion that all is done within language, or even that language is internally related to each world? It does not seem possible that this conclusion itself can be known by just describing a particular world. Their methodology denies that we can go out into the world-in-itself and just observe things as they are, since all such observations are linguistically mediated.

But if language and world are internally related, then that principle, too, does not seem to be knowable just by description. How can it be known without begging the question, if how a particular world is, is due just to how it has been made by the use of a language? On the other hand, we are left with the conclusion that the language-world internal relation is just a particular claim of a discrete way of life (whichever one that is). Therefore, it seems hard to see how they can make their case that others ought to believe their view of the relation of language and a world.

Furthermore, as Kallenberg puts it, "neither 'world' nor 'story' exist independent of the other."[40] Our authors hold that through training within a form of life, language users learn to both see and build the world through their language use. So, language enters into the very "fabric" of "reality," such that reality is fundamentally linguistic.

But whose world is this? If we take their view seriously, it has to be one that each author has helped to construct by the use of his own community's language. Yet these are quite generalized claims, so how do they know that worlds, *generally* speaking, are linguistic? This seems to be what they mean, or else this claim would apply just to their own community's world.

Indeed, other Christian groups do not accept such premises. It seems that those Christians and others outside their particular communities should not necessarily accept this view, and therefore it seems that there is no way to contend that this view should be normative for all believers. At this juncture, however, Hauerwas, Kallenberg, Grenz, and Franke might argue that those Christians are mistaken in their stance, since they have accepted the language-world dichotomy, and thus they have contributed to the philosophical confusion from which Wittgenstein sought to cure us.

Kallenberg, for example, consistently rejects the view that we can get outside of language. If we take him consistently, he does not mean to inform us of the nature of reality when he repeatedly makes this strong claim. Still, how should we interpret his claim that language and world are internally related? Of course, critics likely will interpret him as making claims about the essential nature of reality apart from language, for plainly that seems to be his intent. But if this is not a statement about the way things are apart from language, what then does this claim mean? The only plausible alternative is that it too is just a claim made from within his discrete way of life. If so, the question resurfaces: why should outsiders accept this view? It is just a claim uttered from within his community's world. Supposedly, that claim has been made so according to his community's grammar. But the identity of that community is not specified in its details.

Now that conclusion does not seem to be in accord with the spirit in which Kallenberg, Hauerwas, Grenz, and Franke have argued. They have argued at length and with great force and zeal in many books to convince their readers of many key ideas. Two such ideas are that a world is internally related to a language, and that the confusion that modernity foisted upon us is due to the bifurcation of language and world. But it seems they should write with such passion only if they are writing to fellow members in their own communities.

So it becomes important that we their readers know which are these communities. But besides informing us that they write as Christians, they never specify their particular Christian communities. This is crucial, for, if we take their method consistently, these universal claims are but expressions of some particular linguistic communities. But again, we do not know which ones they are. Rhetorically, this lack of specification of the relevant community works to their advantage, for it enables them to make sweeping, generalized statements as to how Christians should behave or believe.

We are left to speculate as to which community is the relevant one. In Kallenberg's case, it might be some of the evangelical-Christians-who-worshiped-at-Trinity-Evangelical-Free-Church-in-Redlands, California-in-2001. Or, it might be postmodern-evangelicals-at-Fuller-Seminary-in-the-time-of-Nancey-Murphy's-tenure. Or it could be some other local Christian group. Now it might seem that Kallenberg, like Hauerwas, and Grenz and Franke, is very consistent within this linguistic method, since he at least explicitly owns his Christian stance. Each author is quite concerned with making assertions as to how Christians ought to think and live.

Yet, writing simply as Christians still leaves unanswered the critical question as to the identity of their specific communities. Christians are quite diverse. For instance, there are Methodists and Presbyterians, and among them they are diverse geographically, confessionally, and historically. In addition, consider Baptists. There are American and Southern Baptists, to name but two types, the latter of which is a diverse group, too. There are conservative as well as liberal Southern Baptists, and some doctrinal positions vary amongst the seminaries and churches.

There also are Russian Orthodox and Greek Orthodox churches, and there is wide range of kinds of churches in African countries. Some of these African churches have strong leadership by nationals, while others may be more missionary-dominated. Evangelical Christians also are diverse. They share a commitment to the spread of the Gospel, yet they vary in their ethnic mix and musical expression.

So the question remains urgent: what is the relevant, particular Christian community? It makes *all* the difference, if languages are discrete and language use within a community makes its world. Taking them consistently, Hauerwas, Kallenberg, and Grenz and Franke must be telling us how their particular Christian communities see their own worlds. That makes it painfully clear that each one must disclose his relevant community. But on this topic, we are never told. Suppose, though, they were to specify the communities. In this case, we would see that their arguments would be very particular to their respective communities, and thus it would be relatively uninteresting to those outside those communities. Why? Our communities would not hold the exact same commitments as theirs due to their view of the strong particularity of language, even if they all are Christian ways of life.

But surely they want to say much more than just that their particular, historically located communities talk in certain ways. After all, they have written at great lengths about how things are, to get us to see as they do. For example, they argue that we are on the inside of language; that the Enlightenment and a high confidence in universal human reason foisted upon us philosophical confusion; that foundationalism is mistaken and in dire disrepair; that we should learn to see "rightly," as they have; etc. If we take their method consistently, then these claims should be understood for what they are—that is, they are just claims of local, unspecified linguistic communities that happen to have talked and thus constructed their worlds in this way. But this result runs contrary to what they clearly want to say. They strongly argue that we are on the inside of language, which they know to be the truth, and not just for their community, but as the way things *really* are for all of us. Otherwise, their essays lose the force with which they are written. Therefore, it seems most likely they presuppose they can get outside language in order to get their own method off the ground. That is, most likely, they presuppose an epistemic access to an unconstructed, extralinguistic realm.

At this point, let us consider two key objections that seek to rebut my argument. First, as the "grammar" for the Christian communities, the Gospels are indeed the normative standard for the Christian life, and they give us the truth about Jesus. Since the Gospels are common to the many diverse Christian communities, this should suffice to unite them as being Christian. Thus, Hauerwas, Kallenberg, and Grenz and Franke do not need to presuppose access to some essence of Christianity apart from the particularity of the various local expressions of Christianity, including their own.

Despite the attractiveness of this move, if meaning just is use, the meaning of the Gospels is how they are used within particular communities. Accordingly, there will be a multiplicity of meanings of the Gospels, since on their method, each Christian group, while united by a commitment to Jesus, will have its particular use of the Gospels. Each Christian community also must have its own localized, discrete language, lest there be an essence to Christian language. And if there are no essences, even to the meaning of the Gospels or to language, and if there are only particular communities, then the Gospels cannot serve to unify these communities as being Christian. They need to appeal to something beyond the particular to unite them.

But as a second counter, they could reply that even though we are on the inside of language, God has broken through and given us special revelation. If so, then they could argue that they need not presuppose access to a realm outside of language. God knows objective, universal truths and has communicated them in special revelation. Thus Christians are not cut off from knowing the true story, even though, as Hauerwas says, there is no way within history for us to prove it as such. This kind of reply has the advantage for them of preserving both their language-world relationship and the truth of the faith. We will now turn to address this reply, and in so doing we will see a crucial doctrinal implication of their view, one that will undermine a central Christian belief.

An Implication for Christian Doctrine

Truths that God has revealed are true in virtue of their correspondence with an extralinguistic realm that can be known only from a God's-eye viewpoint; hence, God must reveal them by special, as opposed to general, revelation. Now, on Hauerwas's, Kallenberg's, and Grenz and Franke's view, God must have the ability to see things as they are in themselves. Otherwise, he too would be on the inside of something (perhaps the language of the Trinity?) and could not get out. If that were the case, then special revelation would be impossible; God too could see and know things only through his own language, and not in themselves. So, wisely, Grenz and Franke assume that the Holy Spirit can break through human language and speak to the church in all its localities. This move enables them to hold, along with the biblical writers, that we can know and receive special revelation directly from God.

Now, at this stage, we should raise a preliminary concern. If God truly is independent of language, then they face a dilemma. Since they assume that Christians can know God, it seems to be the case that they presuppose that Christians can know and have epistemic contact with something that is unconstructed, namely, God. If that is so, then they presuppose after all that believers do have at least *some* epistemic access to an extralinguistic, unconstructed realm. But that result would seem to be unacceptable to them, since it runs contrary to their *many* claims that we simply do not have such access. Moreover, to grant this point, they would seem to have to concede their premise of the internal relationship of language and world, for something unconstructed (God) would be knowable.

Even so, let us suppose for the sake of argument that they might agree with this position, that Christians can know God in an unconstructed way, but that is the extent of such knowledge. However, then Christians would know reality per se, since God would have revealed such truth. It follows that Christians would have an epistemic vantage point from which they could correctly judge all viewpoints and truth claims. But that result undercuts a central position they have vigorously defended.

In order to treat them as being consistent with their many strong claims, it therefore seems we must interpret them in a way that affirms their clear belief in the human inability to know an unconstructed realm. Given that position, they might reply that, yes, God has given special revelation, and the Holy Spirit does break through Christians' language. But *what they mean* by such claims is just that these are the ways Christians talk according to the rules of their language. They could argue rightly that in giving divine revelation, the Bible makes many universal truth claims, such as that Jesus is the only way to God; that God has spoken through his Son, the prophets, the apostles, etc. Accordingly, they could contend that scripture uses language in ways as to make universal claims and to explain that God has revealed himself. Therefore, it would be proper for them as Christians to make such claims as well.

Now, this possible interpretation holds fast to the internal relationship of language and the world; and on this view, God would not be exempted. The advantage of this interpretation is that it would be consistent with their assertions about our inability to know an unconstructed, extralinguistic realm. On such an account, the claim that God has given special revelation is a particular and internal claim of the Christian community.

But while this is a more consistent position for them to embrace, nonetheless it raises a highly significant problem. Despite their attempts to write in a manner that is consistent with what the scriptural authors wrote, God ends up being a construct of Christians' own language use. This seems to be the case whether or not God is on the inside of language. Consider first if God is not on the inside of language. Even so, *believers* cannot get outside of language; so even if God could get through their language, they cannot know him as he is, or even as he reveals himself, since that would entail that they do indeed know, and have some contact with, an extralinguistic, unconstructed realm. Accordingly, any special revelation from God would have to be interpreted through how Christians use their language, *and this is the critical factor.* If we borrow from the later Wittgenstein the concept that meaning just is use (which is what Kallenberg and Hauerwas both clearly believe, and it seems very consistent with what Grenz and Franke argue), then whatever God meant by his special revelation would be meaningful to people *only* as it is used within the particular linguistic practices of a given community. And this would apply not only to the enscripturated revelation, but also to their appeal to communication by the Holy Spirit as he speaks now to the churches. For if Christians (or anyone else, for that matter) are indeed on the inside of language and cannot get outside to an extralinguistic realm, it seems that the prospects for divine revelation are rather dismal. On the other hand, if God *cannot* escape language, then Christians simply must construct God, and that would be by their language use.

If this is the case, then Christians necessarily would be idolaters on their own terms. Of course, that conclusion would be unacceptable and disastrous for their method. It would require an internal contradiction of scripture. So they might reply that no, God is not a construct made by Christians' language use, meaning that that is not how they talk in their particular communities. How might they counterargue from here? I think they likely will argue that God has been able to break through our language and give us special revelation. Christians know the true story because God has revealed it. Accordingly, they may claim that, after all, they do not presuppose that God is internal to their language. Going further, they could charge that I have been bewitched by the influences of foundationalism to think that I can know things as they truly are, independent of linguistic use, and that I am thereby creating theological confusion. But if they maintain their insistence on (a) the local, discrete character of communities that construct their own worlds by how they use their language, and (b) that we simply do not inhabit (nor can we know) the world-in-itself, then their counterclaim that God is not internal to language is just that: a claim made from within their own discrete, linguistic communities, whichever ones those are. But that conclusion does not fit with the spirit in which they have written, and so, just as we have seen before, they most likely presuppose an access to a realm outside of language to make their own view work.

Conclusion

These are but some of the problems with Kallenberg's, Hauerwas's, and Grenz and Franke's kind of linguistic methodology. But these issues do not apply just to their particular works. To the extent that others accept these same presuppositions, then their views too will suffer from the same problems.[41] These presuppositions include: (1) the internal relation of language and world; (2) the closely related presupposition that we are inside language and cannot get "out" to know an extralinguistic, objective world; (3) language use within a way of life makes that community's world; (4) there is no essence to language, so there are only many languages; and (5) there are as many worlds as there are languages. I have examined these and other issues in greater depth elsewhere.[42] But suffice it to say for present purposes, Hauerwas, Kallenberg, and Grenz and Franke undermine their methodology by presupposing a way outside of language to an extralinguistic realm, and, furthermore, their method does violence to at least one essential Christian doctrine. Thus, this kind of linguistic approach to Christian theology and ethics ought to be rejected. And, to the extent that other Christians adopt these key presuppositions of their linguistic constructionist methodology, those views too will fail.

Notes

1. Brad J. Kallenberg, *Ethics as Grammar: Changing the Postmodern Subject* (Notre Dame, IN: University of Notre Dame Press, 2001), 180.
2. Ludwig Wittgenstein, *Philosophical Investigations*, 3rd ed., ed. G. E. M. Anscombe and Rush Rhees, trans. G. E. M. Anscombe (New York: Macmillan, 1958), §65.
3. Kallenberg, *Ethics as Grammar*, 212.
4. Wittgenstein, *Philosophical Investigations*, §109.
5. Kallenberg, 182.
6. Ludwig Wittgenstein, *Philosophical Grammar*, ed. Rush Rhees, trans. Anthony Kenny (Berkeley and Los Angeles: University of California Press, 1974), §56.
7. Ibid., §55.
8. Ibid., §95.
9. Kallenberg, 234 (emphasis added).
10. Ibid., 51. This concept is the central (and very well-taken) argument of his second chapter.
11. Stanley Hauerwas, *Vision and Virtue* (Notre Dame, IN: Fides, 1974; repr., Notre Dame, IN: University of Notre Dame Press, 1981), 71.
12. Ibid., 20.
13. Ibid., 16.
14. Ibid., 17.
15. Ibid.
16. Jonathan R. Wilson, "From Theology of Culture to Theological Ethics," *Journal of Religious Ethics* 23, no. 1 (Spring 1995): 156.
17. Stanley Hauerwas, *Character and the Christian Life* (San Antonio: Trinity University Press, 1975; repr., Notre Dame, IN: University of Notre Dame Press, 1994), 18.
18. Ibid., 33.
19. Ibid.
20. Ibid., 102.
21. Ibid., 101.
22. Ibid.
23. Stanley Hauerwas, "Ethics and Ascetical Theology," *Anglican Theological Review* 61, no. 1 (Jan. 1979): 97.
24. Stanley Hauerwas, *A Community of Character* (Notre Dame, IN: University of Notre Dame Press, 1981), 96.
25. Kallenberg, 156.
26. Stanley J. Grenz and John R. Franke, *Beyond Foundationalism: Shaping Theology in a Postmodern Context* (Louisville: Westminster/John Knox, 2000), 16.
27. Ibid., 49.
28. Ibid., 53.
29. Ibid.
30. Ibid., 113.
31. Ibid., 226.
32. Ibid., 226–27 (emphases mine).
33. Ibid., 271.
34. Ibid.
35. Ibid., 53.
36. For instance, see ibid., 26, 158, or 161.

37. Alasdair MacIntyre, *Whose Justice? Which Rationality?* (Notre Dame, IN: University of Notre Dame Press, 1988), 357.

38. See page 25 for their initial statement of this concept. But see also page 166, where they summarize what they will unpack in Part 3: that all localized Christian theologies should be "trinitarian in content, communitarian in focus, and eschatological in orientation."

39. Ibid., 229.

40. Ibid., 126.

41. I have argued that Alasdair MacIntyre's views about ethics and traditions land him in a similar problem, although he does not write as a theologian. See my book *Virtue Ethics and Moral Knowledge: Philosophy of Language after MacIntyre and Hauerwas* (London: Ashgate, 2003).

42. In *Virtue Ethics and Moral Knowledge*, I try to develop several lines of critique of MacIntyre, Hauerwas, and Kallenberg. Chapter 4 argues in detail for their presupposition of epistemic access to an extralinguistic realm. Chapter 5 examines the issues with behavior (including that meaning just is use within a way of life), and Chapter 6 argues against MacIntyre's, Hauerwas's, and Kallenberg's idea of the narrative unity of the self. Chapter 7 explores in more detail the implications of their method for several core Christian doctrines, and Chapter 8 attempts to resolve the issue of relativism. See also my article "Some Conceptual Problems for Hauerwas's Virtue Ethics," *Philosophia Christi* 3:1 (2001): 153–64.

3

Pilgrim's Digress: Christian Thinking on and about the Post/Modern Way

Kevin J. Vanhoozer

Introduction: Getting Our Bearings

The Christian thinker this side of the eschaton is always only on the way, a pilgrim passing through other lands heading home. It is therefore fitting that I chart my own position vis-à-vis postmodernity by adding yet another layer of intertextuality to Bunyan's *Pilgrim's Progress*.

A pilgrim's regress

The way has been trod before. C. S. Lewis made his own position vis-à-vis modernity clear in *Pilgrim's Regress*, originally published in 1933, the first book he wrote following his conversion.[1] It is an allegorical tale of how he *unlearned* many of the things he had been taught by modern figures like Mr. Enlightenment and Mr. Sensible (hence, the "regress").

Lewis's allegorical journey takes place between the barren rocks of the North and the fetid swamps of the South. These two hemispheres represent modernity's split personality, the schizophrenic Nietzschean tension between Apollo and Dionysius, objectivity and subjectivity. "The Northerners are the men of rigid systems. . . . The Southerners are by their very nature less definable; boneless souls whose doors stand open day and night to almost every visitant."[2] Roughly speaking, the North stands for reason, the South for romanticism. The Enlightenment project, for example, was manufactured by the epistemological industry that dominates regions north. Lewis took his own age to be predominantly northern, while allowing that many vacationed in the South.

We can also locate academic disciplines on Lewis's map. The natural sciences, together with modernity, dominate the North. Indeed, modernity is to a large extent the attempt to take the instrumental reason that successfully mastered the world of nature and apply it to the human world of ethics, religion, and politics as well. Lewis's map also helps us to represent the postmodern turn in terms of the growing power, numbers, and influence of "southerners." Yet it would be perfunctory simply to equate postmodernity with subjectivism. In the first place, *subjectivity* means something quite different in postmodernity from what is normally described as the "turn to the subject" in modern philosophy. Indeed, it may be more appropriate to associate the postmodern South with *inter*subjectivity. Cities are few and far between in the postmodern South, however; it is rather a region inhabited by scores of rival tribes, many of whom do not speak the same language. Nurture, not nature, accounts for their diversity. The South is the land of the social sciences: history, literary theory, psychology, sociology, and cultural studies, the new kid on the academic block.

The postmodern pilgrim: how (not) to go on

There are several ways in which we can respond to a new phenomenon such as postmodernity: we can *deny* or ignore it. We can refuse to recognize either its importance or its right to exist. Not a few Christians are in denial over postmodernity. Second, we can *defy*, even demonize it as a threat to our security or way of life. Not a few Christians have (in my judgment) overreacted in this direction too. To describe postmodernity as "the latest chapter in unbelief" is both simplistic and self-serving. We can, thirdly, *deify* it, conceding its authority because newer (and more popular) means better. A number of Christian thinkers have sought to "revision" their philosophies and theologies in order to bring them into line with leading postmodern themes. A fourth option is to *discuss* with it. The goal here is to engage it in a mutually edifying conversation. Though clearly preferable to the other strategies, this one may have the disadvantage of playing into its hands. For conversation and rhetoric are largely what postmodernity is about. Yet the concern to make the faith intelligible to contemporary ears—call it "correlation," or the "apologetic" impulse—stands in some tension with the impulse of faith to seek understanding on its own terms.

In the postmodern South, one's self-conception is always already a political affair. It is assumed that there is no such thing as autonomous individuals, hence the postmodern reflex for situating persons in communities and community traditions. I recognize the importance of situatedness yet at the same time resist the notion that one's thinking can be explained merely in terms of the community to which one belongs. Such reductionism eventually leads to a social determinism that ultimately absolves individuals from personal responsibility for their thoughts. Personally, I want to discuss the big questions, not to be dismissed or pigeon-holed as a such-and-such. Don't just look at my identity papers; listen to my reasons! I am barely across the border, and already I am embroiled in dispute. Indeed, my basic stance vis-à-vis postmodernity may ultimately be one of *dispute*—not for what they say so much as for what they do *not* say, or better, for what they deny *can* be said.[3]

Why do I prefer a disputational rather than a conversational model of dialogue? Dispute better captures the seriousness of the encounter; something important is at stake in this discussion. Dispute also suggests that I am contending for my position, not simply sharing it. Better: I am contending for the faith that was once for all entrusted to the saints (Jude 3). Finally, "disputation" has the merit of being a venerable genre of theology, dating from the medieval period. Part of my purpose in the present essay, however, is to revise the notion of disputation so that the focus is on a whole person witness to concrete Christian wisdom rather than a wholly intellectual demonstration of an abstract truth. On this latter point—the necessity of going beyond analysis—I do not dispute with postmodernity but say "amen."

To dispute with postmodernity is also to engage it. Christians thinkers cannot go around postmodernity; we have to go through it. Part of what we are going through, I shall suggest, is modernity in its death throes. We are trying to find our way out of what Paul Ricoeur aptly calls the "desert of criticism." We want meaning and truth, something for which we can live and die, something beyond technical prowess and analytic philosophy. Modernity was clearly and distinctly unfulfilling. But postmodernity begets more criticism—a criticism of criticism or, to be precise, an *ideology* criticism.

To be postmodern is to have a heightened awareness of one's situatedness: in a body, in culture, in tradition, in language. Well and good. It is good to know where you are. But it is even better to know how to go on. The map I shall be following is the one Pascal had sewn into the lining of his jacket, a fragment of paper that read: "God of Abraham, Isaac, and

Jacob. Not the god of the philosophers." What the world needs now, I submit, is Christian wisdom: a demonstration of how to follow biblical maps through the twenty-first century toward the new Jerusalem. But following the biblical maps also leads me to resituate postmodernity.

On Knowing Where We Are: Charting the "Bulverist Turn"

How one reacts to the postmodern depends to a large extent on what one thinks it is; everything thus depends on the way one initially describes postmodernity. One reliable barometer of one's understanding of postmodernity is the way one takes the "post": does the postmodern represent something new or different with regard to the modern and, if so, how? Let me now give my own barometric reading of this epochal change.

The modern architect

Modernity, the so-called Enlightenment project, was an attempt to bring critical rationality and scientific method to bear not only on the natural but on the social world in order to "master" reality. Modern thinkers believed that the universal truths of reason could bring about universal human emancipation through technology, morality, and democracy. The modern university awards students with a "master's" degree; seminaries follow suit by bestowing the improbable title of "master of divinity" on their graduates.

Kant answered his own question "What is enlightenment?" by saying that it is a trust in one's own reasoning powers rather than in authority and tradition. From one perspective, then, modernity was a revolution in first philosophy, whereby epistemology replaced metaphysics as queen of the philosophical sciences. Modernity is thus characterized by a Faustian desire for knowledge that could serve as a certain and universal foundation for one's claims to meaning, truth, and value. The modern intellectual is an architect whose knowledge not only of foundations but of structures enables him to build the City of Man according to the principles of architectonic reason with a single rational blueprint. Modernity is thus a grand exercise in engineering—mechanical, electrical, and social. Surely we are our own masters if we can engineer everything from skyscrapers to the human genome!

The postmodern archaeologist

If architecture is the emblem of modernity, archaeology is its postmodern counterpart. The archaeologist studies the dilapidated remains of what the architect designed. Where the architect viewed blueprints with confidence and hope, the archaeologist sifts among the ruins. It is difficult for the archaeologist to believe in foundations when all that remains are broken fragments. Unlike the modern architect, the post-modern archaeologist is not really interested in building something new; why bother, since no foundation or building material can withstand the ravages of time? So the archaeologist deconstructs, analyzing the process of a thing's original construction, taking special note of the contingencies of its construction and hence of the nonnecessary or arbitrary nature of the final product.

Stipulating: "conditions of impossibility"

Elsewhere I have described postmodernity as a "condition": a state of being or fitness (e.g., a heart condition); a set of circumstances that affects how one functions (e.g., working conditions); a requirement that must be fulfilled in order to do something else (e.g., a condition of entry).[4] The postmodern condition is basically one of disbelief: postmoderns no longer believe in the Enlightenment architectonic project.

Postmoderns excel in specifying the "conditions of impossibility" of truth, of universal reason, even of belief in general. They prefer to do so ironically rather than indicatively. Both Rorty and Derrida have exposed the latent irony in metaphysics: the metaphysician sets out to speak about the real but ends up saying something about himself. This is irony: meaning (expressing) the opposite of what you explicitly say. To speak in the indicative is to offer statements of fact. But *indicating*—making known, referring to—is a gesture that postmoderns are unable to make. The postmodern creed is largely negative: "I *cannot* believe in individual autonomy, in universal reason, in determinate meaning, in absolute truth."

Situating: genealogical analysis as bulverism

One might be tempted at this point to go along with Rorty, and to describe postmodernity as "the linguistic turn." However, rather than seeing postmodernity as a turn in a radically different direction, I view it as a sharper turn in the same direction as modernity's turn to the subject. And, precisely as an extreme turn to the subject, I think postmodernity is an especially virulent strain of what C. S. Lewis calls "bulverism."

Bulverism? The notion stems from a 1944 essay that Lewis entitled "'Bulverism,' or The Foundation of 20th-Century Thought"[5]—an article that is, I believe, prescient in its anticipation of the final outcome of modernity's turn to the subject. Descartes's "discovery" that he exists—"I think, therefore I am"—was disastrous, Lewis thinks, for henceforth we do not simply look, say, at a rose *but at ourselves looking at the rose.*

The temptation is to think that the color of the rose is a product of our optic nerve, and its scent of our noses, so that in the end "there is no rose left."[6]

Lewis christens this skeptical reflex "bulverism," after its imaginary inventor, Ezekiel Bulver. Lewis imagines the moment that bulverism was born, when five-year-old Ezekiel heard his mother say to his father, "Oh, you say that because you are a man."[7] Bulver intuitively grasped the stunning implication: arguments need not be refuted, only *situated*. One rebuts a *thought* simply by calling attention to the genealogy or location of its *thinker*.

Lewis never treated postmodernity directly (he died four years before Derrida published *Of Grammatology*), but he foresaw its coming. His two examples of bulverist thinkers who have anew discovered "that we exist" are Freud and Marx. Instead of examining *what* we think, Freud and Marx explain *why* we think what we do. The celebrated turn to the subject—"that we exist"—is the discovery of human situatedness, perhaps the central insight of postmodernity. Human situatedness—in history, social class, gender, culture, religion—has become the focus of postmodern investigations. The result: every issue is ultimately about identity politics, about where, what, and who one is. *Postmoderns are so preoccupied with the situated self that they cannot get beyond it.* Whatever one is doing—whether reading or speaking or observing or thinking—postmodern attention is invariably riveted on the process of attending, not the object of attention. There is no rose left nor, for that matter, truth, goodness, and beauty.

Lewis acknowledges, anticipating the postmodern penchant for play, that "this is obviously great fun." Yet there are questions that ought soberly to be raised: first, *are* all thoughts contaminated at the source (e.g., reason, language)? Second, is the contamination such so as to render the contaminated thought untrue? The situatedness or contamination of thought is, of course, a two-edged sword. If *all* thoughts are contaminated, then so is postmodern theory.

That Lewis had already detected signs of bulverism in his day suggests to me that postmodernity is an intensification of modernity's turn to the subject. To be precise: postmodernity is a turn to the *archaeology* of the human subject. Instead of thinking that humans can explain the world according to a rational blueprint, as modern architects were wont to do, postmoderns are more interested in what constructs, and constitutes, human subjectivity. Here postmodern opinions vary, with some assigning a greater or lesser role to one or more of the following influences: history, culture, tradition, community, gender—and especially language. To be postmodern is to be aware of the fictive nature of our linguistically constructed worlds. In the words of Ernest Becker: "It is one of the most remarkable achievements of thought, of self-scrutiny, that the most anxiety-prone animal of all could come to *see through himself* and discover the fictional nature of his action world."[8] The postmodern condition can therefore be described as modernity emancipated from false consciousness, as *modernity that has awakened to its own naked-ness.* Hence, my first thesis:

(1) **Postmodernity is the condition of being fully aware of one's** *situatedness.*

Faith and Postmodern Philosophy

Postmodernity is more of a condition than a distinct position, a mood rather than a metaphysic; it nonetheless communicates something about human being-in-the-world. It is a world and life view, not in the sense that it yields a system of propositions, but in the sense that it creates an ethos. Postmodernity may be more than a philosophy, but it is not less; it is a world and life view that is in a relation of codependency with modernity.[9]

"Language" as first philosophy

Whereas Heidegger chided modern philosophers for forgetting the question of Being, postmoderns typically say that we have forgotten the question of language. Human beings have always been language users, of course. Modern thinkers tried to *master* language through scientific study (e.g., linguistics) or through philosophical theories (e.g., structuralism). What postmoderns contribute to the discussion is the awareness of language's irreducibility and plurality. It has become virtually impossible to believe that any one community's language or vocabulary provides a better purchase on reality than another's. This is one thing that almost all postmoderns—nihilist (Derrida), pragmatist (Rorty), hermeneuticist (Gadamer, Ricoeur), and nonfoundationalist (Wittgenstein, MacIntyre)—agree on: that language, in different ways, *situates* us.

Postmodernity is the condition of being so exposed to plurality and otherness that one becomes conscious of the contingency of one's own language, culture, and way of life. Walter Truett Anderson distinguishes the condition from various movements the condition has produced: "Postmodernisms will come and go, but postmodernity—the postmodern condition—will still be here."[10]

Indeed, we may liken the postmodern condition to a third Copernican revolution, a revolution that results in a further decentering of humanity from the center of the universe.[11] Instead of history and culture revolving around reason, reason is now seen to orbit particular cultures and particular times in different ways. If no one set of linguistic and conceptual distinctions is less arbitrary than another, then no one system is deserving of absolute belief. Such is the premise of our distinctly postmodern condition, namely, *the awareness of the deconstructibility and contingency of every text and system of meaning and truth.* Two distinct postmodernisms have worked variations on this postmodern theme of our situatedness in language.

Endless interpretation: language as prison-house

Nietzsche, the patron saint of postmodernity, prophesied accurately: if God is dead, then it's interpretation "all the way down." Formulation never reaches fact. No one interpretation can ever be regarded as final. As in interpretation, so in life: everything becomes undecidable. This is the *Continental* variation on the theme of language as first philosophy. Derrida's claim that "there is nothing outside the text" is not a silly claim about what there is in the world. He is not claiming that "to be is to be textually conceived" or that only writing exists. He is rather making the (bulveristic!) point that what we know about things is linguistically, which is to say culturally and socially constructed.

Christians, I believe, must not merely converse with this view; they must dispute it. Why? Because it makes mincemeat of the scriptures. This does not mean that Derrida has nothing to contribute; he does (see below). Yet biblical interpretation is a crucial barometer and case study that alerts us to both the dangers and the opportunities of modern and postmodern approaches alike. The peril of postmodernity is that of losing the capacity to be informed and transformed by God's Word; the promise of postmodernity is that of rediscovering aspects of God's Word that enable us to get wisdom rather than mere information.

Social interpretation: language as practice

It is too simplistic to tar all forms of postmodernity with the same skeptical brush. For there is another way of conceiving human situatedness in and by language that attempts to bypass the choice between realism and nonrealism (e.g., the choice as to whether our words refer to reality or not) altogether. It is the Anglo-American postmodern way, and it too has to do with the linguisticality of the mind and with the rootedness of language in social life.

According to Wittgenstein, modern philosophers tend mistakenly to associate words to mental concepts. Thinking is not simply some process that takes place in our heads.[12] On the contrary, meaning is a function of how human beings use language in concrete social practices: "what is real for humans is shown by the way human beings . . . speak with one another."[13] How do I know that the two-footed feathered creature flying overhead is a bird? By being socialized into the use of the English language; by learning the "grammar" of "bird."

Anglo-American postmodern theologians want to say something similar about the term *God,* hence the importance of being *socialized* into church practices, and hence the phenomenon of ecclesiology becoming "first theology." Recall my earlier point about postmodern being "southern" (i.e., oriented to the social sciences and nurture rather than to the natural sciences and nature). To locate ecclesiology as a "special" instance of a "general" pragmatics, however, is to miss the sui generis nature of our union with Christ. Christianity is not something that the church invented; on the contrary, the church is a "creature of the Word" (Luther). The church is not a particular instance of some general phenomenon such as communitarianism, but rather a scandalous particular that cannot be encompassed by the categories of secular thought, whether modern or postmodern.

Ironic interpretation: language as persuasive tool

Richard Rorty makes points similar to both the above varieties of postmodernism. Because language is an arbitrary social construction, Rorty recommends giving up the misguided attempt to "get it right," that is, to speak about the world as it is. "One cannot transcend language; that is, one cannot find a point of view outside of all linguistic frameworks from which the world will appear 'as it is.'"[14] The postmodern philosopher is not a metaphysician but an ironist for whom the only practical question is not "Which language gets reality right?" but "Which language best suits our present purpose?"

Rorty's ironist knows that "anything can be made to look good or bad by being redescribed."[15] The postmodern pragmatist's challenge, therefore, is to solve problems by describing a course of action so persuasively as to secure intersubjective agreement. Rorty believes that the notion of a community striving for intersubjective agreement is just as useful as the idea of "objectivity" or "transcendence." Of course, the ironist cannot really *believe* in what he says; his descriptions are not true, but expedient.[16] Rorty thus helps bring the peculiarly postmodern form of bulverism into focus. We no longer simply talk about roses but about ourselves talking about roses. "Philosophical problems are problems about what language to speak in order to best suit our purposes."[17] But can Rorty's own rhetoric withstand the withering scrutiny of the bulverist: "You say that because you're a clever white male liberal democrat"?

What Christians can learn from postmodernity

There is a certain providential parallel between what postmodernity is doing for the church today and what Persia did for ancient Israel (Ezra 1:1; Isa. 44:28). As Cyrus released Israel from her Babylonian captivity and encouraged the rebuilding of the Jerusalem temple, so postmodernity releases the church from its Athenian captivity to modernity and enables the return of certain exiled themes, religion and transcendence among them.[18] What postmodernity teaches, however, is primarily a *negative* lesson, one moreover that we should have already known, namely, that we are situated, limited, contingent.[19]

Cleansing the temple

Modernity sired biblical criticism in its numerous forms: source, form, redaction, structuralist, etc. The postmodern's emphasis on situatedness, however, makes possible a new kind of critique, a critique of *impure* reason. Postmoderns contend that claims to meaning and truth are all too often simply masks for what Nietzsche called the will to power. To say that my reading of the Bible is "true" is in fact a disguised way of saying, "This is what I *will* the Bible to mean."

What postmodernity bequeaths to the world is ideology criticism: the criticism of isms. Here we have what is in my opinion the single most helpful contribution of postmodernity to Christian thinkers: a thoroughgoing iconoclasm, a radical protest against oppressive systems of thought.[20] Irony in particular is a powerful tonic against conceptual idolatry, namely, the tendency to treat any one vocabulary or conceptual scheme as "final." The postmodern prophets to whom I hearken are those that offer words of critique: *de*construction. Theirs is a negative ministry of casting down what Bruce Benson refers to as "graven ideologies."[21]

(2) Christians can and should learn something from postmodernity, namely, the criticism of isms.

My most charitable reading of postmodern thinkers like Derrida and Rorty, therefore, casts them in the heroic role of outraged prophets seeking to cleanse, sometimes playfully and sometimes painfully, the modern philosophical temples of knowledge. Overturning the economies of the knowledge changers is an ethical gesture on behalf of marginalized others whose voices and vocabularies have been systematically suppressed. To the extent that we can identify with such repressed minorities, Christian thinkers too should applaud these iconoclastic gestures and perhaps wonder why we had not cleansed the temple of modernity earlier ourselves.[22]

Returning the exiled and the repressed

Postmoderns want to think the unthought of modernity. Many therefore evince "a predilection for the plural, the multiple, a valorization of everything that had been suppressed by earlier systematicity, everything that had been left out or relegated to the margins."[23] David Tracy goes so far as to describe postmodernity as "the turn to the other," where the "other" is whatever has been systematically excluded by various modern isms.[24] The postmodern critique of ideologies has paved the way for the return to academic respectability of other forms of literature and thought than that of the concept. The net gain: it is possible once again to speak of *transcendence*.[25]

Why postmodernity should not set the Christian agenda

Should postmodernity be allowed to set the agenda for Christian thought simply because it makes space for transcendence? I think not. While postmodernity is a kind of liberation, it is nevertheless important to distinguish *freedom from* and *freedom for*. Postmodernity sets the captives free *from* certain aspects of modern thought, but not from the bondage of sin and death nor from meaninglessness and despair, nor does postmodernity set them free *for* others or the wholly other (God). Moreover, precisely because it is a reaction to modernity, postmodernism inadvertently risks letting *modernity* set the agenda, even if only in a negative fashion.

I do not understand why certain thinkers who bemoan theology's captivity to modern philosophy are so anxious to exchange masters. Nancey Murphy and Brad Kallenberg, for example, appear to advocate a correlation between theology and Anglo-American postmodern philosophy: "We count as postmodern . . . theologians who either explicitly appropriate these philosophical developments [viz., those of Wittgenstein, Quine, Kuhn, MacInytre, et al.] or who have arrived at similar propositions by alternate routes."[26] The prior question, however, is whether Christian thought should seek to "correlate" at all.

The method of correlation puts theology in thrall to questions posed outside the community of faith and forces theology to play by other disciplinary rules. Note well: my dispute is not with philosophy per se, only with the pretensions of philosophy as a discourse that aspires to metanarrative status. As a discipline philosophy, like physics and psychology, has a legitimate place; however, again like physics and psychology, *this place is not that of the governing framework of Christian thought*.

The danger in correlating theology with this or that philosophy (or any other discipline) is that of domesticating the divine, of reducing the strange new world of the Bible to this-worldly terms, of exchanging the scandal of the cross for the pottage of intellectual respectability. This is as much a danger in postmodernity as in modernity. Whereas the modern inclination was to exaggerate divine immanence, postmodern theologies tend to stress the "otherness" of God and to exaggerate divine transcendence. Their "God" is so "beyond" language and categories as to become amorphous, the "woolly other" about whom nothing definite can be said. Yet Christians confess that Jesus Christ is God in human form (Phil. 2:5–7; Heb. 1:3); far from being amorphous, God has taken the form of a servant. The life of the man Jesus Christ is the criterion for understanding the identity of God.[27]

Christian thinkers from all disciplines would do well to heed Plantinga's advice to Christian philosophers: what we need is "less accommodation to current fashion and more Christian self-confidence."[28] I submit that we take what Plantinga says as less a suggestion than a mandate ("Plantinga's law"): "Thou shalt not let others set the Christian agenda."[29]

(3) Christians must not "correlate" with postmodernity or let concerns and frameworks other than Christ and canon set faith's credenda and agenda.

Obviously, Christians need to keep their eyes and ears open. However, as we shall see, there are distinctly Christian ways of thinking about human situatedness and even language, not to mention meaning, knowledge, and truth.

Faith Seeking Theological Understanding

South by southwest

The late Hans Frei also engaged in a bit of map making in order to locate modern theology. The result was an insightful typology of the ways in which philosophy relates to theology or, to put it a bit differently, the ways in which *Christian* thought relates to *current* thought. Frei distinguished two basic types of Christian thought that we, for the sake of charting pilgrim's postmodern peregrinations, can label "East" and "West."[30] Frei's West is a land ruled by philosophy, whose citizens manufacture universal categories or extratextual schemes that can be used to describe just about anything, including Christianity.[31] Frei's East, by contrast, is distinctly Christian; people there live differently from Westerners, speak their own language and, just as importantly, describe their way of life with their own domestically produced categories.

(4) Christian thought is faith seeking understanding and thus specifically Christian, that is, biblical and trinitarian.

If we superimpose Frei's typology on that of C. S. Lewis, we get something like the following:

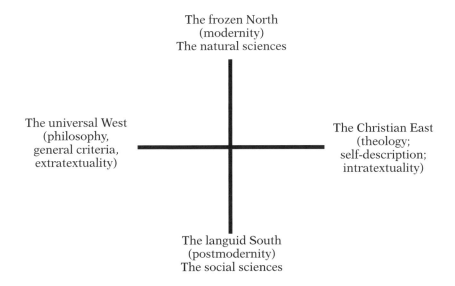

The frozen North
(modernity)
The natural sciences

The universal West
(philosophy,
general criteria,
extratextuality)

The Christian East
(theology;
self-description;
intratextuality)

The languid South
(postmodernity)
The social sciences

Most people, especially intellectuals, live in the West, and increasing numbers, including Christians, are migrating south. For to the extent that postmodern concerns are allowed to set the agenda, people will continue to inhabit the Western Hemisphere. It may be that a good many Christians believe they are dwelling in the Southeast, but according to my plat of survey they have actually pitched their tents in the arid Southwest. It's not quite the land of Mordor, but it's not Jerusalem either. Christians who dwell in the West are "mediators" who seek to make the faith intelligible in terms of the surrounding culture even at the risk of modifying or revising it. It is my considered conviction that Christian thinkers should move East; people of faith can and must pursue faith's own agenda for the sake of the church, the academy, and the world alike. At the same time, I think it is important to maintain diplomatic relations with Westerners.

The postmodern always comes late

Implausible though it sounds, I believe that the Bible anticipated many of postmodernity's central claims. Take, for example, the crucial postmodern insight that human reason is *situated*. From scripture we already know that human beings are finite, rooted in the dust of the earth (Gen. 2:7), yet at the same time "a little lower than the heavenly beings" (Ps. 8:5). Situated between heaven and earth, we lack the knowledge of angels. Or take ideology criticism. Christians do not need postmoderns to know about the many ways in which the will to power distorts knowledge claims and the quest for truth; we have the narrative of the fall and the doctrine of original sin for that. Moreover, we have the Hebrew prophets: their idolatry critique, and their irony, antedates postmodernity by a few millennia. As to the postmodern "discovery" of language, here too Christian thinkers are not without their own resources. Apophatic and analogical theology acknowledge the inadequacy of human language for naming or understanding God. And the plurality of languages associated with Babel represents a standing critique of any one human vocabulary that aspires to be the language of heaven.[32]

(5) Postmodernity has not discovered anything that was not already available, at least implicitly, in Christian scripture and tradition.

Imagination and the biblical mythos

The imagination, together with its linguistic offspring (e.g., metaphor), is another of those repressed themes in modernity. Rationalists held the imagination in low regard, while romantics understood its importance but failed to discipline it. By *imagination* I mean the power of synoptic vision—the ability to synthesize heterogeneous elements into a unity. The imagination is a cognitive faculty by which we see as whole what those without imagination see only as unrelated parts. Stories display the imagination in action, for it is the role of the plot (mythos) to unify various persons and events in a single story with a beginning, middle, and end.

The truth of Christianity is not like the universal truths of reason. The cradle of Christian faith is a story rather than a system. Though the Bible includes many literary genres, what holds it together is a narrative unity: the story of what God is doing in the world through Israel, through Jesus Christ, through the church. Christian thought inhabits the biblical mythos—not cleverly devised modern or postmodern myths, but *myth become redemptive history*. This is the mythos that serves as our framework for interpreting God, the world, and the self.

C. S. Lewis insists that the imagination is a truth-bearing faculty whose bearers of truth are not propositions but *myths*. Myths enable us both to "taste" and to "see": to experience "as a concrete what can otherwise be understood only as an abstraction."[33] What gets conveyed, therefore, is not simply the proposition but something of the reality itself: not simply information about God, but God's triune identity itself as this is displayed in and through his creative and redemptive work. Further, the words of scripture do not simply inform us about God but act as the medium of divine discourse. It is these words—the stories, the promises, the warnings, etc.—that ought to orient Christians vis-à-vis reality.

Theology should have the courage of its convictions. In particular, Christians should think—as well as live, and move, and have their being—within the biblical mythos. The creation-fall-redemption-consummation schema is a comprehensive (and canonical) interpretative framework that should govern Christian thinking about everything, including—nay, especially!—truth, goodness, and rationality.

(6) Thinking in a distinctly Christian way means thinking out of the mythopoetic framework of scripture (e.g., in terms of creation, fall, redemption, consummation).

Engaging Postmodernity I: Matters of Substance

How do I respond to specific postmodern views concerning knowledge, truth, ethics, and language? I take these challenges seriously, not simply as threats but as opportunities to display the rich resources of Christian doctrine.

Knowledge, metanarratives, and rationality

Situating reason: scripture as exploratory framework

Lyotard famously defines the postmodern condition as one of "incredulity towards metanarratives." Largely because of bulverism, we cannot believe in the "one true story" that explains every other story. We are too aware that other groups have their own stories that claim to be equally comprehensive. Metanarratives thus dwindle into *mere* narratives; "reason" is situated, deuniversalized. Consequently, the burning question becomes: Whose story (and whose interpretation of it) counts, and why? It is as hard for postmoderns to believe in metanarratives as it was for Victorians to believe in fairies (if you believe in metanarratives, clap your hands!). How can Christians respond to this legitimation crisis?

What is knowledge? Merely to exchange metaphors, substituting *web* or *raft* for *foundation,* is no guarantee against correlationism. The masters may have changed, but philosophers are still instructing theologians in how to make epistemological bricks out of the mud and straw of human experience or creativity. Having issued this caution, I nevertheless wish to propose the following metaphor for knowledge: the map. Metanarratives, I submit, are not so much explanatory as *exploratory* frameworks.

The map also has the advantage of situating knowledge claims in the context of everyday life: our *walk*.

You are here. I agree with the postmodern insight that human reasoning is situated. I also agree with Lesslie Newbigin that the postmodern critique of foundationalism has shown that human thinking always takes place within "fiduciary" frameworks. Even the Enlightenment project began with a "faith" in the omnicompetence of reason, with a faith in a certain way of mapping the world and our way in it. The question, then, is not whether we can avoid subscribing to some fiduciary framework or another, but rather, which one enables us to make cognitive contact with reality?

All human thinking takes place within fiduciary frameworks, but only the biblical frameworks enable us rightly to interpret the nature of ultimate reality. To be sure, the biblical maps do not explain everything. They may tell us how to go to heaven, but they do not tell us how the heavens go; we need Galileo and Einstein for that. Similarly, they tell us how humans should live, but not everything that life consists of; we need Crick and Watson for that. These supplementary maps drawn up by other disciplines do not contradict the biblical maps but identify previously unknown or uncharted features. The point is that we need multiple maps for multiple purposes. We can map the same terrain according to a variety of different keys and scales. In this respect, Rorty is right: our vocabularies (maps) are related to our interests, to what we want to do. A road atlas need not contradict a map that highlights topography, or a map that highlights historical landmarks and points of scenic interest, or a plat or survey that shows where properties begin and end.

Reason does not stand over the gospel, deciding which map to accept and what to reject. Here Christians and postmoderns agree: reason itself is always already situated. Postmodern philosophy is never "from above." Christians are therefore entitled to assume the gospel as the ultimate interpretative framework with which to make sense of all other knowledge and experience. To reason Christianly is to negotiate the real world with the aid of biblical maps. Reason here plays a *ministerial* role. But are we rational in accepting *just these maps?* I believe that rationality is less a matter of starting points or neutral ground than it is a matter of being willing to put one's faith commitments to any number of critical, even existential, tests.[34]

To construe knowledge as a map and to contend that the biblical maps chart certain aspects of reality correctly is to subscribe to what we may term a *confessing* epistemology. To say "I know" is, for Christians, a way of saying "I believe rationally," and rational belief is part and parcel of the larger Christian project of bearing witness. I believe in the epistemic primacy of the gospel and its canonical context, not as a base on which to build a pyramid of knowledge, but as a map that reliably guides us in the way of truth and life.

Doctrine and rationality

Situating knowledge in the biblical creation-fall-redemption schema yields specifically Christian perspectives on the nature of rationality. Plantinga appeals to the doctrine of creation when he speaks of the "design plan" of the human mind, which is to produce true beliefs. The doctrine of creation is a compelling warrant for affirming the reliability of our cognitive faculties. The doctrine of the fall, however, reminds us that our cognitive faculties are distorted—out of order. Accordingly, we need to complement reliabilism with a fallibilism that insists on rationality as a willingness to submit one's belief to critical testing. It is easier for a camel to pass through the eye of a needle, however, than for an academic to admit that he or she was wrong! Our account of knowledge needs a third moment. In order to practice criticizability, the knower must become intellectually honest and evince epistemic humility. Honesty and humility are not functions of methodological procedures but personal virtues. The rational person must be a person of intellectual virtue.[35] And to acquire intellectual virtue, we need to undergo a transformation of our hearts and minds alike. As the doctrines of creation and fall lend support to reliabilism and fallibilism in the domain of epistemology, so here too the doctrine of redemption confirms and deepens virtue epistemology's point that rationality has less to do with following scholarly procedures and more to do with becoming a saint.

Creation (reliabilism), fall (fallibilism), redemption (intellectual virtue): a threefold epistemological cord is not easily broken. In sum: "I believe in reason, but I reason in belief." *I believe in reason.* Reason is a God-designed cognitive process of inference and criticism, a discipline that forms virtuous habits of the mind. *I reason in belief.* Reasoning—giving warrants, making inferences, analyzing critically—does not take place in a vacuum but in a fiduciary framework, a framework of belief.

Being, metaphysics, and reality

Nonrealism and metaphysical idolatry

If metaphysics is the attempt to think all of reality by means of a single set of categories (e.g., "being"), then the postmodern condition is as antimetaphysical as it is antisystematic. Though everyone has some kind of informal metaphysic or "final vocabulary"—"a set of words which they employ to justify their actions, their belief, and their lives"[36]—the postmodern ironist is aware of other vocabularies that purport to be final and are equally as impressive.

The challenge is not whether we can find the words to describe the world, but whether any of our descriptions get beyond *self*-description. The bulverist turn is especially damaging to metaphysics. Is what we say ever indicative of the world, or is what we say always about us: about our preferences, our interests, our abilities? This general worry becomes even more acute when the reality we are trying to think is God. Must we conclude that the metaphysical quest for God, like the quest for the historical Jesus, is simply the story of people looking into a deep well and seeing their own reflections?

Realism with a human-divine face

Christian faith compels me to dispute certain nonrealist postmodern claims. To confess belief in a creator God is to confess that what there is—reality—does not depend on *my* language and thought. At the same time, I agree that no one language or vocabulary carves up reality at its joints. One could say the same thing about the gospel: no one Gospel carves up the gospel at its joints. We need a quadraphonic witness—Matthew, Mark, Luke, and John—rightly to perceive what God was doing in Jesus Christ. I agree with Mikhail Bakhtin that some truths are "dialogical" because they can only be grasped by employing more than one conceptual scheme. Such pluralistic metaphysics is best seen not as a relativism but as a moderate realism, and this for two reasons.

First, the plurality of descriptions may be due to different levels of complexity in reality. The point is that each level gives a correct description as far as it goes. For example, one can describe the same occurrence—say, a person's falling in love—on a variety of levels: biochemical, psychological, cultural, sociological, and theological.[37] Second, we need a variety of descriptions or vocabularies in order to highlight the different levels or *aspects* of reality. Such an *aspectival realism* has nothing to do with a perspectivalism that holds that what we see is *constructed* by our theories. No, *the world is there, mind-independent and differentiated, yet indescribable apart from human constructions and only partially accessible to any single theory.* The moderate realist insists that though our knowledge of the world is partial it can still be true: "we need a pluralism of vocabularies in order to give an adequate account of how matters stand"[38] for the same reason that we need a plurality of maps (e.g., historical, topographical, geological, political) in order to navigate our way through the world.

At the same time, not just any map will do. The requirement for plurality is not a license for an anything-goes relativism; reliable maps must ultimately correspond with this or that aspect of what is really there, *and* they must be compatible with one another. Note that cartographic compatibility is not quite as stringent a criterion as coherence. Things that *cohere* are united in a single conceptual framework; things that are *compatible* have only not to contradict one another. The number of maps I have in mind, then, is plural but not infinite. As Kant rightly insisted, reason does strive for a certain unity of thought. On the view presented here, however, the unity for which Christian thinkers should be working is a function not of a single metaphysic (for this would require us to make one conceptual scheme into a metanarrative) but rather of a single *atlas:* a *canon,* as it were, of authoritative maps.[39]

I am arguing not for a social constructivism, then, but for a critical or moderate realism that, while affirming a reality independent of our language and theories, nevertheless acknowledges the necessity of language and theories for making contact with reality. Certain aspects of reality come to light only under particular descriptions. One cannot describe the workings of Parliament, for example, with the categories of particle physics. Nor can one describe the reality of faith with psychological categories alone.

(7) Christian faith is realist but insists that some truths can adequately be grasped only by means of a plurality of vocabularies or conceptual schemes oriented to different levels or aspects of reality.

With regard to the reality of God, however, *no* vocabulary, especially no *single* vocabulary, is entirely adequate. Here we must heed Jean-Luc Marion's caution not to construct a god after our own metaphysical images. Even a "perfect being" is simply an extrapolation from our culturally conditioned human thoughts about "perfection." The divine reality must present itself. Reinhard Hütter rightly reacts against constructivism in modern theology, especially the idea that theology is poetic (via., a species of *creative* discourse), by stressing the pathos of theology: "Rather than theology creating its object, the object forces itself upon theology; indeed . . . that object constitutes both theology and the theologian."[40] I take it that the "object" to which Hütter refers is the Word of God. In an important sense, therefore, we *are* constituted by language: *God's* language. Better: we, and everything that is, are constituted (and situated) by divine speech acts: "Let there be"; "Samuel"; "Thou shalt not kill"; "where two or three are gathered, there I am in the midst of you."

The Word of God is God-in-communicative-action. God's Word is true because, whatever it is doing—representing states of affairs, promising, commanding, warning, etc.—it can be relied on ultimately. It is the Word of God that creates, sustains, and governs the universe. God's Word is thus the measure of truth and reality. The *logos* of *theos* precedes any human *logos:* "In place of onto-theo-logy we have theo-onto-logy."[41] The Bible as theodrama not only recounts the acts of God but is itself part of the economy of God's communicative action. It is the means by which God creates, sustains, and governs that part of reality we call the church. Reality just is the playing out of this theodrama: the God-world active relation. It follows that Christians must acknowledge a realism with a human-divine face, a christological realism that sees the reality of God and man alike, as well as the future of creation, summed up in the face of Jesus Christ: God's Word made personal.

The ethos of the mythos: attention to the fitting "in Christ"

For the Christian, ethics is about our responsible response to the gift of Christian freedom, about giving appropriate form to freedom. I agree with postmoderns that universal moral rules go only so far in helping us determine how to act in specific situations. Appropriate action requires understanding, seeing a particular situation aright: "The capacity to see what is there . . . is integrally related to the capacity to love."[42] Ethics demands what Simone Weil calls "attention": the ability to transcend oneself in order to see things as they are. It is precisely for the sake of attending to the salient features of particular situations that we need to get beyond postmodern solipsism—the bulveristic preoccupation with ourselves. For wisdom is the ability to see what is right and fitting in a particular situation given one's understanding of the larger whole of which it is a part. In particular, we need the evangelical imagination: the ability to see situations in light of what God is doing for the world in Jesus Christ.

Theological wisdom is a matter of learning how to read and relate to reality rightly. The wise person is the one who understands and participates fittingly in the created order.[43] We get wisdom by letting the biblical texts train our imaginations to see how things fit together theodramatically as ingredients or moments in the drama of redemption. Scripture depicts the world as created and redeemed; this picture generates a certain ethos that in turn shapes our moral character. Scripture also depicts the love of God—which is the summation of the law and hence the essence of Christian ethics—in the face of Jesus Christ. Ethics is about how to participate fittingly in the form of the good personified in Jesus Christ. Christianity thus represents an alternative way of doing justice to the other. Thanks to the theodramatic imagination, we see the other not as an unknowable, and hence unlovable, cipher, but as Jesus sees the other, as *neighbor*. In sum, the Bible *situates* both me and the other in a larger theodrama that orients right action by calling us to love others as God has loved us.

(8) The aim of Christian thinking about the true, the good, and the beautiful is wisdom, the ability to participate rightly in reality; the norm for Christian thinking about the true, the good, and

the beautiful is the wisdom of God reflected in the face, and life, of Jesus Christ.

Language, history, and culture

But we began with language as the postmodern emblem for our situatedness in history, culture, and tradition.

The death of God put into writing

Language—"writing" (Derrida) or "vocabulary" (Rorty)—is the postmodern poster child, the symbol and symptom of all that is wrong with the Enlightenment project. Far from being a transparent medium that mediates the mind-world relation, language is rather a social construction or system of differences that acts as a filter or screen between the mind and the world. No one language or vocabulary or conceptual scheme is universal or absolute; on the contrary, every language is contextual and contingent. At the limit, this insight results in a certain despair of language. Wretched man that I am! Who will deliver me from this bondage to partiality, irony, and a limited vocabulary? Writing situates us because, for postmoderns, there is nothing that escapes or transcends the play of signifiers. We should not miss the significance of Derrida's comment that deconstruction is "the death of God put into writing."

The providence of God put into writing

Instead of deciding on what language is and making the Bible conform to that, Christians should attend to how scripture itself depicts the significance of language use. If they do, they will see that language looks quite different in biblical and theodramatic perspective; indeed, language becomes "the providence of God put into writing." In the first place, language in theodramatic perspective is a God-ordained means of communicative agency.[44] Scripture depicts speakers, human and divine, doing such diverse things as making promises, issuing warnings, giving commands, counsel, and comfort, all by means of language. *Language is not a prison-house from which we cannot escape, but rather the means through which we exercise responsible personal agency.*

The second point follows from the first. *Language is providential not only as a means of divine action, but also as a medium of divine care.* For language is not only a communicative but a *covenantal* medium, a divinely created means for relating to human others (e.g., conversation), to the world (e.g., observation, statements, theories), and to God himself (e.g., praise, prayer). Furthermore, there is a "presumption of covenantal relation" in every speech act, namely, a tacit plea or demand to understand. It is impossible to think about language for very long from a Christian perspective without considering it in covenantal terms: privilege and responsibility.

The notion of covenantal relation characterizes not only our thinking about language but, in a certain sense, our thinking about knowledge, reality, and ethics too. The covenantal nature of interpersonal relations is easiest to see in ethics, where we recognize obligations to others in our church community, to our neighborhood, even to our natural environment. Knowledge, too, is a covenantal affair insofar as it involves epistemic virtues such as humility and honesty and proceeds from an initial personal commitment to a fiduciary framework. Finally, there is a quasicovenantal relation even in the realm of metaphysics. Christians believe that God upholds the universe by his Word: being itself depends on the bond that is God's Word. For ultimate reality is personal: "Fatherhood is the principle that runs the universe" (George MacDonald). To be human, then, *is* to be situated in language in a sense, for God's covenantal word structures creation, gives understanding, and directs freedom.

Now we can better understand why I have seen fit not simply to correlate but to dispute with postmodernity: *Scripture and Christian doctrine afford unique resources for thinking, about language as well as everything else.*

Engaging Postmodernity II: Matters of Style

The postmodern challenge is a salient reminder to Christian thinkers to give an account of the hope that is in us and to do so nonviolently, in a way that is beyond reproach (1 Pet. 3:15–17). Christian thinkers must distance themselves from ideologies wherein meaning and truth stand at the service of individual or institutional power. Here too, I believe, the Christian thinker can make use of resources intrinsic to the faith, for not only the matter, but the *manner* of Christian thought should be derived from scripture and church tradition. In particular, I believe the four traditional marks of the church also characterize the essential features of Christian thought: one, holy, catholic, and apostolic.

"One"

Christian thinking should be "one," but not in the sense of uniformity. Lévinas rightly criticizes "Greek" thinking (e.g., metaphysics, epistemology) for its totalitarian tendency to swallow up recalcitrant particulars in grand theory. Yet the unity of Christian thinking need no more issue in conceptual uniformity than church unity need result in unvarying sameness. The unity of the church is a unity-in-diversity, for God has given different gifts to its many members.

I advocate a "holistic" oneness. Thinking is holistic when it avoids reductionism. Even in reading scripture, we must acknowledge that the whole—the literary genre—is greater than the sum of its parts and pericopes.[45] Christian thinking is holistic, secondly, in emphasizing the integral and personal nature of knowing. Knowledge is not a disembodied but a whole-person affair.[46] On this point, postmoderns and incarnational Christian faith agree. Like the unity of the church, however, the unity of truth presently eludes us. All things were indeed created through Christ, but we shall see Christ as he is only at the eschaton. At present, therefore, the unity of truth remains a matter of hope as much as sight.

We can tie together a number of the above emphases by calling Christian thought to be imaginative. The imagination, as we have seen, is the cognitive capacity for synoptic vision, the ability creatively to discern wholes. The unities it grasps—especially the mythopoetic gospel account of what God was doing in Jesus Christ—are both thought and felt. Indeed, only the imagination can perhaps perceive that ultimate unity of truth, goodness, and beauty that is embodied in Jesus Christ.

"Holy"

Christian thinking should be holy, first, in the formal sense of the term: "set apart." I have argued that Christians should not feel beholden to secular theories. We are not to be slaves to any one theory or philosophical system. Indeed, what Luther says concerning the freedom of the Christian—"lord of all, subject to none"—pertains also to the relation of Christian thinking to those systems that would subdue it. The Christian mind is a bondservant to the revelation of God in Jesus Christ. No mind can serve two masters.

Christian thinking ought also to be characterized as "holy" in the ordinary sense too: that which is morally and spiritually excellent. Here we simply may recall what was said earlier concerning the intellectual virtues and reiterate that Christian thinking has nothing to do with violence. Genuine knowledge is not won by forcing recalcitrant data, whether the results of lab work or of exegesis, into preconceived interpretative schemes. "Mastery" is an inappropriate image for depicting epistemological success; knowledge is an exercise not of power but of virtue.

Knowing, I have suggested, is a covenantal affair. The object to be known—biblical text, physical world, historical events, God—in a certain sense *gives* itself to be known, thus incurring privileges and responsibilities on the part of the knower. To know, therefore, is to enter into *covenantal* as well as correspondence relations with the object to be known by attending with due intellectual virtue to the object in its particularity. There is thus a connection between intellectual and spiritual formation.

"Catholic"

Christian thinking should be catholic, not in the Roman sense of according magisterial authority to the official tradition of the institutional church, but rather in recognizing what we might call the ministerial authority of the consensus tradition of the global church. Catholicity is the antidote to the tribalism and parochialism that can infect Christian thinking that never leaves its ghetto.

Christian thinkers, like everyone else, must accept their situatedness in language (i.e., history, culture, tradition). But they must also dispute the implication that such situatedness justifies either irresponsible play or joyless despair, for the story of language ends not with Babel but with Pentecost. Pentecost is especially important for understanding catholicity: the Spirit did not create church unity by creating a common tongue but ministered the Word of God to the assembled crowd in such a way that each person heard it in his or her own native language (Acts 2:8). Apparently there is not one language of heaven but many.

Missiologists Andrew Walls and Lamin Sanneh argue from the translatability of the gospel to the conclusion that no single human language or tradition exhausts the Word of God, and that no one language (or culture) has a monopoly on what form the gospel can take.[47] There never was a commentary written that rendered the biblical text superfluous. Once again, postmodernity reminds us of something we should have known from scripture and theology, namely, that we need the *many* human interpretations to hear the *one* Word of God. The Word-ministering Spirit has not been given to one person, denomination, or interpretative tradition, but to the whole church. Seen in the light of Pentecost, plurality need not be the enemy of meaning and truth, but their enabling condition.

Contemporary Christian thinkers ought therefore to be aware of what Christian thinkers in other times and places have thought. They ought also to beware of being too closely associated with any one philosophical school. Monogamy is not a virtue when Christian thinkers are so wed to one conceptual scheme that they cannot appreciate or appropriate wisdom from other systems of thought. If Christian thinkers are successfully to resist letting extratextual theories set the agenda, they had better view philosophy not as a single handmaid but as the *harem* of theology.[48]

"Apostolic"

Credulity—the willingness to believe what one is told—is under normal conditions a reliable belief-producing mechanism. Apostolicity means faithfulness to what Christians have been told by the apostles, the "ones sent" throughout the world with the message of the gospel. It was the apostles who first proclaimed the theodrama and passed it on to others, and the apostles themselves were only passing on what they had been told by the Spirit of God. Kierkegaard's distinction between a genius and an apostle is a salient reminder that what makes thought distinctly Christian is its rootedness in apostolic testimony. We call that person a genius, says Kierkegaard, who arrives at the truth first. However, the truth so arrived at is a truth of reason and applies only to the sphere of "immanence," to that which can be deduced from this-worldly phenomena. By contrast, the apostle proclaims a truth that is not of his own devising, a truth that is transcendent because it pertains to something that human beings could not even in principle find out.

Christians must eventually dispute with postmodernity because they know something postmoderns do not know. Christians know something about the true end of life: the *summum bonum*. They know this not because they are cleverer or more worthy than postmoderns but because they have been told it. What Christians know is not apodictic but *apostolic* truth. What Christians know is actually *someone:* Jesus Christ, the wisdom of God. Christian thinkers are Knights of the Lord's Table—servants, not lords, of that concrete representation of the theodrama's climax, the demonstration of the wisdom of God on the cross of Christ.

(9) Christian thinking is one (holistic, integrative, imaginative), holy (distinct, virtuous, covenantal), catholic (demonstrating awareness of the length and breadth of the Christian tradition, philosophically eclectic), and apostolic (biblical, christocentric).

Conclusion: Two Roads Diverge in a Harrowed World

Christian pilgrims may be knights, but not Crusaders, for those who follow the way of Jesus Christ must renounce using truth claims as instruments of oppression. (Postmoderns prefer genealogical undoing, a weapon of class destruction.) How, then, may we construe the Christian pilgrim's journey through postmodernity? It is not a sentimental journey, for postmoderns are acutely aware of the contingency of the past as well as the present; only carry-on nostalgia allowed! Nor can we say that the postmodern pilgrim has made progress, for most of the gains (i.e., incredulity toward metanarratives, ideology critique) have been negative. No, from a Christian perspective we must conclude that postmodernity is ultimately the story of pilgrim's *digress*. There is perhaps no better metaphor for postmodernity than that. For a digression is a temporary departure from the main subject, which, in the case of Western civilization, was *wisdom* and *well-being:* the discourse on the True, the Good, and the Beautiful.

Pilgrim's digress

For Christians, of course, the main subject is Jesus Christ, for he is the truth and the life, and the way to be right with God and neighbor. Seen in this light—in the light of him who is the light of the world—*both* modernity and postmodernity are digressions, departures from the main subject and from the main road, that narrow yet royal way to eternal life. Make no mistake: modernity and postmodernity alike are *ways,* not merely intellectual positions—ways that cannot help but be means of spiritual as well as intellectual formation.

The Enlightened pilgrim, like the proverbial American tourist, wonders why everyone else does not do things the modern way. Or, to change metaphors, the modern pilgrim is a traveling salesman convinced of the superiority of electric vacuum cleaners, even for Bedouin tents. The postmodern pilgrim is right to poke fun at such hubris. As we have seen, postmodernity at its best represents a potent, even prophetic blast against the intellectual and cultural pretensions of modernity. If one had to associate modernity with one of the seven deadly sins, it would surely be pride: pride in human reason, human goodness, and human potential.

The preference for the creature over the Creator takes many forms, however, and postmoderns have their own stratagems for evading the divine summons. Whereas the modern stratagem was to inflate the sense of self (pride), postmoderns tend to deflate our sense of self (sloth). In this respect, the postmodern pilgrim resembles a vagrant; his way leads nowhere in particular. Indeed, it is not even clear that postmodern pilgrims have even embarked on the journey. Perhaps they are waiting for Godot. Like Vladimir and Estragon in Beckett's play, the postmodern pilgrim says "Let's go" but remains sitting in the seat of the scoffer (Ps. 1:1–4). "The postmoderns sometimes seem more determined by ennui than by ethics."[49] The postmodernist does not say "I believe in order to understand" but "I *stand back* in order to understand belief" or "I *stand by* in order to defer belief." The self as a responsible and answerable agent is as far from being established in postmodernity as in modernity.

Sloth—that reluctance to make any effort—is the besetting temptation of the postmodern pilgrim. It is also a deadly sin. According to Dorothy Sayers, sloth is the sin "that believes in nothing, enjoys nothing, hates nothing, finds purpose in nothing, lives for nothing, and remains alive because there is nothing for which it will die."[50] *The form of postmodernity I dispute is that which acts as a corrosive to conviction and commitment, a bulverism that deprives the will of anything in which to believe ultimately through an exaggerated focus on the motives and mechanisms of belief.* By paying excessive attention to ourselves and our situatedness—to our body, our class, our language, our ethnicity, our culture—we fail to attend adequately to the world and to the Word.

Oddly enough, there is a certain pride hidden beneath this sloth. For the postmodern pilgrim insists that *all* pilgrims must follow the same digression. All pilgrims must take a detour, for the way forward is blocked by postmodern "conditions of impossibility." Unfortunately, it is hard to make much forward progress during a digression (though to the extent that postmodernity derails us from the false track of modernity, it is a kind of progress). But if we can truly love only what we know, and if we can never meet the conditions for knowledge, then we are relieved of the responsibility of having to love intelligently. This is convenient, the perfect excuse for those who do not wish to answer the beck and call of their fellow creatures, much less their Creator. Such sloth is perhaps the ultimate conceit.

10. Modernity and postmodernity alike are ultimately digressions from the main subject, namely, the way of wisdom and of life summed up in Jesus Christ.

Concluding unironic postscript: the via crucis

Christian pilgrims, not vagrants. The Christian wayfarer, unlike the postmodern wanderer, is a disciple with a destination, and a path. The Christian way of staking claims to meaning, knowledge, truth, and rightness is not the way of the will to power but of the will to weakness. It is, in sum, the way of Jesus Christ, a way that leads to and from the divine truth claim staked on a cross. Those who follow Christ must also suffer for the truth, enduring all forms of criticism, epistemic and existential, for the sake of a rational, and righteous, witness. The way of Jesus Christ is the way of a wisdom and witness that is both bold yet humble: the *via crucis*.

The Christian pilgrim-thinker is ultimately on a missionary journey. Jesus's mission was to be God's truth claim to the world; similarly, the mission of Christian thinkers is to bear witness to the truth of Jesus Christ in all that they say and do. It is ultimately because of one's commitment to the truth of Jesus Christ that the Christian must part ways with postmodern vagrants and return to the main road, heading East, toward Jerusalem.

The present challenge to Christian thought—to establish truth claims—involves demonstrating Christian wisdom in and to and against other forms of wisdom. This is not a matter of epistemological foundationalism but of demonstrating the integrity and uniqueness of the Christian world and life view. Christian thinkers are engaged in a project of comparative wisdoms: the wisdom of the crucified God vs. the wisdom of the self-glorifying world. To demonstrate the wisdom of the cross, however, is to be willing to be both fool and martyr. Staking a Christian truth claim can be a costly affair, requiring us to bear faithful witness in word and way. Indeed, in the final analysis, our understanding of faith is displayed not merely in thought but in life. Our way of life is our most important form of biblical interpretation. *The vocation of the Christian thinker is to respond to the provocation of reality in the light of divine revelation.*

The postmodern digression is helpful to the extent that it enables us to recover the main road. I have suggested that it does so, at least partially, insofar as it shows the inadequacy of the high road of modernity. Absolute knowledge is indeed beyond our grasp; the postmoderns have rightly called attention to human situatedness in history, on the *hither side* of the eschaton. What postmodernity fails to grasp, however, is the *eschatological* nature of the otherness that is "to come," together with the New Testament claim that this transcendent otherness has already/not yet come in the person of Jesus Christ and, subsequently, in the pouring out of Christ's Spirit.

This is not Platonism but theodramatic (eschatological) realism. The gospel is the good report that the eternal God has himself made a pilgrimage into history. The Father has sent his Son and his Spirit—what Irenaeus calls God's "two hands"—on missions into the far country. It is precisely because the eternal has entered into history—because God has got his hands dirty—that we do not have to rely on speculation to determine the way to truth and life. God has found a way to us; it suffices that we follow it back to him. It is precisely this realization that Christians are beneficiaries of the eschatological work of the triune God that enables them to walk the way of Jesus Christ with boldness and humility. Christian disciples are not the masters of meaning and truth but its humble servants. We have not devised the theodrama, but we have been accorded the dignity of playing a part in it. The wise witness is willing to dispute on behalf of the gospel and, precisely because she is wise, will temper her witness with appropriate measures of boldness and humility. Christian pilgrims evince humble yet joyful confidence that, thanks to the guidance of Word and Spirit, we are indeed on the way to truth and life.

Christian thought means making the way of Christ intelligible, both theoretically and practically. It means living a life that embodies the

Word in the power of the Spirit in such a way that it is able to meet, and pass, the critical tests of human reflection and human existence. It means being able to pass the greatest test of all: the test of time. Endurance may well be one of the most important criteria for truth. Even the Son of Man had to suffer before entering into his glory. God has staked his truth claim in the same manner that we must stake ours: the way of the bold yet humble witness.

Is the above a charter for autonomous Christian individuals who think for themselves and walk their own way? Individuals are answerable, but not autonomous, agents. I have argued that Christian thinking is characterized by humility: an acceptance of, and dedicated service to, a wisdom greater than our own. Moreover, if we are to be holistic, we must relate the life of the mind to the distinctive qualities of Christian life in general: obedience, thanksgiving, joy. The joyful Christian plays without ceasing: not the postmodern game of arbitrary juxtaposition (which drains our words and acts of significance), but the dramatic play of the gospel, in which we participate in the joy of the Christian mythos. For the darkened cruciform way of Jesus Christ is only the penultimate stage of the journey; the road ultimately opens onto a clearing lit by resurrection brightness. That light is already beginning to shine, and not in the mind only. The Christian thinker is at the service of a joyful company of pilgrim-players who not only walk the way of Jesus Christ but embody and perform it, creating parables of the kingdom wherever two or three are gathered in Jesus's name.

Summary of Theses

1. Postmodernity is the condition of being fully aware of one's situatedness, and hence of one's contingency and deconstructibility.
2. Christians can and should learn something from postmodernity, namely, the criticism of isms.
3. Christians must not "correlate" with postmodernity or let concerns and frameworks other than Christ and canon determine faith's credenda and agenda.
4. Christian thought is faith seeking understanding and thus specifically Christian, that is, biblical and trinitarian.
5. Postmodernity has not discovered anything that was not already available, at least implicitly, in Christian scripture and tradition.
6. Thinking in a distinctly Christian way means thinking out of the mythopoetic framework of scripture (e.g., in terms of creation, fall, redemption, and consummation).

7. Christian faith is realist but insists that some truths can adequately be grasped only by means of a plurality of vocabularies or conceptual schemes oriented to different levels or aspects of reality.

8. The aim of Christian thinking about the true, the good, and the beautiful is wisdom, the ability to participate rightly in reality; the norm for Christian thinking about the true, the good, and the beautiful is the wisdom of God reflected in the face, and life, of Jesus Christ.

9. Christian thinking is one (holistic, integrative, imaginative), holy (distinct, virtuous, covenantal), catholic (demonstrating awareness of the length and breadth of the Christian tradition, philosophically eclectic), and apostolic (biblical, christocentric).

10. Modernity and postmodernity alike are ultimately digressions from the main subject, namely, the way of wisdom and of life summed up in Jesus Christ.

Notes

1. C. S. Lewis, *The Pilgrim's Regress: An Allegorical Apology for Christianity, Reason and Romanticism* (Grand Rapids: Eerdmans, 1981).

2. Ibid., p. 206.

3. My dispute with postmodernity is actually somewhat more complex. While I concede much of the postmodern discourse on situatedness and the limits of language and thought, I see this as making only a penultimate point inasmuch as it describes the human situation *apart from the Christian contention that God has spoken and acted in the world.* Hence, postmodernity says both too little and too much: too little, because apart from Christian assumptions, reason, history, hope, and values are left hanging over the abyss; too much, because postmoderns typically insist that the limits of the human situation are intractable, thus claiming to know more than they actually can. In short: my dispute with postmodernity is *ex post facto revelatio:* after the fact of Christian revelation.

4. See my "Theology and the Condition of Postmodernity: A Report on Knowledge (of God)," in *The Cambridge Companion to Postmodern Theology*, ed. Kevin J. Vanhoozer, pp. 3–25 (Cambridge University Press, 2003).

5. Reprinted in Lewis, *God in the Dock: Essays on Theology and Ethics* (Grand Rapids: Eerdmans, 1970), 271–77.

6. Ibid., 271.

7. Ibid., 273. Note that Lewis here anticipates the postmodern critique of patriarchy!

8. Ernest Becker, *The Birth and Death of Meaning*, cited in Walter Truett Anderson, ed., *The Truth about the Truth: De-confusing and Re-constructing the Postmodern World* (New York: Penguin/Putnam, 1995), 359. Editor's note: There is a summary of the theses presented in this essay, located at the end of the chapter, just before the endnotes.

9. "Philosophy" has typically been the discourse that focuses on addressing the enduring conceptual problems of language and life, for example, "What is truth?" and "What is time?" Postmodern philosophers too address these questions and either give new answers or explain why the question cannot be an-

swered. As an academic discipline, "philosophy" also refers to certain tools and practices (e.g., conceptual analysis) that are more diagnostic than prescriptive. The present essay deals primarily with the former aspect.

10. Walter Truett Anderson, "Introduction: What's Going on Here?" in Anderson, *Truth about the Truth*, 7.

11. Copernicus's original revolution was to suggest that the earth orbits the sun, rather than vice versa. Kant compared this revolution to his own proposal that objects conform to the categories of the mind rather than vice versa. Ricoeur's "second Copernican revolution" contends that human subjectivity is not self-constituting but is itself dependent on a poetic word—symbol, story—that precedes it. What I am calling the third, properly postmodern, Copernican revolution puts into question this poetic word, as previous revolutions had called objectivity and subjectivity respectively into question.

12. See Fergus Kerr, *Theology after Wittgenstein* (Oxford: Basil Blackwell, 1988).

13. Nancey Murphy and Brad Kallenberg, "Anglo-American Postmodernity: A Theology of Communal Practice," in Kevin J. Vanhoozer, ed., *Cambridge Companion to Postmodern Theology*, 32.

14. Richard Rorty, "Realism, Categories, and the 'Linguistic Turn,'" *International Philosophical Quarterly* 2 (1962): 310.

15. Richard Rorty, *Contingency, Irony, and Solidarity* (Cambridge: Cambridge University Press, 1989), 73. Interestingly, the one exception Rorty makes to this rule is human suffering. As Christians, we might agree with this sentiment, but we maintain that it applies before all else to the suffering of Christ. Christian faith is based on the distinctly nonironic passion narratives of Jesus.

16. Rorty follows William James in viewing "the true" as "expedient belief" in *Philosophy and Social Hope* (London: Penguin, 1999), xvi.

17. Rorty, "Realism, Categories, and the 'Linguistic Turn,'" 310.

18. Intriguingly, God uses Cyrus even though Cyrus is unaware of it; indeed, Cyrus is actually called God's anointed (Messiah) in Isaiah 45:1.

19. See thesis 5 below.

20. Cf. my *Is There a Meaning in This Text?* (Grand Rapids: Zondervan, 1998), 38–40.

21. Bruce E. Benson, *Graven Ideologies: Nietzsche, Derrida & Marion on Modern Idolatry* (Downers Grove, IL: InterVarsity Press, 2002).

22. In fact, there have been such attempts, by Kierkegaard, Barth, Plantinga, and Wolterstorff, among others.

23. Robert Stam, *Film Theory: An Introduction* (Malden, MA: Blackwell, 2000), 299.

24. "Theology and the Many Faces of Postmodernity," *Theology Today* 51 (1994): 108.

25. Three examples: Derrida speaks of justice as "beyond" deconstruction; Marion speaks of the "gift" of God's self-revelation that is "beyond" economies of exchange; a number of biblical scholars now speak of a theological interpretation of scripture that is "beyond" typical forms of biblical criticism. If there is a faith proper to postmodernity, it is this: a faith in these "impossibilities"—impossible, that is, in terms of modern forms of thinking.

26. Murphy and Kallenberg, "Anglo-American Postmodernity," 40.

27. See, in this regard, Richard Bauckham, *God Crucified: Monotheism and Christology in the New Testament* (Grand Rapids: Eerdmans, 1998).

28. From "Advice to Christian Philosophers," inaugural lecture to the John A. O'Brien Chair of Philosophy at the University of Notre Dame on Nov. 4, 1983.

I have tried to follow Plantinga's advice with regard to the question of textual meaning in my *Is There a Meaning in This Text?*

29. This law has practical ramifications too: it rules out the church growth movement that seeks to "correlate" styles of worship with what the audience/consumer/seeker wants.

30. See Hans Frei, *Types of Christian Theology* (New Haven: Yale University Press, 1992), ch. 3.

31. *Extratextual* refers to those readings where the Bible is interpreted in terms of some framework derived from elsewhere than the biblical text. The "world" thus explains the "Word" rather than vice versa.

32. I argue below that scripture and Christian theology afford new insights into the nature of language as a covenantal medium through which humans can engage God, others, and the world.

33. Lewis, "Myth Became Fact," *God in the Dock*, 66.

34. Of course, what is actually tested is not simply the reliability of the maps themselves but our *reading* of them.

35. See, for example, W. Jay Wood, *Epistemology: Becoming Intellectually Virtuous* (Downers Grove, IL: InterVarsity Press, 1998), and Linda T. Zagzebski, *Virtues of the Mind* (Cambridge: Cambridge University Press, 1996).

36. Cited in Anderson, *Truth about Truth*, 100.

37. Something similar may pertain to the experience of coming to faith.

38. Frank Farrell, *Subjectivity, Realism, and Postmodernism: The Recovery of the World* (Cambridge: Cambridge University Press, 1994), 129.

39. The Bible, on my view, is similarly a unified atlas composed of a variety of different kinds of maps or literary genres.

40. Reinhard Hütter, *Suffering Divine Things: Theology as Church Practice* (Grand Rapids: Eerdmans, 2000), 77–78.

41. Benson, *Graven Ideologies*, 236.

42. Richard Harries, *Art and the Beauty of God: A Christian Understanding* (London and New York: Mowbray, 1993), 106.

43. For a fuller presentation of doctrine as "direction for fitting participation in the drama of redemption," see my *The Drama of Doctrine: A Canonical-Linguistic Approach to Theology* (Louisville: Westminster/John Knox, 2005).

44. For a fuller exposition of the ideas presented here, see my "From Speech Acts to Scripture Acts: The Covenant of Discourse and the Discourse of the Covenant," in *First Theology: God, Scriptures, & Hermeneutics* (Downers Grove, IL: InterVarsity Press, 2002), 159–203.

45. Interestingly, Murphy observes that holism is an intellectual strategy that is "essential for an understanding of language, the justification of knowledge claims, the relation between individuals and society, and, finally, the relations among the sciences" and goes on to suggest that it is the quintessential mark of postmodern thinking (Murphy and Kallenberg, "Anglo-American Postmodernity," 35).

46. Cf Polanyi, *Personal Knowledge: Towards a Post-Critical Philosophy* (Chicago: University of Chicago Press, 1962). See also Colin Gunton: "Knowledge of the Other Is Mediated by All the Five Senses," in his *A Brief Theology of Revelation* (Edinburgh: T & T Clark, 1995), 22–23.

47. Lamin Sanneh, *Translating the Message: The Missionary Impact on Culture* (Maryknoll, NY: Orbis, 1989); Andrew Walls, *The Missionary Movement in Christian History: Studies in the Transmission of Faith* (Maryknoll, NY: Orbis, 1996), esp. ch. 3. Note that Walls ultimately bases his faith in the possibility of translation on God's prior act of translation: the Incarnation.

48. As some maps are more helpful and reliable than others, so too with schools of philosophy. The point is that the Christian thinker may employ any number of such maps, provided that they are compatible with scripture, the canonical atlas: just those maps that enjoy epistemic primacy.

49. David Tracy, "Theology and the Many Faces of Postmodernity," *Theology Today* 51 (1994), 107.

50. Dorothy L. Sayers, *Christian Letters to a Post-Christian World* (Grand Rapids: Eerdmans, 1969), 152.

4

Christian Faith and Postmodern Theory: Theology and the Nonfoundationalist Turn

John R. Franke

As we enter into the twenty-first century, the discipline of Christian theology is in a state of transition and ferment brought about by the breakdown of the assumptions of the modern world spawned by the Enlightenment. This breakdown has given rise to the emergence of postmodern theory, with its withering critique of the modern, scientific quest for certain, objective, and universal knowledge and its attempt to engage in new forms of discourse in the aftermath of modernity's demise. However, this situation is not restricted by any means to the discipline of theology. One observer notes that when we survey "the panorama of contemporary thought it is evident in field after field, in discipline after discipline, that a significant critique of modernity has arisen along with a discussion of a paradigm change. The upshot is that the kind of change under discussion is not incremental or piecemeal, but structural and thoroughgoing."[1]

One common response among Christian thinkers to the emergence of postmodern thought has been to view it primarily as a threat to Christian faith. Catholic theologian Richard John Neuhaus sums up the reaction of many to postmodernity by connecting it with relativism and subjectivism and calling it the enemy of basic thinking about moral truth.[2] This sort of response has been characteristic of thinkers across the theological spectrum. At the heart of this critique is the consistent identification of postmodern thought with relativism and nihilism. In this conception postmodernism is viewed as fundamentally antithetical to Christian faith. Merold Westphal comments that at "varying degrees along a spectrum that runs from mildly allergic to wildly apoplectic" many Christian thinkers "are inclined to see postmodernism as nothing but warmed-over Nietzschean atheism, frequently on the short list of the most dangerous anti-Christian currents of thought as an epistemological relativism that leads ineluctably to moral nihilism. Anything goes."[3] This view has been particularly characteristic among evangelicals, who, according to Mark McLeod, "tend to think that postmodernism opposes the truth, and in particular, the absolute truth of the gospel."[4] In contrast, this essay will focus on the promise of postmodern theory, particularly with respect to the nonfoundationalist turn, for the task of Christian theology.

The Postmodern Situation

The introduction of postmodern theory at this stage raises the question as to the proper conception of the postmodern situation. It is important to realize that a precise understanding of postmodernity is notoriously difficult to pin down. Despite the fact that there is no consensus concerning the meaning of the term, it has become almost a commonplace to refer to the contemporary cultural situation as postmodern. The lack of clarity about the term has been magnified by the vast array of interpreters who have attempted to comprehend and appropriate postmodern thought. Paul Lakeland observes that there are "probably a thousand different self-appointed commentators on the postmodern phenomenon and bewildering discrepancies between the ways many of these authors understand the term *postmodern* and its cognates."[5] In the context of this lack of clarity about the postmodern phenomenon, the term has come to signify widely divergent hopes and concerns among those who are attempting to address the emerging cultural and intellectual shift implied by the term.

As we have already mentioned, one of the common tendencies has been to dismiss postmodernity as nothing more than nihilistic relativism. However, such an identification of postmodern thought is simply too narrow to do justice to the actual breadth of the phenomenon and fails to account for the many postmodern thinkers who do not pursue the more radical implications of poststructural and deconstructive thought. The Reformed epistemology of Alvin Plantinga and Nicholas Wolterstorff offers a vigorous defense and affirmation of truth as well as a telling critique of modernity.[6] Moreover, postanalytical philosophers such as Cornel West,[7] Jeffrey Stout,[8] and Hilary Putnam[9] provide extensive critiques of modernity and move in postmodern directions. In ethics, the constructive communitarian approach of Alasdair MacIntyre may be called postmodern.[10] Thomas Kuhn[11] and Stephen Toulmin[12] have sought to develop contextual, postmodern approaches to the philosophy of science. In theology, the postliberalism associated with Hans Frei[13] and George Lindbeck[14] is indebted to postmodern theory and the later work of Wittgenstein.[15] Given the variety of intellectual endeavor that may be described as postmodern, we must conclude that postmodern thought cannot be narrowly associated with only a few select interpreters. The breadth of postmodern thought suggested by the few examples offered here raises the question as to what gives unity and cohesion to postmodern thought. Dan Stiver points out that we should not expect postmodernism to be characterized by a tight conformity to particular categories and patterns of thought. He reminds us that we "use terms like analytic philosophy, existentialism, phenomenology, structuralism, process philosophy, and pragmatism with meaning but also with awareness that it is notoriously difficult to come up with demarcation criteria that will tell us in any and every case who is and is not in the pertinent group. Postmodernism is that kind of term."[16]

This situation presses the question as to whether any similarity can be found within the diversity of postmodern thought so as to make sense of the movement, while moving beyond the narrow understanding that sees it only as a synonym for radically deconstructive relativism. To address this circumstance it will be helpful to see postmodernism as a label that identifies an ongoing paradigm shift in Western culture. Almost without exception, those who are engaged in the pursuit of this paradigm shift use the term *postmodern*. This engagement generally involves the vigorous critique of the modern paradigm and some general and tentative suggestions concerning the shape of an alternative. This observation enables us to suggest a basic, minimalist understanding of *postmodernism* as referring primarily to the rejection of the central features of modernity, such as its quest for certain, objective, and universal knowledge, along with its dualism and its assumption of the inherent goodness of knowledge. It is this critical agenda, rather than any proposed constructive paradigm to replace the modern vision, that unites postmodern thinkers. Nancey Murphy employs the term *postmodern* to describe emerging patterns of thought and to "indicate their radical break from the thought patterns of Enlightened modernity."[17] As Diogenes Allen puts it, postmodern thought is discourse in the aftermath of modernity.[18]

This broad construal of postmodern thought as a critique and rejection of modernity leads to a central dimension of postmodern theory that is particularly significant. At the heart of the postmodern ethos is the attempt to rethink the nature of rationality in the wake of the modern project. This rethinking has resulted not in irrationality, as is often claimed by less informed opponents of postmodern thought, but rather in numerous redescriptions and proposals concerning appropriate construals of rationality and knowledge after modernity. In spite of their variety, these attempts can be broadly classified as producing a chastened rationality that is more inherently self-critical than the constructions of rationality common in the thought-forms of modernity.[19]

Several common features serve to distinguish this chastened rationality from the modernist conceptions it seeks to replace. Chastened rationality is marked by the transition from a realist to a constructionist view of truth and the world.[20] Postmodern thinkers maintain that humans do not view the world from an objective vantage point but structure their world through the concepts they bring to it, such as language. Human languages function as social conventions that describe the world in a variety of ways depending on the context of the speaker. No simple, one-to-one relationship exists between language and the world, and thus no single linguistic description can serve to provide an objective conception of the "real" world. Chastened rationality is also manifest in the "loss of the metanarrative" and the advent of "local" stories. Postmodern thinkers assert that the all-encompassing narratives of scientific progress that shaped and legitimated modern society have lost their credibility and power. Further, they maintain that the very idea of the metanarrative is no longer credible.[21] This is not to suggest that narratives no longer function in the postmodern context. Rather, the narratives that give shape to the postmodern ethos are local rather than universal. Above all, however, the chastened rationality of post- modernity entails the rejection of epistemological foundationalism and the adoption of a nonfoundationalist and contextual approach to the theological enterprise. The centrality of this approach to the concerns of postmodern theory gives rise to the assertion that postmodern theology is nonfoundationalist theology. With this in mind we will now turn our attention to the case for such an approach to theology before offering a brief construal of its formal principles.

The Case for a Nonfoundationalist Theology

In the modern era, the pursuit of knowledge was deeply influenced by Enlightenment foundationalism. In its broadest sense, foundationalism is merely the acknowledgment that not all beliefs are of equal signifi- cance in the structure of knowledge. Some beliefs are more "basic" or "foundational" and serve to give support to other beliefs that are derived from them. Understood in this way, nearly every thinker is in some sense a foundationalist, rendering such a description unhelpful in grasping the range of opinion in epistemological theory found among contemporary thinkers. However, in philosophical circles foundationalism refers to a much stronger epistemological stance than is entailed in this general observation about how beliefs intersect. At the heart of the foundationalist agenda is the desire to overcome the uncertainty generated by the tendency of fallible human beings to error and the inevitable disagreements and controversies that follow. Foundationalists are convinced that the only way to solve this problem is to find some means of grounding the entire edifice of human knowledge on invincible certainty.

This quest for complete epistemological certitude, often termed "strong" or "classical" foundationalism, has its philosophical beginnings in the thought of the philosopher René Descartes. Descartes sought to reconstruct the nature of knowledge by rejecting traditional medieval or "premodern" notions of authority and replacing them with the modern conception of indubitable beliefs that are accessible to all individuals. This conception of knowledge became the dominant assumption of intellectual pursuit in the modern era. In terms of a philosophical conception of knowledge, foundationalism is a theory concerned with the justification of knowledge. It maintains that beliefs must be justified by their relationship to other beliefs and that the chain of justifications that results from this procedure must not be circular or endless, but must have a terminus in foundational beliefs that are immune from criticism and cannot be called into question. The goal to be attained through the identification of indubitable foundations is a universal knowledge that transcends time and context. In keeping with this pursuit, the ideals of human knowledge since Descartes have tended to focus on the universal, the general, and the theoretical rather than on the local, the particular, and the practical.

In spite of the hegemony of this approach to knowledge, Nancey Murphy notes that it is "only recently that philosophers have labeled the modern foundationalist theory of knowledge as such."[22] This means that while this approach to knowledge has been widely influential in intellectual thought, it has been assumed by modern thinkers rather than explicitly advocated and defended. In light of this Murphy suggests two criteria in the identification of foundationalism: "first, the assumption that knowledge systems must include a class of beliefs that are somehow immune from challenge; and second, the assumption that all reasoning within the system proceeds in one direction only—from that set of special, indubitable beliefs to others, but not the reverse."[23] The goal of this foundationalist agenda is the discovery of an approach to knowledge that will provide rational human beings with absolute, incontestable certainty regarding the truthfulness of their beliefs. The Enlightenment epistemological foundation consists of a set of incontestable beliefs or of unassailable first principles on the basis of which the pursuit of knowledge can proceed. These basic beliefs or first principles must be universal, objective, and discernable to any rational person apart from the particulars of varied situations, experiences, and contexts.[24]

This conception of knowledge came to dominate the discipline of theology as theologians reshaped their construals of the Christian faith in accordance with its dictates. In the nineteenth and twentieth centuries, the foundationalist impulse produced a theological division in the Anglo-American context between the "left" and the "right." Liberals constructed theology upon the foundation of an unassailable religious experience, whereas conservatives looked to an error-free Bible as the incontrovertible foundation of their theology.[25] It is interesting to note that, for all their differences, both groups were drawing from commonly held foundationalist conceptions of knowledge. In other words, liberal and conservative theologians can often be viewed as working out theological details from two different sides of the same modernist, foundationalist coin.

In the postmodern context, however, foundationalism is in dramatic retreat, as its assertions about the objectivity, certainty, and universality of knowledge have come under fierce criticism.[26] Merold Westphal observes, "That it is philosophically indefensible is so widely agreed that its demise is the closest thing to a philosophical consensus in decades."[27] J. Wentzel van Huyssteen agrees: "Whatever notion of postmodernity we eventually opt for, all postmodern thinkers see the modernist quest for certainty, and the accompanying program of laying foundations for our knowledge, as a dream for the impossible, a contemporary version of the quest for the Holy Grail."[28] And Nicholas Wolterstorff offers this stark conclusion: "On all fronts foundationalism is in bad shape. It seems to me there is nothing to do but give it up for mortally ill and learn to live in its absence."[29] The heart of the postmodern quest for a chastened rationality lies in the rejection of the foundationalist approach to knowledge.

Postmodern theory raises two related but distinct questions to the modern foundationalist enterprise. First, is such an approach to knowledge *possible?* And second, is it *desirable?* These questions are connected with what may be viewed as the two major branches of postmodern hermeneutical philosophy: the hermeneutics of finitude and the hermeneutics of suspicion. However, the challenges to foundationalism not only are philosophical, but also emerge from the context of Christian theology. Merold Westphal suggests that postmodern theory, with respect to hermeneutical philosophy, may be properly appropriated for the task of explicitly Christian thought on theological grounds: "The hermeneutics of finitude is a meditation on the meaning of human createdness, and the hermeneutics of suspicion is a meditation on the meaning of human fallenness."[30] In other words, many of the concerns of postmodern theory can be appropriated and fruitfully developed in the context of the Christian doctrines of creation and sin. Viewed from this perspective, the questions that are raised by postmodern thought concerning the possibility and desirability of foundationalism are also questions that emerge from the material content of Christian theology. They both lead to similar conclusions. First, modern foundationalism is an impossible dream for finite human beings, whose outlooks are always limited and shaped by the particular contexts from which they emerge. Second, the modern foundationalist emphasis on the inherent goodness of knowledge is shattered by the fallen and sinful nature of human beings, who desire to seize control of the epistemic process in order to empower themselves and further their own ends, often at the expense of others. The limitations of finitude and the flawed condition of human nature mean that epistemic foundationalism is neither possible nor desirable for created and sinful persons. This double critique of foundationalism, emerging as it does from the perspectives of both postmodern philosophy and Christian theology, suggests the appropriateness and suitability, given the current intellectual situation, of the language of nonfoundationalism as descriptive of an approach to the task of theology that is both postmodern and faithful to the Christian tradition.

A nonfoundationalist or antifoundationalist approach to knowledge does not demand that knowledge systems include a class of beliefs that are immune from criticism; rather, all beliefs are subject to critical scrutiny. It also maintains that reasoning within the system proceeds not in only one direction, but rather moves conversationally in multiple directions. This suggests a metaphorical shift in our understanding of the structure of knowledge from that of a building with a sure foundation to something like a web of interrelated, interdependent beliefs.[31] Further, the ideals of human knowledge in nonfoundational and contextual approaches place emphasis on the local, the particular, and the practical rather than on the universal, the general, and the theoretical. According to William Stacy Johnson, nonfoundationalist approaches to theology "share a common goal of putting aside all appeals to presumed self-evident, non-inferential, or incorrigible grounds for their intellectual claims."[32] They reject the notion that among the many beliefs that make up a particular theology there must be a single irrefutable foundation that is immune to criticism and provides the certain basis upon which all other assertions are founded. In nonfoundationalist theology all beliefs are open to criticism and reconstruction. This does not mean, as is sometimes alleged, that nonfoundationalists cannot make assertions or maintain strong convictions that may be vigorously defended. As Francis

Schüssler Fiorenza says, to engage in nonfoundationalist theology is to accept that "it is a self-correcting enterprise that examines all claims, all relevant background theories" without demanding that these be completely abandoned all at once.[33] Nonfoundationalist theology does not eschew convictions; it simply maintains that such convictions, even the most longstanding and dear, are subject to critical scrutiny and therefore potentially to revision, reconstruction, or even rejection.

The adoption of a nonfoundationalist approach to theological method has raised concerns for many who see the abandonment of foundationalism as little more than a potential (or actual) slide down the proverbial "slippery slope" into nihilistic relativism.[34] We will touch on this concern at a later point. At this stage, let us note that one of the significant benefits of a nonfoundationalist theology is its inherent commitment to contextuality that requires the opening of theological conversation to the voices of persons and communities who have generally been excluded from the discourse of Anglo-American theology. It maintains without reservation that no single human perspective, be it that of an individual or a particular community or theological tradition, is adequate to do full justice to the truth of God's revelation in Christ. Richard Mouw points to this issue as one of his own motivations for reflecting seriously about postmodern themes: "As many Christians from other parts of the world challenge our 'North Atlantic' theologies, they too ask us to think critically about our own cultural location, as well as about how we have sometimes blurred the boundaries between what is essential to the Christian message and the doctrine and frameworks we have borrowed from various Western philosophical traditions."[35] The adoption of a nonfoundationalist approach to theology mandates a critical awareness of the role of culture and social location in the process of theological interpretation and construction. From the perspective of the ecumenically orthodox Christian tradition, nonfoundationalist theology seeks to nurture an open and flexible theology that is in keeping with the local and contextual character of human knowledge while remaining thoroughly and distinctly Christian.

The Shape of a Nonfoundationalist Theology

A theology that seeks to take seriously postmodern and nonfoundationalist sensitivities views itself as conversation. This constructive theological conversation involves the interplay of three sources: scripture, culture, and tradition. We will now turn our attention to the role of each in theological construction, focusing on the work of the Spirit in order to develop a nonfoundationalist and contextual approach to theology by means of a thoroughly pneumatological theological method.[36] While the Christian tradition has been characterized by its commitment to the authority of the Bible, much debate has been engendered in the church as to the precise way in which its authority ought to be construed. This leads us to consider how the Bible ought to function in theology by pursuing the traditional assertion that scripture is theology's "norming norm." By this we mean that among the various sources involved in the shaping of theological judgments and conclusions, scripture functions as the norm, or authority, with no other norm over it; hence, it is theology's norming norm. By way of contrast, the Christian tradition also functions in theology as a norm, but always as a "normed norm." Some theological conclusions and interpretations of scripture that have emerged in the history of the Christian tradition have been accorded authoritative status by the Christian community. However, their authority, as normed norms, is dependent on their congruity with scripture, the norming norm.

The point of departure for this affirmation of scripture as norming norm lies in the Protestant principle of authority articulated in confessions such as the Westminster Confession of Faith, which states: "The Supreme Judge by which all controversies of religion are to be determined, and all decrees of counsels, opinions of ancient writers, doctrines of men, and private spirits, are to be examined, and in whose sentence we are to rest, can be no other than the Holy Spirit speaking in the Scripture."[37] This statement reflects the Protestant concern to bind Word and Spirit together as a means of providing the conceptual framework for authority in the Christian faith and brings into focus the sense in which the Bible is viewed as norming norm: scripture holds this position because it is the instrumentality of the Spirit. The Bible is the instrumentality of the Spirit in that the Spirit appropriates the biblical text in order to speak to the church for the purpose of creating a "world" that finds its coherence in Jesus Christ. As Walter Brueggemann maintains, the biblical text "has generative power to summon and evoke new life" and holds out an eschatological vision that "anticipates and summons realities that live beyond the conventions of our day-to-day, take-for-granted world."[38] This points to the capacity of the text to speak beyond the context in which it was originally composed. In short, as John Goldingay declares, the text "calls a new world into being."[39] However, the point that needs to be stressed here is that this capacity for world construction, while bound closely to the text, does not lie in the text itself. Instead, this result is ultimately the work of the Spirit speaking through the text as the instrumentality of world creation. Further, the world the Spirit creates is not simply the world surrounding the ancient text or the contemporary world, but rather the eschatological world God intends for creation as disclosed, displayed, and anticipated by the text.

While the ultimate authority in the church is the Spirit speaking in and through scripture, this speaking always comes to its hearers within a specific social, historical context. This points to the role of culture in theology. The specificity of the Spirit's speaking means that the conversation with culture and cultural context is crucial to the theological task. Because theology must be in touch with life in the midst of present circumstances, the questions, concerns, and challenges it brings to the scriptures are not necessarily identical with those of contemporary exegetes or even the ancient writers themselves. Douglas John Hall states that what theology seeks "from its ongoing discourse with the biblical text is determined in large measure by its worldly context," in order that it might address that setting from "the perspective of faith in the God of Abraham, Isaac, and Jacob."[40]

In addition to listening for the voice of the Spirit speaking through scripture, theology must also be attentive to the voice of the Spirit speaking through culture. While Western theology has tended to focus on the church as the sole repository of all truth and the only location in which the Spirit is operative, scripture appears to suggest a much broader understanding of the Spirit's presence, a presence connected to the Spirit's role as the life-giver. The biblical writers speak of the Spirit's role in creating and sustaining life as well as enabling it to flourish. Because the life-giving Creator Spirit is present in the flourishing of life, the Spirit's voice resounds through many media, including the media of human culture. Because Spirit-induced human flourishing evokes cultural expression, we can anticipate in such expressions traces of the Spirit's creative and sustaining presence. Consequently, theology should be alert to the voice of the Spirit manifest in the artifacts and symbols of human culture. However, it should be added that the speaking of the Spirit through the various media of culture never comes as a speaking against the text. Setting the Spirit's voice in culture against the text is to follow the foundationalist agenda and elevate some dimension of contemporary experience or thought as a criterion for accepting or rejecting aspects of the biblical witness. Darrell Jodock notes this danger: "The problem here is not that one's world view or experience influences one's reading of the text, because that is inescapable. The problem is instead that the text is made to conform to the world view of codified experience and thereby loses its integrity and its ability to challenge and confront our present priorities, including even our most noble aspirations."[41]

Therefore, while being ready to acknowledge the Spirit's voice wherever it may be found, we must still uphold the primacy of the text as theology's norming norm. While we cannot hear the Spirit speaking through the text except by listening within a particular social-historical setting, the Spirit speaking through scripture provides the normative context for hearing the Spirit in culture. Having said this, it must be affirmed that the speaking of the Spirit through scripture and through culture does not constitute two different communicative acts, but rather one unified speaking. Consequently, theology must listen for the voice of the Spirit who speaks normatively through scripture, but also particularly in the variegated circumstances of diverse human cultures.[42]

Scripture, theology's norming norm, is always in conversation with culture, theology's embedding context. In this way the Spirit continually speaks to the believing community in its present situation through the witness of scripture to the paradigmatic events of God's revelation in Jesus Christ as a means of providing ongoing guidance for the church as it grapples with constantly changing circumstances. This raises implicitly the question of the role of the Christian tradition, as the historical witness to the speaking of the Spirit, in the task of contemporary theological construction. A nonfoundationalist conception views the tradition of the church above all as the hermeneutical trajectory in the context of which the theological task of the community is pursued. From this perspective the Christian tradition provides a hermeneutical trajectory for theology that is open-ended, eschatologically directed, and performatively operative.

A helpful distinction may be drawn between "open" and "closed" confessional traditions. Closed traditions hold a particular statement of beliefs to be adequate for all times and places. In contrast, an open tradition, in the words of Jack Stotts, "anticipates that what has been confessed in a formally adopted confession takes its place in a confessional lineup, preceded by statements from the past and expectant of more to come as times and circumstances change."[43] An open confessional tradition understands its obligation to develop and adopt new confessions in accordance with shifting circumstances. Although such confessions are "extraordinarily important" for the integrity, identity, and faithfulness of the church, "they are also acknowledged to be relative to particular times and places."[44] Throughout the course of the ebb and flow of the history of the church the Spirit is at work completing the divine program and bringing the people of God as a community into a fuller comprehension of the implications of the gospel. This activity of the Spirit will reach consummation only in the eschatological future. Until then the church must grapple with the meaning and implications of the biblical message for its context as it listens patiently and expectantly for the voice of the Spirit speaking afresh through scripture and yet in continuity with the Spirit-guided trajectory of Christian tradition.

This ongoing dynamic and eschatological orientation that characterizes the nature of the Christian tradition is summarized by Gabriel Fackre: "The circle of tradition is not closed, for the Spirit's ecclesial Work is not done. Traditional doctrine develops as Christ and the Gospel are viewed in ever fresh perspective. Old formulations are corrected, and what is passed on is enriched. The open-endedness, however, does not overthrow the ancient landmarks. As tradition is a gift of the Spirit, its trajectory moves in the right direction, although it has not arrived at its destination."[45] In short, at the heart of tradition and of the role of tradition in theology is the eschatological directedness of the Spirit's work in guiding the community of faith into the purposes and intentions of God, which constitute a divinely given *telos* that is ultimately realized only at the consummation. The eschatological-directedness of the community as a whole gives a similar character to the theological reflection that becomes church tradition.

Another aspect of the function of tradition as hermeneutical trajectory emerges through the metaphor of performance.[46] Tradition provides an interpretive context for the task of living out or "performing" the deepest intentions of an established, historical community. The purpose of theology is to facilitate and enable authentic "performance" of the Christian faith by the community of Christ's disciples in its various cultural locations. Tradition provides an essential component in this process. Like the performance of a symphony that has only one score but many possible interpretations, so the text of scripture has been subject to numerous interpretations over the centuries. While the score of the symphony is authoritative, it demands performance in order to realize the intention for which it was produced, and performance requires interpretation. However, not all interpretations have equal integrity; some are too radical or idiosyncratic. Determinations as to the legitimacy or illegitimacy of particular interpretations and performances emerge in the context of tradition. Frances Young offers a helpful perspective on the performative metaphor. She writes, "For classic performance, tradition is indispensable. A creative artist will certainly bring something inspired to the job, but an entirely novel performance would not be a rendering of the classic work. Traditions about appropriate speed and dynamics are passed from master (or mistress) to pupil, from one generation to another, and a radical performance will be deliberate reaction against those traditions if it violates them."[47] The tradition of the Christian community functions in much the same manner. It establishes a context for authentic interpretation and performance of the biblical message and its implications, which allows for creativity in addressing new situations while providing a basis for identifying interpretation that is not consonant with the historic position of the community.[48]

N. T. Wright suggests a model of biblical authority that moves along similar lines.[49] He uses the analogy of a five-act Shakespeare play in which the first four acts are extant, but the fifth has been lost. In this model the performance of the fifth act would be facilitated not by the writing of a script that "would freeze the play into one form" but by the recruitment of "highly trained, sensitive, and experienced Shakespearean actors" who would immerse themselves in the first four acts and then be told *to work out a fifth act for themselves*."[50] The first four acts would serve as the "authority" for the play, but not in the sense of demanding that the actors "should repeat the earlier parts of the play over and over again." Instead, the authority of these extant acts would consist in the fact of an "as yet unfinished drama, which contained its own impetus, its own forward movement, which demanded to be concluded in the proper manner but which required of the actors a responsible entering in to the story as it stood, in order to first understand how the threads could appropriately be drawn together, and then to put that understanding into effect by speaking and acting with both *innovation* and *consistency*."[51] Wright then suggests that this model closely corresponds to the pattern of the biblical narratives. Such a model brings the role of Christian tradition in the task of theology into sharp relief. A key component of Wright's model, although not one he emphasizes, is the role of tradition. His actors were not only immersed in the first acts of the play, the textual authority, but also in the Shakespearean interpretive *tradition*, which also functions in an authoritative fashion in the performance of the final act. In this conception, the Christian tradition provides a spiritually animated, historically extended, and socially embodied context in which to interpret, apply, and live out the communally formative narratives contained in the canonical texts.

Conclusion: Nonfoundationalist Theology and "Foundations"

This nonfoundationalist conception envisions theology as an ongoing conversation between scripture, tradition, and culture in which all three are vehicles of the one Spirit through which the Spirit speaks in order to create a distinctively Christian "world" centered on Jesus Christ in a variety of local settings. In this way theology is both one, in that all truly Christian theology seeks to hear and respond to the speaking of the one Spirit, and many, in that all theology emerges from particular social and historical situations. Such a theology is the product of the reflection of the Christian community in its local expressions. Despite its local character, such a theology is still in a certain sense global in that it seeks to explicate the Christian faith in accordance with the ecumenical tradition of the church throughout its history and on behalf of the church throughout the world.

Further, despite its particularity as specifically Christian theology, such a theology is also public and carries an implicit claim to be articulating a set of beliefs and practices that are "universal" in the only way that any claim to universality can be made, as the faith of a particular believing community. In this way, such a theology calls for a response beyond the confines of the particular community from which it emerges, and is set forth as a contribution to the wider public conversation about the nature of ultimate reality, meaning, and truth. As Kathryn Tanner explains, there is no reason to think that a specifically Christian context rules out theological claims that are universal in scope or that a Christian context means that theologians are discussing matters that concern only Christians. Instead, theologians seek to "proclaim truths with profound ramifications for the whole of human existence; that they do so from within a Christian cultural context simply means that the claims they make are shaped by that context and are put forward from a Christian point of view. Indeed, if, as an anthropologist would insist, assertions always show the influence of some cultural context or other, following a procedure like that is the only way that universal claims are ever made."[52]

We will conclude by responding to a question raised earlier. Does not such an approach finally amount to a theological relativism that allows for anything? We might first respond that no theological method can secure truth and that all is subject to distortion in the hands of finite and fallen human beings. A nonfoundationalist approach to theology seeks to respond positively and appropriately to the situatedness of all human thought and therefore to embrace a principled theological pluralism. It also attempts to affirm that the ultimate authority in the church is not a particular source, be it scripture, tradition, or culture but only the living God. Therefore, if we must speak of "foundations" for the Christian faith and its theological enterprise, then we must speak only of the triune God who is disclosed in polyphonic fashion through scripture, the church, and even the world, albeit always in accordance with the normative witness to divine self-disclosure contained in scripture. Put another way, nonfoundationalist theology means the end of foundationalism but not "foundations." However, these "foundations" are not "given" to human beings. As Bruce McCormack notes, they "always elude the grasp of the human attempt to know and to establish them from the human side," and they cannot be demonstrated or secured "philosophically or in any other way."[53] Hence, human beings are always in a position of dependence and in need of grace with respect to epistemic relations with God. Attempts on the part of humans to seize control of these relations are all too common throughout the history of the church and, no matter how well intentioned, inevitably lead to forms of oppression and conceptual idolatry. Nonfoundationalist theology seeks to oppose such seizure through the promotion of a form of theology and a theological ethos that humbly acknowledges the human condition of finitude and fallenness and that, by grace if at all, does not belie the subject of theology to which it seeks to bear faithful witness.

Notes

1. Dan R. Stiver, "The Uneasy Alliance between Evangelicalism and Post-modernism: A Reply to Anthony Thiselton," in *The Challenge of Postmodernism: An Evangelical Engagement*, ed. David Dockery (Wheaton: BridgePoint, 1995), 243.

2. Richard John Neuhaus, "A Voice in the Relativistic Wilderness," *Christianity Today*, February 7, 1994, 34.

3. Merold Westphal, *Overcoming Onto-theology: Toward a Postmodern Christian Faith* (New York: Fordham University Press, 2001), ix.

4. Mark McLeod, "Making God Dance: Postmodern Theorizing and the Christian College," *Christian Scholar's Review* 21, no. 3 (March 1992): 281.

5. Paul Lakeland, *Postmodernity: Christian Identity in a Fragmented Age* (Minneapolis: Fortress, 1997), ix–x.

6. Alvin Plantinga and Nicholas Wolterstorff, eds., *Faith and Rationality: Reason and Belief in God* (Notre Dame, IN: University of Notre Dame Press, 1983).

7. Cornel West, *Prophetic Thought in Postmodern Times* (Monroe, MN: Common Courage, 1993).

8. Jeffrey Stout, *Flight from Authority: Religion, Morality, and the Quest for Autonomy* (Notre Dame, IN: University of Notre Dame Press, 1981).

9. Hilary Putnam, *Reason, Truth, and History* (Cambridge: Cambridge University Press, 1981).

10. Alasdair MacIntyre, *Whose Justice? Which Rationality?* (Notre Dame, IN: University of Notre Dame Press, 1988).

11. Thomas Kuhn, *The Structure of Scientific Revolutions*, 2nd ed. (Chicago: University of Chicago Press, 1970).

12. Stephen Toulmin, *Cosmopolis: The Hidden Agenda of Modernity* (Chicago: University of Chicago Press, 1990).

13. Hans Frei, *The Eclipse of Biblical Narrative: A Study in Eighteenth and Nineteenth Century Hermeneutics* (New Haven: Yale University Press, 1974).

14. George Lindbeck, *The Nature of Doctrine: Religion and Theology in a Postliberal Age* (Philadelphia: Westminster, 1984).

15. Ludwig Wittgenstein, *Philosophical Investigations*, trans. G. E. M. Anscombe (New York: Macmillan, 1953). On the implications for theology of Wittgenstein's later writings, see especially the account of Fergus Kerr, *Theology after Wittgenstein*, 2nd ed. (London: SPCK, 1997).

16. Stiver, "Uneasy Alliance," 242.

17. Nancey Murphy, *Anglo-American Postmodernity: Philosophical Perspectives on Science, Religion, and Ethics* (Boulder, CO: Westview, 1997), 1.

18. Diogenes Allen, "The End of the Modern World," *Christian Scholar's Review* 22, no. 4 (June 1993): 341.

19. For a helpful discussion of this rethinking of rationality, see J. Wentzel van Huyssteen, *The Shaping of Rationality: Toward Interdisciplinarity in Theology and Science* (Grand Rapids: Eerdmans, 1999).

20. See, for example, Walter Truett Anderson, *Reality Isn't What It Used to Be: Theatrical Politics, Ready-to-Wear Religion, Global Myths, Primitive Chic, and Other Wonders of the Postmodern World* (San Francisco: Harper & Row, 1990).

21. Jean-François Lyotard, *The Postmodern Condition: A Report on Knowledge*, trans. Geoff Bennington and Brian Massumi (Minneapolis: University of Minnesota Press, 1984), xxiv.

22. Nancey Murphy, *Beyond Liberalism and Fundamentalism: How Modern and Postmodern Philosophy Set the Theological Agenda* (Valley Forge, PA: Trinity, 1996), 13.

23. Ibid., 13.

24. For a more detailed description of foundationalism, see W. Jay Wood, *Epistemology: Becoming Intellectually Virtuous* (Downers Grove, IL: InterVarsity Press, 1998), 77–104.

25. On this liberal/conservative debate concerning the proper foundation for theology, see Murphy, *Beyond Liberalism and Fundamentalism*, 11–35.

26. John E. Thiel, *Nonfoundationalism* (Minneapolis: Fortress, 1994), 37.

27. Merold Westphal, "A Reader's Guide to 'Reformed Epistemology,'" *Perspectives* 7, no. 9 (November 1992): 10–11.

28. J. Wentzel van Huyssteen, "Tradition and the Task of Theology," *Theology Today* 55, no. 2 (July 1998): 216.

29. Nicholas Wolterstorff, *Reason within the Bounds of Religion* (Grand Rapids: Eerdmans, 1976), 52.

30. Westphal, *Overcoming Onto-theology*, xx.

31. See, for example, Willard V. O. Quine and J. S. Ullian, *The Web of Belief* (New York: Random House, 1970).

32. William Stacy Johnson, *The Mystery of God: Karl Barth and the Postmodern Foundations of Theology* (Louisville: Westminster/John Knox, 1997), 3.

33. Francis Schüssler Fiorenza, *Foundational Theology: Jesus and the Church* (New York: Crossroad, 1986), 287.

34. See, for example, Douglas Groothuis, *Truth Decay: Defending Christianity Against the Challenges of Postmodernism* (Downers Grove, IL: InterVarsity Press, 2000).

35. Richard Mouw, "Delete the 'Post' from 'Postconservative,'" *Books & Culture* 7, no. 3 (May/June, 2001): 22.

36. For a more detailed discussion of the approach summarized here, see Stanley J. Grenz and John R. Franke, *Beyond Foundationalism: Shaping Theology in a Postmodern Context* (Louisville: Westminster/John Knox, 2001), 57–166.

37. The Westminster Confession of Faith, 1.10, in John H. Leith, ed., *The Creeds of the Churches*, 3rd ed. (Atlanta: John Knox, 1982), 196.

38. Walter Brueggemann, *Finally Comes the Poet* (Minneapolis: Fortress, 1989), 4–5.

39. John Goldingay, *Models for Scripture* (Grand Rapids: Eerdmans, 1994), 256.

40. Douglas John Hall, *Thinking the Faith: Christian Theology in a North American Context* (Minneapolis: Fortress, 1991), 263.

41. Darrell Jodock, "The Reciprocity between Scripture and Theology: The Role of Scripture in Contemporary Theological Reflection," *Interpretation* 44, no. 4 (October 1990): 377.

42. For an example of the interpretive plurality that such a model seeks to authorize theologically, see John R. Levison and Priscilla Pope-Levison, eds., *Return to Babel: Global Perspectives on the Bible* (Louisville: Westminster/John Knox, 1999).

43. Jack L. Stotts, "Introduction: Confessing after Barmen," in Jan Rohls, *Reformed Confessions: Theology from Zurich to Barmen*, trans. John Hoffmeyer (Louisville: Westminster/John Knox, 1998), xi.

44. Ibid.

45. Gabriel Fackre, *The Christian Story: A Narrative Interpretation of Basic Christian Doctrine*, 3rd ed. (Grand Rapids: Eerdmans, 1996), 18–9.

46. For the development of the metaphor of performance with respect to scripture and theology, see Frances Young, *The Art of Performance: Towards a Theology of Holy Scripture* (London: Darton, Longman and Todd, 1990).

47. Ibid., 45.

48. Ibid., 45–65.

49. N. T. Wright, "How Can the Bible Be Authoritative?" *Vox Evangelica* 21 (1991): 7–32.

50. Ibid., 18.

51. Ibid., 19.

52. Kathryn Tanner, *Theories of Culture: A New Agenda for Theology* (Minneapolis: Augsburg Fortress, 1997), 69.

53. Bruce L. McCormack, "What Has Basel to Do with Berlin? The Return of 'Church Dogmatics' in the Schleiermacherian Tradition," *Princeton Seminary Bulletin* 23, no. 2 (2002): 172.

5

A Little Story about Metanarratives: Lyotard, Religion, and Postmodernism Revisited

James K. A. Smith

The preoccupation with "the present"—our contemporaneity—that characterizes current philosophical discourse is not particularly new, though it is certainly a modern project whose origin is Kantian. Indeed, the posing of the question "What is Enlightenment?"[1] raised the tone of philosophy[2] to reflection on the present as a critical interrogation of "our time" and its significance: the question of what is happening, now. More than just an attempt to situate the present in relation to its past and future, Kant's question probes the meaning of the present and what it means to be "us"—to be here, now, contemporary. Arguing that Kant's essay "introduces a new type of question into the field of philosophical reflection," Foucault remarks that "with this text on the *Aufklärung* we see philosophy—and I don't think I'm exaggerating when I say that it is for the first time—problematizing its own discursive contemporaneity."[3] In modernity, philosophy has redoubled itself insofar as it has put modernity into question; in other words, this critical philosophy could be characterized as "the discourse of modernity on modernity."[4] Originating with modernity, the question of who we are becomes a question of our present, our "now."

While "we postmoderns" may have abandoned any "idea for a universal history from a cosmopolitan point of view," our preoccupation with naming the present betrays our modern filiation and Enlightenment genealogy. Though this original philosophical reflection on the present, encapsulated in the query "What is Enlightenment?" is, in *our* present, formulated as a different query—"What is postmodernism?"[5]—the questioning itself is modern. And so, to "we postmoderns," I might pronounce: "My fellow postmoderns, there are no postmoderns," insofar as our penchant to describe our present—even as rupture—is indicative of a modern project.[6]

We might understand Jean-François Lyotard's own project in his *Postmodern Condition: A Report on Knowledge* within this Kantian tradition of naming the present. Faced with the question, Lyotard picked up the gauntlet and tackled the challenge early on: "Simplifying to the extreme," he remarks, "I define *postmodern* as incredulity toward metanarratives [*grands récits*]."[7] And for various reasons,[8] his answer has been quickly seized upon as a succinct formulation of our present condition, particularly by scholars operating within the Christian tradition.[9] Christian scholars (particularly those within the evangelical tradition), when challenged by the pluriform phenomenon of postmodernism, quickly appropriated Lyotard's 'definition' and thus consider the challenge of postmodernism in terms of Lyotard's definition and the viability of metanarratives.[10] Richard Middleton and Brian Walsh, for instance, devote two chapters of their important and original book, *Truth Is Stranger Than It Used To Be*, to the question of how biblical faith, which they understand to be grounded in a metanarrative, could be viable in postmodernity, which is characterized by an incredulity toward metanarratives.[11] A similar concern is expressed in the work of Catholic theologian Frederick Christian Bauerschmidt, who, in contesting Lyotard's notion of the "end" of metanarratives, seeks to offer "the possibility of a true (or real) metanarrative presentation (or presence) of the sublime" as a viable theological alternative in a postmodern context.[12] For both, the biblical story *is* a metanarrative; however, they argue that it is not implicated in the violence of metanarratives—which they consider to be the concern of the postmodern critique—because it contains within itself an "antitotalizing" and "ethical thrust" which undermines just such totalization and violence.[13]

But *is* the biblical story a "metanarrative?" Is the scriptural narrative a "metanarrative" in the way that Lyotard speaks of the Hegelian system, or Marx's historical materialism, or the modern scientific narrative of progress? It is here that I think we would profit from carefully reading Lyotard's analysis. For Lyotard, the term *metanarrative* [*grand récit*] does not simply refer to a "grand story" in the sense of stories that have grand or universal pretensions, or even make universal claims.

What is at stake is not the *scope* of these narratives but the *nature* of the claims they make. For Lyotard, metanarratives are a distinctly *modern* phenomenon: they are stories which not only tell a grand story (since even premodern and tribal stories do this), but also claim to be able to *legitimate* the story and its claims *by an appeal to universal Reason*. On Lyotard's account, the *Enuma Elish,* though telling a story that is universal or grand in scope, is nevertheless not a metanarrative because it does not claim to legitimate itself by an appeal to scientific Reason. On the other hand, Lyotard sees classical Marxism as a metanarrative insofar as it claims to be a system legitimated by Reason, and therefore to be universally accepted on that basis. What is wrong with this is that such a modern *grand récit* fails to see that it, too, is grounded in a myth and faith-commitments.[14] As a result, postmodernity's "incredulity toward metanarratives" ought to be understood as an *opportunity* for religious thought in a contemporary context—an ally rather than a foe.

Given this more precise definition of metanarratives, I will argue (contra Middleton and Walsh, and others) that the biblical story is *not* a metanarrative in Lyotard's sense. Yes, it makes grand, even universal claims (e.g., that every person is created in the image of God); but it does not—at least within a broadly conceived "Augustinian" tradition—claim to be legitimated by Reason, but rather trusted in faith. To accomplish this, Part I will catalogue and outline a number of engagements with postmodernism (and Lyotard in particular) by Christian philosophers and theologians, in order to point out a common misreading of Lyotard and hence a prevailing misconstrual of "our present": *viz.*, postmodernity. To attempt to correct this, Part II will offer a close reading of Lyotard's argument in *The Postmodern Condition.* Part III will then offer a rereading of postmodernism as a unique opportunity for religious thought in "our time."

I

Like *deconstruction,*[15] the term *metanarrative* has become a word that has never lacked employment, but unfortunately has been put to work doing jobs for which it never asked.[16] In other words, the term *metanarrative* has been subject to equivocation and thus displaced from the very specific context of Lyotard's employment of the concept. The result, it seems, is a straw man.

We see this confusion, for instance, in Middleton and Walsh's discussion, where Lyotard's notion of a metanarrative is misconstrued in three ways. First, concerning the very definition of "metanarratives": after citing Lyotard's definition of postmodernism as incredulity toward metanarratives, they go on to explain what they suggest are, "[f]rom a postmodern perspective, [the] two central problems with metanarratives": (a) that they are "universal" stories, (b) that they are totalizing or marginalizing.[17] In other words, they argue that the problem with metanarratives is their *scope:* a metanarrative "purports to be not simply a local story (an ad hoc, first-order account of a community's experience) but the universal story of the world from *arche* to *telos,* a grand narrative encompassing world history from beginning to end."[18] They then go on to suggest—even though they concede Lyotard never says this[19]—that incredulity toward metanarratives entails "widespread suspicion of any comprehensive metanarrative of world history that makes 'total' claims" because such claims inevitably lead to violence.[20] The problem with this explanation of metanarratives (and hence postmodernism) is that it lacks any grounding in *Lyotard's* discussion of metanarratives, and thus seriously misconstrues what "postmodernism" would be. As we will see in Part II, the problem with metanarratives has nothing to do with the *scope* of their claims—that they are "large-scale" stories of "universal scope"[21]—but the nature of their *legitimation.*

Second, in Middleton and Walsh the term *metanarrative* is conflated with other discourses concerning the "social construction" of meaning: "If metanarratives are social constructions, then, like abstract ethical systems, they are simply particular moral visions dressed up in the guise of universality."[22] So on their accounting, what's wrong with metanarratives from a postmodern perspective is the fact that they are merely social constructions masquerading as universal truths: local claims with universal pretensions. "To the postmodern mind," they conclude, "metanarratives are mere human constructs, fictive devices through which we impose an order on history and make it subject to us (hence they may be termed "master" narratives)."[23] However, once again they are importing something into the notion of metanarrative that is absent from Lyotard's discussion.[24]

Third, as indicated above, Middleton and Walsh consider the second major problem with metanarratives to be an *ethical* one: as universal narratives, metanarratives are hegemonic, violently excluding any who are "different" or reject the dominant story.[25] While concerns with totalizing violence, marginalization, and oppression are certainly important aspects of postmodern critique,[26] it must again be noted that this is *not* something that Lyotard advances with respect to metanarratives. We do well to recall (as we will do below) that the *Postmodern Condition* is *A Report on Knowledge*, which thus revolves around the epistemological problem of *legitimation* or justification.

However, given their reading of Lyotard, postmodernism, and metanarratives, Middleton and Walsh pose the problem as follows:

> The problem, from a postmodern point of view, is that the Scrip-
> tures, in which Christians claim to ground their faith and in which
> we will seek answers to the worldview questions we have raised,
> constitute a metanarrative that makes universal claims. [. . .] So
> the question we are confronted with . . . is whether the Christian
> faith, rooted as it is in a metanarrative of cosmic proportions, is
> subject to the postmodern charge of totalizing violence.[27]

As they note, this is to assume that Christian faith *is* grounded in a
metanarrative: "The important question, then, would not be *whether*
the Christian faith is rooted in a metanarrative, but *what sort of* metanarrative the Scriptures contain."[28] My goal in this essay is to argue
that *whether* Christian faith is rooted in a metanarrative is *precisely* the
important question. Because Middleton and Walsh have misunderstood
the notion of metanarrative, they end up conceding that the biblical story
is a metanarrative, and thus pose the challenge of postmodernism in a
way that is misleading, or at least, misguided. When we turn to a close
analysis of *The Postmodern Condition,* we must conclude that when we
properly understand "metanarratives," the biblical narrative does not
constitute a metanarrative and thus Christian faith is not subject to the
postmodern critique in the way that Middleton and Walsh suggest.

Middleton and Walsh are not alone in their rendering of postmodernism in general, or metanarratives in particular. While grounded in a much
closer reading of Lyotard, in his *Primer on Postmodernism* Stanley Grenz
also misconstrues Lyotard's discussion by suggesting that postmodernism finds fault with the mere universality of "metanarratives." In other
words, Grenz also seems to think that it is the *scope* of metanarratives
that is the problem:

> What makes our condition "postmodern" is not only that people
> no longer cling to the myths of modernity. The postmodern out-
> look entails the end of the appeal to any central legitimating myth
> whatsoever. Not only have all the reigning master narratives lost
> their credibility, but the idea of a grand narrative is itself no longer
> credible. [. . .] Consequently, the postmodern outlook demands
> an attack on any claimant to universality—it demands, in fact, a
> "war on totality."[29]

And if metanarratives are simply orienting stories with universal claims,
then it must be the case that the biblical narrative that grounds Christian faith is also a metanarrative. As a result, we are put in a position
of choosing between postmodernism—which, of course, is defined by
"incredulity toward metanarratives"—and Christian faith. Thus, like
Middleton and Walsh, Grenz concludes that Christian scholars must

ultimately part ways with the postmodern critique of metanarratives, though they might adopt it to a certain extent:

> To put this in another way, we might say that because of our faith in Christ, we cannot totally affirm the central tenet of postmodernism as defined by Lyotard—the rejection of the metanarrative. We may welcome Lyotard's conclusion when applied to the chief concern of his analysis—namely, the scientific enterprise. . . . Contrary to the implications of Lyotard's thesis, we firmly believe that the local narratives of the many human communities do fit together into a single grand narrative, the story of humankind. . . . As Christians, we claim to know what that grand narrative is.[30]

But isn't that trying to have our cake and eat it, too? To arbitrarily say that the postmodern critique applies to Enlightenment or scientific claims but not Christian claims by appealing to the fact that we believe the one and not the other is to beg the question. Further, and more to my point here, Grenz paints himself into a corner by failing to understand what really constitutes a metanarrative.[31] It seems we need to read Lyotard again (for the first time).

By failing to appreciate Lyotard's very specific meaning of *metanarrative,* Christian philosophers and theologians have created a phantom problem that ultimately proposes a false dichotomy: *either* postmodernism *or* Christian faith. Invoking Luther's notion of *theologia crucis* (versus *theologia gloriae*), Brian Ingraffia poses this bifurcation in the starkest of terms: "The theology of the cross pronounces an either/or: either biblical revelation or philosophical speculation. The same either/or must be proclaimed to the present age: either biblical theology or postmodern theory."[32] While more nuanced in Grenz and Middleton and Walsh, the proposed dichotomy remains operative precisely because of a misinterpretation of Lyotard on postmodernism and metanarratives. As a corrective, we will engage in a closer reading of the *The Postmodern Condition* in Part II.

II

In postmodernity, the rules of the game have changed. In particular, changes have taken place "since the end of the nineteenth century" which "have altered the game rules for science, literature, and the arts." In other words, postmodernism is characterized by a shift in the criteria of knowledge; it is an epistemological matter.[33] Lyotard sets the stage for his discussion by chronicling a conflict between "science" and "narratives": when judged by the criteria of modern science, stories and narratives are little more than "fables." When pushed, however, science must *legitimate* itself: it must produce a "discourse of legitimation" which Lyotard simply calls "philosophy." So before determining what *postmodern* would mean, he first defines what he means by "modern": "I will use the term *modern* to designate any science that legitimates itself with reference to a metadiscourse of this kind making an explicit appeal to some grand narrative, such as the dialectics of Spirit [Hegel], the hermeneutics of meaning [Schleiermacher?], the emancipation of the rational [Kant] or working subject [Marx], or the creation of wealth [Smith]."[34] The question of the relation between modernity and post-modernity revolves around this issue of "legitimation."

The process of legitimation or justification must be thought within the pragmatics of communication: Every discourse of legitimation is "sent" by a "sender" to an "addressee." In order for there to be legitimation, there must be a *consensus* between sender and addressee. But in order for this to occur, sender and addressee must already agree upon the rules of the game—must already have committed themselves to language and meanings that will be shared and agreed upon. Thus, while purporting to legitimate or justify itself to another who does not agree, a discourse of legitimation must presume an original consensus. So legitimation occurs only for those who agree to play the game by the same rules. While not exactly preaching to the choir, it is a matter of preaching to those who have agreed to come to church. What this means, however, is that the great discourses of legitimation in, say, the Enlightenment, are in fact predicated upon an agreed upon *narrative* that established the rules of the game.

In order to appreciate this infiltration of narrative into science, we need to consider more closely Lyotard's account of what he describes as "narrative knowledge" and "scientific knowledge." As we have already noted, this unfolds within a framework of language theory and an analysis of the pragmatics of discourse.[35] Unpacking the triad of sender, message, and addressee, and noting the consensus that is required for such communication to take place, Lyotard (*pace* Wittgenstein) refers to such shared pragmatics as "language games" in which the rules of the game are agreed upon by those who choose to play. Of each game he notes: "their rules do not carry within themselves their own legitimation, but are the object of a contract, explicit or not, between players."[36] Further, these shared rules both require and produce a social bond; this is why "the question of the social bond, insofar as it is a question, is itself a language game."[37]

With this methodological framework of language game pragmatics in place, we can now consider the pragmatics of "narrative" knowledge as distinguished from the pragmatics of "scientific" knowledge—a distinction between "myth" and "science"[38] (or, I would suggest, "faith" and "reason"). "Narrative" knowledge (which Lyotard also refers to as "traditional" knowledge, or what we might describe, given his categories, as *pre*modern knowledge) is grounded in the "custom" of a culture and, as such, does not require legitimation. Lyotard links this to a kind of "tribal" paradigm in which the homogeneity of "a people" (*Volk*), coupled with the "authority" of a narrator, produces a kind of immediate auto-legitimation. "The narratives themselves have this authority," he notes. In a sense, "the people are only that which actualizes the narratives."[39] Legitimation is not demanded but rather is implicit in the narrative itself as a story of the people.

In contrast to this auto-legitimation, modern scientific culture externalizes the problem of legitimation. The two pragmatic poles of sender and addressee are distinguished, and the addressee demands of the sender justification for messages sent her way. I must now provide "proof."[40] However, the homogeneity of the premodern *Volk* has dissolved; therefore, we have no immediate or previously agreed upon consensus; we do not all share the same language game. As such, modern legitimation has recourse to a *universal* criterion: Reason. It is this move that generates what Lyotard famously describes as "metanarratives": appeals to criteria of legitimation that are understood as standing outside any particular language game and thus guarantee "universal" truth.

And it is precisely here that we locate postmodernity's incredulity toward metanarratives: they are just another language game, albeit masquerading as the game above all games. Or as Lyotard puts it, scientific knowledge, which considered itself to be a triumph over narrative knowledge, covertly *grounds itself in a narrative* (i.e., an originary myth).[41] In particular, Lyotard analyzes two modern "narratives of legitimation": first, the humanistic metanarrative of emancipation (as found in Kant and Marx), and second, the metanarrative concerning the life of the Spirit in German Idealism.[42] But we can see this infusing of myth in knowledge as far back as Plato, where "the new language game of science posed the problem of its own legitimation at the very beginning."[43] In Books VI and VII of the *Republic,* for instance, the answer to the question of legitimation (here both epistemological and sociopolitical) "comes in the form of a narrative—the allegory of the cave, which recounts how and why men yearn for narratives and fail to recognize knowledge. Knowledge is thus founded on the narrative of its own martyrdom."[44] In a similar way, Lyotard argues, modern scientific knowledge, when called upon (by itself) to legitimate itself, cannot help but appeal to narrative—this "return of the narrative in the non-narrative" is "inevitable."[45] Whenever science attempts to legitimate itself, it is no longer scientific but narrative, appealing to an orienting myth which is not susceptible to scientific legitimation.[46] Science demands of itself the impossible: "the language game of science desires its statements to be true but does not have the resources to legitimate their truth on its own."[47] The appeal to "Reason" as the criterion for what constitutes knowledge is but one more language game among many, shaped by founding beliefs or commitments which determine what constitutes "knowledge" within the game; reason is grounded in myth. *Metanarratives,* then, is the term Lyotard ascribes to these false appeals to universal, rational, scientific criteria—as though they were divorced from any particular game and transcend all language games.

Here we must return to the question posed at the close of Part I: If postmodernity is "incredulity toward metanarratives," then would postmodernism signal a rejection of Christian faith insofar as it is based on the "grand story" of the scriptures? I think the answer is clearly negative, since the biblical narrative and Christian faith do not claim to be legitimated by an appeal to a universal, autonomous Reason, but rather by an appeal to *faith* (or, to translate, "myth" or "narrative").[48] Lyotard very specifically defines metanarratives as universal discourses of legitimation that mask their own particularity; or to put it another way, metanarratives deny their narrative ground even as they proceed upon on it as a basis. In particular, we must note that the postmodern critique is not aimed at metanarratives because they are really grounded in narratives; on the contrary, the problem with metanarratives is that they do not own up to their own mythic ground.[49] Postmodernism is not incredulity toward narrative or myth; on the contrary, it unveils that all knowledge is grounded in such. Once we appreciate this, the (false) dichotomy which Middleton and Walsh, Grenz, Ingraffia, and others propose is dissolved insofar as the biblical narrative is not properly a "metanarrative." As a result, new space is opened for a Christian appropriation of the postmodern critique of Enlightenment rationality.[50]

What characterizes the postmodern condition, then, is not a rejection of grand stories in terms of *scope* or the sense of epic claims, but rather an unveiling of the fact that all knowledge is rooted in *some* narrative or myth. The result, of course (and here I note one of the genuine problems of postmodernity), is what Lyotard describes as a "problem of legitimation"[51] (or what Habermas describes as a "legitimation crisis") since what we *thought* were universal criteria have been unveiled as just one game among many.[52] If we consider, for instance, the reality of deep *moral* diversity and competing visions of the Good, postmodern society is at a loss to adjudicate the competing claims. There can be no appeal to a higher court that would transcend a historical context or language game, no neutral observer or 'God's-eye-view' that can *legitimate* or *justify* one paradigm or moral language game above another. If all moral claims are conditioned by paradigms of historical commitment, then they cannot transcend those conditions; thus, every moral claim operates within a 'logic' that is conditioned by the paradigm. Or, in other words, every language game has its own set of rules. As a result, *criteria* that determine what constitutes 'evidence' or 'proof' must be *game-relative*: they will function as rules only for those who share the same paradigm or participate in the same language game. Arguments or defenses of moral claims operate on the basis of *intra*-paradigm or *intra*-game criteria; as such, the arguments carry force only insofar as the addressee shares the same paradigm; in this case there would be a consensus between the sender and addressee of a statement. If, however, the sender of the argument and the addressee live in different language games, then the argument is bound to be lost in the mail.[53] The incommensurability of language games means that there is a plurality of logic*s* that precludes any demonstrative appeal to a "common reason." Or again, in the model of language games, the rules for distinct games are not proportional.[54] The pragmatics of justification, which requires a reversibility (i.e., consensus) between the sender and addressees, is precisely that which is denied *between* language games. "[T]he problem," Lyotard notes, "is indeed one of translation and translatability. It so happens that languages are translatable, otherwise they are not languages; but language games are not translatable, because if they were, they would not be language games."[55] Recognition of the incommensurability of language games means that there is no consensus, no *sensus communis.*[56]

In the face of this problem, we must not lose sight of the fact that what constitutes the postmodern condition is precisely a *plurality* of language games—a condition in which no *one* story can claim either auto-legitimation (because of the plurality of "the people") or appeal to a phantom universal "Reason" (because Reason is just one game among others, which is itself rooted in a narrative).[57] And this plurality is based on the fact that each game is grounded in different "narratives" or myths (i.e., founding *beliefs*). Whether we understand this as a new Babel or a new Pentecost, I shall argue in the final section that this situation—though posing a challenge—also presents a unique opportunity for religious thought.

III

At root, I would argue that what is at stake in postmodernism is *the relationship between faith and reason.* When Lyotard describes postmodernism as "incredulity toward metanarratives," he indicates a suspicion and critique of the very idea of an autonomous Reason—a universal rationality without commitments. Modernity's metanarratives cannot disengage themselves from narratives as their ultimate ground, and thus cannot divorce themselves from "myth"—orienting beliefs which themselves are not subject to rational legitimation. In this light, consider, for instance, Kuhn's analyses concerning the role of paradigms in scientific research. Dominated by the language of faith,[58] Kuhn's *The Structure of Scientific Revolutions* points out the role of paradigms, as "constellations of belief,"[59] in orienting how we perceive our world and what we consider knowledge and truth. In other words, science finds itself grounded in prior beliefs that do not admit of legitimation, but rather function as the basis for further legitimation. The paradigm itself is a "belief"—a matter of faith. It is also at this level that Wittgenstein notes: "If I have exhausted the justifications I have reached bedrock, and my spade is turned. Then I am inclined to say: 'This is simply what I do.'"[60] To this list we could add Gadamer, Polanyi, Derrida, and others;[61] common to all of them is a delimitation of rationality, particularly Enlightenment ideals of scientific, objective rationality.

In this sense, the postmodern critique described by Lyotard as "incredulity toward metanarratives" represents a displacement of the notion of autonomous Reason as itself a myth.[62] And that, it seems to me, is a project with which Christian scholars ought to ally themselves, particularly once we have clarified that such an alliance does not require jettisoning the biblical narrative. By calling into question the idea of an autonomous, objective, neutral rationality, I have argued that postmodernity represents the retrieval of a fundamentally Augustinian epistemology that is attentive to the structural necessity of faith preceding reason, believing in order to understand.[63] While this Augustinian structure is formalized—in the sense that there is a plurality of faiths, as many as there are language games— the structure (of faith preceding reason) remains in place, in contrast to modern (and perhaps even Thomistic)[64] epistemologies. The incredulity of postmodernity toward metanarratives is due to the fact that modernity denies its own commitments, renounces its faith, while at the same time never escaping it. Postmodernism refuses to believe the Enlightenment is without a creed. But note: the postmodern critique does not demand that modern thought relinquish its faith (a modern gesture to be sure), but to own up to it—to openly confess its *credo*. Thus we might consider the postmodern critique as a revaluing of myth, of orienting faith, providing new spaces for religious discourse—and in particular, an integrally Christian philosophy—in a climate where it has been demonstrated that everyone's "got religion."

How will this insight be helpful to Christian philosophers? My point is not to suggest that Lyotard's analysis concretely helps us to understand Christian faith; in other words, I am not arguing that we look to Lyotard for assistance in helping us to understand Christian faith commitments. Rather, I think that "Christian philosophers"—whose faith is an integral aspect of their philosophy and their philosophizing[65]—should find in Lyotard's critique of metanarratives and autonomous Reason an ally that opens up the space for a radically Christian philosophy. By calling into question the very ideal of a universal, autonomous Reason (which was, in the Enlightenment, the basis for rejecting "religious thought"), and further demonstrating that all knowledge is grounded in "narrative" or "myth," Lyotard relativizes (secular) philosophy's claim to autonomy, and so grants the legitimacy of a philosophy which grounds itself in Christian faith. Previously, such a distinctly "Christian philosophy" would have been exiled from the "pure" arena of philosophy because of its "infection" with bias and prejudice. Lyotard's critique, however, demonstrates that no philosophy—indeed, no knowledge—is untainted by prejudice or faith-commitments. In this way the playing field is leveled, and new opportunities to voice a Christian philosophy are created. So Lyotard's postmodern critique of metanarratives, rather than being a formidable foe of Christian faith and thought, can in fact be enlisted as an ally in the construction of a Christian philosophy.[66]

Notes

Originally published as James K. A. Smith, "A Little Story about Metanarratives: Lyotard, Religion, and Postmodernism Revisited," *Faith and Philosophy* 18: 3 (July 2001): 353–68. Reprinted by permission of the editors of *Faith and Philosophy* journal.

1. Immanuel Kant, "What Is Enlightenment?" in *On History*, ed. Lewis White Beck (New York: Macmillan, 1963), 3–10.

2. This is the focus of Derrida's gloss on Kant's "On a Newly Arisen Superior Tone in Philosophy." See Jacques Derrida, "On a Newly Arisen Apocalyptic Tone in Philosophy," in *Raising the Tone of Philosophy: Late Essays by Immanuel Kant, Transformative Critique by Jacques Derrida*, ed. Peter Fenves (Baltimore: Johns Hopkins University Press, 1993).

3. Michel Foucault, "The Art of Telling the Truth," found in a helpful context in *Critique and Power: Recasting the Foucault/Habermas Debate*, ed. Michael Kelly (Cambridge: MIT Press, 1991), 139–40.

4. Ibid., 141. In his own reflection on Foucault's reflection on Kant, Habermas offers the same evaluation: "Foucault discovers in Kant the *first* philosopher to take aim like an archer at the heart of a present that is concentrated in the significance of the contemporary moment, and thereby to inaugurate the discourse of modernity" (Habermas, "Taking Aim at the Heart of the Present: On Foucault's Lecture on Kant's *What Is Enlightenment?*" in ibid., 151). See also Habermas, *The Philosophical Discourse of Modernity: Twelve Lectures*, trans. Frederick G. Lawrence (Cambridge: MIT Press, 1987), 1–22. One of the implications of my argument in this paper is to open a space for a renewed dialogue between contemporary French philosophy's understanding of "postmodernism" and Habermas's discussion of the "unfinished project of modernity."

5. Jean-François Lyotard, "Answering the Question: What Is Postmodernism?" trans. Regis Durand, as an appendix to *The Postmodern Condition: A Report on Knowledge*, trans. Geoff Bennington and Brian Massumi (Minneapolis: University of Minnesota Press, 1984), 71–82.

6. Lyotard is attentive to this, later posing the question: "Are 'we' not telling, whether bitterly or gladly, the great narrative of the end of great narratives? For thought to remain modern, doesn't it suffice that it think in terms of the end of

some history?" See Lyotard, *The Differend: Phrases in Dispute*, trans. Georges Van Den Abbeele (Minneapolis: University of Minnesota Press, 1988), 135–36.

7. Lyotard, *Postmodern Condition*, xxiv.

8. Among which I would include its early appearance in both French (1979) and English (1984), its deceiving simplicity, its appearance in the Preface, and its largely epistemological definition of postmodernism. All of these factors make it prime real estate for academic squatters who get there first, don't have to read much, and find it "easy."

9. The other major focus of Christian scholars with respect to postmodernism has been the challenge of hermeneutics, particularly posed by Derrida and deconstruction. The slogan seized upon in that context is Derrida's claim, "There's nothing outside of the text" (Jacques Derrida, *Of Grammatology*, trans. Gayatri Spivak [Baltimore: Johns Hopkins University Press, 1976], 158). I will not address this question explicitly here. For a discussion, see my *Fall of Interpretation: Philosophical Foundations for a Creational Hermeneutic* (Downers Grove, IL: InterVarsity Press, 2000), and my forthcoming piece "Limited Inc/arnation: Revisiting the Searle/Derrida Debate in Christian Context." Here I would just briefly note that Derrida is not denying reference, or the existence of a world outside of books. He is not some kind of linguistic Berkeleyan. I hope to be able to engage these issues further in Part II of this book.

10. In *The Postmodern Condition*, Lyotard himself did not generate a critique of Christianity as a metanarrative. Nor does he do so in his recent engagement with Christianity in Jean-François Lyotard and Eberhard Gruber, *The Hyphen: Between Judaism and Christianity*, trans. Pascale-Anne Brault and Michael Naas (Amherst, NY: Humanity Books, 1999).

11. J. Richard Middleton and Brian J. Walsh, *Truth Is Stranger Than It Used to Be: Biblical Faith in a Postmodern Age* (Downers Grove, IL: InterVarsity Press, 1995), chs. 4 and 5. In the structure of the book, these two chapters form the fulcrum of the text (see the table of contents for a visual aid on this point). We should note a careful distinction here: their contention is that the "the Scriptures . . . constitute metanarratives that make universal claims" and that Christian *faith* "is undeniably *rooted in* [this] metanarrative" (emphasis added, 83). I will not contest that Christian faith is grounded in the scriptures; the question is whether the scriptures really constitute a "metanarrative" in Lyotard's sense. If not, then the so-called "problem" of "biblical faith in a postmodern age" (Middleton and Walsh's subtitle) will not revolve around its alleged complicity with metanarratives.

12. Frederick Christian Bauerschmidt, "Aesthetics: The Theological Sublime," in *Radical Orthodoxy: A New Theology*, ed. John Milbank, Catherine Pickstock, and Graham Ward (New York: Routledge, 1999), 204.

13. Middleton and Walsh, *Truth Is Stranger*, 87–107. This is engaged more extensively below.

14. In other words, I would suggest that Lyotard's specific critique of metanarratives in *The Postmodern Condition* is analogous to Gadamer's unveiling of the Enlightenment *prejudice* against prejudice: "The fundamental prejudice of the Enlightenment is the prejudice against prejudice itself." See Hans-Georg Gadamer, *Truth and Method*, 2nd ed., trans. Joel Weinsheimer and Donald G. Marshall (New York: Continuum, 1989), 273. For a further discussion of postmodernism within the context of hermeneutics, see my *The Fall of Interpretation: Philosophical Foundations for a Creational Hermeneutic* (Downers Grove, IL: InterVarsity Press, 2000). It is in this sense that even deconstruction can be, to an extent, an ally of Christian scholarly witness. See my "Is Deconstruction an

Augustinian Science?: Augustine, Derrida, and Caputo on the Commitments of Philosophy," in *Religion with/out Religion: The Prayers and Tears of John D. Caputo*, ed. James H. Olthuis (New York: Routledge, 2001), 50–61.

15. Derrida discusses the fact that the word *deconstruction* is "already attached to very different connotations, inflections, and emotional or affective values" in his "Letter to a Japanese Friend," trans. David Wood and Andrew Benjamin in *A Derrida Reader: Between the Blinds*, ed. Peggy Kamuf (New York: Columbia University Press, 1991), 270. "This word," he continues, "at least on its own, has never appeared satisfactory to me (but what word is), and must always be girded by an entire discourse" (272).

16. Again, since such misunderstandings are so common with respect to contemporary French philosophy, which *we* call "postmodern" (they do not), I would again refer to Derrida's reception in the United States. Concerning the caricature of his work in North America, at Villanova University (in 1994), Derrida took the opportunity "to reject a commonplace, a prejudice, that is widely circulated about deconstruction. That is, not only among bad journalists, and there are many of them, but among people in the academy who behave not like good journalists—I have the deepest respect for good journalists—but like bad journalists, repeating stereotypes without reading the text." See "The Villanova Roundtable: A Conversation with Jacques Derrida," in *Deconstruction in a Nutshell: A Conversation with Jacques Derrida*, ed. John D. Caputo (New York: Fordham University Press, 1997), 8–9. In a similar way, I think Lyotard has gotten "bad press"; the goal of my paper is to push us beyond the stereotype of postmodernism by actually reading the text of *The Postmodern Condition*.

17. Middleton and Walsh, *Truth Is Stranger*, 70–71.

18. Ibid., 70.

19. Ibid., 214 n. 32.

20. Ibid., 71.

21. Ibid., 76.

22. Ibid., 70. They, of course, are not endorsing this position; this is their summary of postmodernism, to which they respond in ch. 5.

23. Ibid., 71. Their favorite authority in this regard (indicated even in the title of their book) seems to be Walter Truett Anderson, *Reality Isn't What It Used to Be: Theatrical Politics, Ready-to-Wear Religion, Global Myths, Primitive Chic, and Other Wonders of the Postmodern World* (San Francisco: Harper & Row, 1990). I have reservations about Anderson functioning as an authority on contemporary French philosophy. If Middleton and Walsh were to reply that their concern is in fact not postmodern*ism* as an intellectual movement but postmoder*nity* as a pop cultural phenomenon (in which case Anderson would seem an appropriate adjudicator of evidence), then it is hard to understand why Lyotard's definition would function as the fulcrum of their book.

24. Let us recall the relative humility of my thesis, here: my primary objective is to clarify a misreading of Lyotard and thus a common misunderstanding of postmodernism and its relationship to narratives. However, "postmodernism" is by no means a monolithic phenomenon. As such, I can't fairly grapple with its many aspects in the space provided here, but I do hope to take up this question elsewhere. Suffice it to say that Christians would have legitimate concerns about more "Nietzschean" strains (as in the work of Deleuze).

25. Middleton and Walsh, *Truth Is Stranger*, 71–73.

26. As evidenced, for instance, in the work of Levinas and in Derrida's later work. For a discussion of these matters, see my "Determined Violence: Derrida's Structural Religion," *Journal of Religion* 78 (1998): 197–212, and "Alterity,

Transcendence, and the Violence of the Concept," *International Philosophical Quarterly* 38 (1998): 369–81.

27. Middleton and Walsh, *Truth Is Stranger*, 83. My goal here is not to engage their response in ch. 5, since, on my account, it is a misguided response at best, and at worst, responding to a straw man because of their misconstrual of Lyotard's discussion of metanarratives.

28. Ibid., 84.

29. Stanley J. Grenz, *A Primer on Postmodernism* (Grand Rapids: Eerdmans, 1996), 45.

30. Ibid., 164. Of particular concern here is Grenz's use of the word *know* in the final sentence. How that is defined would be the crux of whether the Christian narrative really is a metanarrative in Lyotard's sense.

31. Henry Knight also misunderstands Lyotard on this point, defining a metanarrative as simply an "overarching explanatory story." See Henry H. Knight III, *A Future for Truth: Evangelical Theology in a Postmodern World* (Nashville: Abingdon, 1997), 58.

32. Brian Ingraffia, *Postmodern Theory and* [it seems to me this conjunction should be a disjunction: *or*] *Biblical Theology: Vanquishing God's Shadow* (Cambridge: Cambridge University Press, 1995), 241 (cp. 14). While space does not here permit a full critique, the naïveté of Ingraffia's thesis and argument is frustrating. His book begins with a protest against the "synthesis" of biblical theology and philosophy, which he traces to "the early Church fathers" who "often used Greek conceptuality and philosophy to articulate their faith," and thus diluted biblical truths (14)—as though Greek conceptuality was not the framework for articulating biblical ideas in the New Testament itself! Describing this synthesis as "ontotheology," Ingraffia (echoing Barth) proposes to separate the two, distilling a purely biblical theology (is the New Testament "theology"?). And lest we ignore Ingraffia's claims in this regard as uncommon or insignificant in contemporary discourse, I would note that similar appeals to "revelation" are heard in the work of Jean-Luc Marion. I hope to take this up in another context, however.

33. Lyotard, *Postmodern Condition*, xxiii. He goes on to consider the "computerization" of knowledge, indicating a condition wherein any knowledge that cannot be translated into "code" or reduced to "data" will be abandoned (4). His analysis (in 1979, it should be noted) of the way in which knowledge is transformed into "information" and commodified is both insightful and instructive.

34. Ibid.

35. See especially ibid., 9–11. Here Lyotard places his work within the tradition of Wittgenstein, Peirce, and Morris.

36. Ibid., 10.

37. Ibid., 15.

38. We must note that when Lyotard speaks of "science" it must be understood in the broad sense of a "theoretical" discourse (*Wissenschaft*), not the narrow North American sense of the natural sciences.

39. Ibid., 23.

40. Ibid., 23–24.

41. "The state spends large amounts of money to enable science to pass itself off as epic" (Ibid., 28).

42. Ibid., 31–37.

43. Ibid., 28.

44. Ibid., 28–29. Following Lyotard's lead, from the *Republic* alone we could multiply ad infinitum examples of the way in which knowledge is grounded in myth, or how the discourse of reality is presented in images, or the way in which philosophy is grounded in religion (since the battle of philosophy and poetry, staged in the *Republic*, is really a battle between philosophy and religion—or better, one religion and another).

45. Ibid., 27–28.

46. One can see, then, how logical positivism constituted the final naïveté of modernity: rejecting all that could not be legitimated until it recognized its own collapse. (Incidentally, Lyotard applauds Wittgenstein for not falling into this positivist trap [Ibid., 41].)

47. Ibid., 28.

48. That said, I would however concede that some might argue that the Christian faith *can* be legitimated by reason. In evangelical apologetic discussions, for instance, "classical" or "evidential" apologists (versus "presuppositionalists") might perhaps argue that Christian faith is grounded in reason and thus constitutes a metanarrative. Without rehearsing the history of debates regarding apologetic method, I would argue that classical or evidential apologetics would fall prey to Lyotard's critique of metanarratives (since it consorts with a notion of universal Reason), and that such a critique would be welcomed by presuppositionalists. One of the constructive engagements with Lyotard would be to consider his discussion of language games and critique of metanarratives and its correlation with presuppositional discourses on "worldviews" and critique of "autonomous Reason." For a nuanced discussion of the latter, see Herman Dooyeweerd, *In the Twilight of Western Thought: Studies in the Pretended Autonomy of Theoretical Thought*, ed. James K. A. Smith, The Collected Works, B/4 (Lewiston, NY: Edwin Mellen Press, 1999).

49. Again, as I noted earlier, I am using "myth" here in a benign way as "orienting commitments" or "fundamental beliefs." It makes no evaluation regarding the "truth" or "falsity" of such beliefs (which would be to understand such narratives precisely on a "scientific" register where "myth" is opposed to "fact").

50. Grenz and Middleton and Walsh both note that Christian scholars can participate in the postmodern critique of modernity but then always add the proviso that we can't go "all the way" with postmodernism, because that would entail critique of the biblical (meta)narrative. My point is to show that such provisos are unnecessary, because the biblical narrative is *not* a metanarrative. (That is not to say, of course, that the biblical narrative is immune from critique, even postmodern critique. But the criterion will be ethical, not epistemological.)

51. Lyotard, *Postmodern Condition*, 8.

52. There is also a second sense in which "legitimation" is at issue here: with respect not only to *how* metanarratives are legitimated, but also to *what* is legitimated—which, all too often, is an oppressive status quo. Thus, not only do metanarratives appeal to a universal Reason to legitimate themselves, they do so in order to legitimate a present order. While this "ethical" concern is more developed by Lyotard elsewhere (in *Just Gaming* and *The Differend*), it is not unrelated to the epistemological critique of metanarratives in *The Postmodern Condition*. In this respect, I think Middleton and Walsh are suggestive insofar as they argue that the biblical story carries within itself an "antitotalizing thrust" and an inherent "counterideological dimension" by which the biblical story comes as a challenge and disruption to every society—"de-legitimizing" our social practices. For a careful exposition of these elements within the biblical canon, see Middleton and Walsh, *Truth Is Stranger*, 87–107.

53. Cp. Derrida's analysis of these problematics in "Envois," in *The Post Card*, trans. Alan Bass (Chicago: University of Chicago Press, 1987).

54. See Lyotard and Jean-Loup Thébaud, *Just Gaming*, trans. Wlad Godzich (Minneapolis: University of Minnesota Press, 1985), 22.

55. Ibid., 53. This point is contested by Rorty, who claims that while language games are incommensurate, they are not "unlearnable"; or, in other words, Rorty's position (and hope) is that no *differend* is a priori untranslatable—that every differend could be turned into a litigation (see Rorty, "Cosmopolitanism without Emancipation: A Response to Jean-François Lyotard," in *Essays on Heidegger and Others* [Cambridge: Cambridge University Press, 1991], 215–17). Apart from an interpretive disagreement regarding Wittgenstein, I think Rorty also misses Lyotard's careful distinction between "languages" and "language games"; throughout this discussion, Rorty uses the two interchangeably. Lyotard is emphasizing (in a better reading of Wittgenstein, I think) that to change games is to change rules, and hence to change criteria for evidence, etc.

56. Lyotard and Thébaud, *Just Gaming*, 14. In this context, I can only outline this ethicopolitical problem posed by postmodernity, since it is not central to the argument of this paper. I have formulated a response to it in my "The Limits of Paralogistics: Yahweh's Paganism and Lyotard's Body" (forthcoming). For an instructive discussion of plurality and the challenge of pluralism, see Richard J. Mouw and Sander Griffioen, *Pluralisms and Horizons: An Essay in Christian Public Philosophy* (Grand Rapids: Eerdmans, 1993).

57. For Lyotard, justice is precisely recognizing and creating space for this plurality, though not without limits. He describes this postmodern sense of justice as "paganism," in contrast to the "piety" of those who think their (language) game is the only game in town, which usually results in "terror." These themes are most systematically explored in *Just Gaming*. On the limits to this paganism, on Lyotard's own register, see my "The Limits of Paralogistics."

58. For just a selective example of such passages from Thomas Kuhn, *The Structure of Scientific Revolutions,* 2nd ed. (Chicago: University of Chicago Press, 1970), on "belief," see 2, 4, 17, 43, 113; on "commitments," see 4–5, 7, 11, 40–43; on "tradition," see 6, 10, 39, 43.

59. Ibid., 175.

60. Ludwig Wittgenstein, *Philosophical Investigations,* trans. G. E. M. Anscombe (New York: Macmillan, 1959), § 217.

61. For a discussion, see James K. A. Smith and Shane R. Cudney, "Postmodern Freedom and the Growth of Fundamentalism: Was the Grand Inquisitor Right?" *Studies in Religion/Science Religieuses* 25 (1996): 41–44.

62. For an earlier Christian critique in this vein, see Dooyeweerd, *In the Twilight of Western Thought.* For a discussion, see my introduction, "Dooyeweerd's Critique of 'Pure' Reason," v–xiii.

63. See my "The Art of Christian Atheism: Faith and Philosophy in Early Heidegger," *Faith and Philosophy* 14 (1997): 71–81, and "Is Deconstruction an Augustinian Science?" (op. cit.).

64. That is, it seems to me that the notion of an autonomous reason is not unique to the Enlightenment, but already can be located in Thomas's understanding of "natural reason." Thomas and Augustine disagree on this point, as seen in Aquinas's commentary on Boethius's *De trinitate,* Q. 1, art. 1. My goal here is not to mediate that debate, but to raise a question that demands further consideration. For an argument to the contrary, see John Milbank and Catherine Pickstock, *Truth in Aquinas,* Radical Orthodoxy Series (New York: Routledge, 2001).

65. Not all that goes under the rubric of "Christian philosophy" operates on the basis of an integral understanding of the relationship between faith and philosophy wherein all philosophy proceeds from *some* faith commitments. As I have argued in "The Art of Christian Atheism," much "Christian" philosophy accepts the dogma regarding the autonomy of philosophical thought. It is the rejection of such a dogma that characterizes what I am describing as an "Augustinian" understanding of the relationship between faith and reason, which concludes that there is no reason that is not grounded in at least *a* faith. Permit me to again refer to Dooyeweerd, *In the Twilight of Western Thought,* chs. 1 and 2.

66. My thanks to Christopher Kaczor and an anonymous referee of *Faith and Philosophy* for their helpful comments, and Bil Van Otterloo for his assistance.

6

Onto-theology, Metanarrative,
Perspectivism, and the Gospel

Merold Westphal

Some of the best philosophers whom I count among my friends are postmodernists. But they do not share my faith. Others of the best philosophers whom I count among my friends share my faith. But they are not postmodernists. Decidedly not. At varying degrees along a spectrum that runs from mildly allergic to wildly apoplectic, they are inclined to see postmodernism as an enemy of the gospel of Jesus Christ, frequently on the short list of the most dangerous anti-Christian currents of thoughts at the beginning of the new millennium. Relativism, nihilism, cynicism, anything goes. It is in terms like these that postmodern philosophy is portrayed as the enemy of all things bright and beautiful.

I often find myself *philosophically* closer to my postmodern friends who do not share my faith than to the Christian philosophers who do. I hope that in trying to explain why I'll be able to open some helpful perspectives for discussion and debate. But first, two caveats and a preamble.

Caveat One. I shall not talk about the "postmodern world" but only that part of it about which I am qualified to speak, postmodern philosophy. Some speak about a very broad cultural change when they speak of a "postmodern world." They often focus on the transition from a modern world in which science was king to a postmodern world in which science has lost its hegemony; and they often suggest that this change is not limited to intellectual elites but is a broad-based, popular trend attested by a variety of phenomena lumped together under the heading *New Age* and by what we might call the new supernaturalism in story telling, narratives filled with angels and vampires taking their place alongside of *science* fiction.

Without denying the reality and importance of either these phenomena or the postpositivistic philosophies of science that challenge the simplistic concepts of scientific objectivity that were part of the Enlightenment project, I have reservations about this analysis of the "postmodern world." From the seventeenth century on, as Bacon, Hobbes, and Descartes (and now Heidegger) have made especially clear, the Enlightenment project was one of science in the service of technology. And the human race has never lived more completely under the hegemony of its scientifically grounded technologies than at present. Quibbles about the nature of scientific rationality and fascination with angels and vampires are like a little Zen meditation in the midst of a multinational corporation—purely epiphenomenal. The computer at which I write about postmodernism declares the glory of modernity, and its modem, which gives me instant communication with my Christian friend in Moscow and my postmodern friend in Melbourne, shows its handiwork.

Caveat Two. I shall speak of three central themes emerging from postmodern philosophers and of their relation to Christian faith. In a wide variety of academic departments, mostly in the humanities and social sciences, these and related issues are lively topics of discussion and debate. But outside the bookway (analogue: beltway) that encircles the intellectual elites, it is not clear to me that there has been much substantive trickle-down (even if Woody Allen has moved on from erotic existentialism to *Deconstructing Harry*). The "many" (hoi polloi) about whom the academy speaks and to whom the church tries to speak are not fledgling deconstructionists, though many are suspicious of anyone, personal or institutional, who claims to have all the answers.

Still, Christian mission, whether it involves worship, evangelism, catechesis, spiritual formation, theology and biblical interpretation, or whatever, needs to be thoughtfully in touch with the intellectual as well as the socioeconomic, political, and popular cultural contexts in which it occurs. The church needs to know more about postmodernism than what it can gain from reading the weekly news magazines or hearing a few po-mo shibboleths tossed around carelessly.

Preamble. The strategy that I now employ in relation to the postmodern philosophies of thinkers such as Nietzsche, Heidegger, Derrida, Foucault, Lyotard, and Rorty was developed in an earlier book entitled *Suspicion and Faith: The Religious Uses of Modern Atheism*. There I examine the critiques of religion (mostly Christianity) to be found in Marx and Freud (quintessentially modern thinkers with an unquestioning faith in scientific rationality) and in Nietzsche (a postmodern thinker who sees the will to power as more basic than the love of truth professed by the Enlightenment project but undermined by interests it hides from itself).

My argument goes something like this. These three are probably the three most widely influential atheists of the last couple centuries. But looked at closely, their arguments about the various ways in which religious beliefs and practices can be put, with the help of systematic self-deception, in the service of quite irreligious interests, both personal and social, have two striking characteristics: (1) they are all too true all too much of the time (even if they are not the whole story about religion, as this trio is all too eager to assume), and (2) they have striking similarities of substance, in spite of diametrically different motives, to the critiques of the piety of the covenant people of God to be found on the lips and in the writings of the Old Testament prophets and of Jesus, Paul, and James.

So I found myself accusing Marx and Freud of shameless plagiarism (Nietzsche acknowledges the link between his critique and Jesus's critique of the Pharisees) and proposing that instead of denouncing these thinkers, we acknowledge the painful truths to which they point and use them for personal and corporate self-examination. The opening chapter is entitled "Atheism for Lent," and at least a couple of churches developed Lenten studies around this suggestion.

I recently had the opportunity to summarize this argument to an audience that included a very fine Christian theologian. Having spent too long a time in contexts where "theology" consisted very largely of debunking Christianity with the help of this terrible trio and then replacing the gospel with some currently fashionable social or therapeutic agenda, he was toward the apoplectic end of the spectrum. He just couldn't imagine any authentically religious uses of modern atheism.

Having no desire to defend the kind of "theology" against which he was quite rightly reacting, I was disappointed that he couldn't see the difference between it and what I was saying. My response consisted in reminding him of Balaam's ass. Better known for his braying than for his praying, this humble servant of the Lord (by no design of his own) nevertheless spoke God's word of rebuke to another (this time self-professed) servant of the Lord, who needed to hear it just as badly as he wished not to hear it.

◆◆◆

Turning to the major postmodern philosophers, I adopt the same strategy, refusing to assume that the enemies of faith (a question of motive) never speak the truth (a question of content). The thinkers in question, including the Gang of Six mentioned above, are no friends of historic Christianity. Most are overtly atheistic, and even when this is not the case, God is conspicuously absent from the world as they present it to us. The atheistic or at least nontheistic character of their thought is not modified by the religious motifs that emerge in the later thought of Nietzsche, Heidegger, and Derrida. So it is widely assumed, by friend and foe alike, that the central themes of the postmodern philosophers and the central loci of orthodox Christian theology are mutually exclusive. I propose to examine three cases.

First, Heidegger's critique of onto-theology. The term is often used by assistant professors who have appointed themselves campus terrorists and, alas, by senior scholars who should be more careful, as a kind of sci-fi conceptual zapper. You aim it at any theology archaic enough to affirm a transcendent, personal creator and vaporize it by intoning the magic word, "onto-theology."

But what do we find in Heidegger's text? He derives the term from Aristotle and applies it to Hegel. Aristotle had sought to develop a science of being as such, not this dimension of being or that region, but being qua being. But to carry out his project, subsequently known as ontology, Aristotle discovered that he needed to posit God, not the God of Abraham, Isaac, and Jacob, to be sure, but the impersonal, oblivious Unmoved Mover. With this, ontology becomes theology, or, as Heidegger puts it, onto-theology. The key idea is that there is a highest being who is the key to the meaning of the whole of being. Surely every Christian theology makes this affirmation in relation to the triune God, just as Spinoza makes it in relation to the all-encompassing energy/process he calls Nature, and Hegel makes it in relation to the all-encompassing energy/process he calls Spirit. So, it is assumed, every Christian theism falls prey, along with these modern pantheisms, to Heidegger's critique of onto-theology.

But what is the critique? In the first place, Heidegger describes onto-theology a bit more specifically than as the claim that there is a highest being who is the key to the meaning of the whole of being. Onto-theology occurs when philosophy allows God to become a theme of its discourse on its terms and in the service of its project. That project is spelled out in complex detail in terms of the closely interrelated concepts of representative thinking and calculative thinking.

It is not possible in this context to follow Heidegger's analysis of these two concepts in detail. But the upshot can be expressed quite simply. Philosophy's project is to render the whole of being fully intelligible to human understanding, to have the world at its disposal, first conceptually and then practically. Thus onto-theology may begin in metaphysical systems like Aristotle's, Spinoza's, and Hegel's, but it is in modernity's wedding of science and technology that onto-theology has its greatest triumph, placing the world at its disposal, first conceptually and then practically.

Although we now have a more detailed account of onto-theology, we have not yet identified Heidegger's critique. What is wrong with onto-theology in his view? Three things. First, it deprives the world of its mystery. Second, it gives us a God not worthy of worship. In a famous passage, Heidegger complains that before the *causa sui* (a name for the God of onto-theology that emphasizes the need for an explainer that doesn't need to be explained) no one would be tempted to pray or to sacrifice and that this God evokes neither awe nor music and dance. Onto-theology is hostile to piety.

Finally, having deprived the world of both its mystery and of a God worthy of worship, onto-theology opens the way for the unfettered self-assertion of the will to power in the form of modernity, namely the quest of science and technology to have everything at human disposal. This is the ultimate *hubris* of Western humanity, in which, under the banner of Modernity, it arrogates to itself the place of Plato's Good and the Christian God. Heidegger describes this self-coronation as an "attack," an "assault," an "uprising," an "insurrection."

Against whom? Against Being. Heidegger's attempt to think Being (which is not to be confused with God) is anything but clear, and he succeeds in restoring mystery to the world perhaps more than he intends. Moreover, he launches a powerful critique of the will to power embedded in modern technology, though it is not clear that any force or substance is added to his critique by invoking the name of Being in the process. Where Heidegger doesn't seem to meet his own criteria is in giving us a God worthy of worship, someone to whom to pray and sacrifice and before whom to sing and dance. Even the truest of the Heideggerian true believers have not been caught, to my knowledge, relating to Being in these ways.

But our question is not about Heidegger's own thought but whether his critique of onto-theology is a critique of Christian theism. What is wrong with onto-theology is that it involves an inappropriate human posture toward the Sacred, toward that ultimacy in proper relation to which alone humankind can flourish. For the theist this would obviously be God.

Is Christian thinking then inevitably onto-theological by virtue of positing a highest being who is the key to the meaning of all being? It is worth noting that Heidegger does not name Christian thinkers in his critique. Along with Aristotle and Hegel and modern technology, already mentioned, he cites the tradition that stretches from Anaxagoras to Nietzsche! But of course he might be assuming that the Abrahamic monotheisms are somehow part of this tradition, that Jerusalem, as Nietzsche would have it, is simply Athens for the many. So our question stands. Two questions indicate a negative reply. First, does Christian thinking, in the search for total intelligibility, give us a universe deprived of mystery and a God who evokes neither prayer, nor sacrifice, nor awe, nor music, nor dance? Second, does Christian thinking legitimize that will to power (Heidegger's modernity) which seeks to place the whole of reality, including God, at its disposal, making all beings, including God (and, ironically, human beings), into means to human ends?

Obviously not, in both cases. But some further observations may be in order. (1) In his critique of onto-theology's assault on mystery in the name of reason Heidegger sounds a lot like Pascal contrasting the god of the philosophers with the God of Abraham, Isaac, and Jacob, and a lot like Kierkegaard contrasting the Paradox with the System. In other words, one could quite legitimately have religious rather than secular motives for offering a critique like Heidegger's.

But it is important to notice that these are not the only Christian thinkers eager to preserve the mystery of God and the limits of human understanding. That is also fundamental to the theologies of Augustine and Aquinas, of Luther and Calvin, and, not to be too Western, of every orthodox theology I have ever encountered. Each of these traditions, to mention only some, refuses in its own distinctive way to make total transparency to human understanding the condition for God's entry into human discourse. They affirm that to posit God is to affirm mystery, not to make everything clear. Christian theology, taken as a (very complex) whole, is more a sustained critique of onto-theology than an instance of it. On this point Christianity has been "postmodern" from the start, not a precursor of the Enlightenment project.

(2) This is true in relation to the second question as well.

Nowhere is this clearer than in those theologies that follow Augustine in seeing pride as the essence of sin. (Heidegger is also a plagiarist, and his critique of modern technology needs some footnotes to Augustine.) But all Christian thinking places a check on the unconstrained will to power of human desire and affirms that we get it sinfully (and tragically) wrong when instead of placing ourselves at God's disposal we make God a means to our ends.

(3) Still, we need to listen to Heidegger's critique as a critique, not only of Aristotle, Spinoza, Hegel and the like, but of our own thinking as well. For in spite of what has just been said, Christian theology, against its better judgment, often has strong onto-theological tendencies. Our philosophical theologies, especially when they focus on the "metaphysical" attributes of God and marginalize the "moral" attributes of a personal God, can easily lapse, both in appearance and in fact, into

trying to make everything clear, thereby producing a God not obviously related to prayer, worship, and witness.

Even when our systematic theologies subordinate philosophical analysis to biblical exegesis, they can and sometimes do become systems in an onto-theological sense. I am reminded here of Camus's definition of the world of myth as a world of all answers and no questions. Just to the degree that our theologies become mythical in this sense, perhaps with the aid of a high view of scripture, they become onto-theological. In them, no doubt against our conscious intentions, God becomes the One Who Makes Our System Work, who sees to it that we are never at a loss conceptually, that we always have THE ANSWERS. Although Thomistic theology has deep anti-onto-theological substance, the format of the *Summa Theologiae* pictures what I have in mind here. Questions have no function other than to introduce our answers.

(4) We also need to hear Heidegger's critique as a critique of our systems of practice and not only of our theories. For when these systems involve the degradation of the environment or the oppression of other humans they take on an onto-theological character. They put nature and other humans at our disposal and God as well, for it becomes God's assignment to legitimize our practices. Even indifference has an onto-theological character. For when our practices reduce God and the world to means to our ends, those who are not useful to us fall off our radar screens. Here again Christian traditions have powerful resources for resisting these tendencies. But all too often we have succumbed to such temptations and we can never be too vigilant. Postmodernism here speaks, if we will hear it, a prophetic warning.

◆◆◆

Among the most frequently cited apothegms of postmodernism is Lyotard's definition (but no one else's) of the postmodern condition as "incredulity toward metanarratives." In my experience no other theme from our Gang of Six, not even Derrida's (in)famous "There is nothing outside the text," generates as much apoplexy among Christian scholars or as high a degree of certainty that Christianity and postmodernism represent a dyad like truth and error, light and darkness, good and evil, and so forth.

There aren't many senior Christian scholars as knowledgeable about Derrida as one I once heard give a paper exploring possible points of convergence between his own Christian thinking and deconstruction. Ignoring the fact that the paper was about Derrida and not Lyotard, another senior Christian scholar of considerable repute (like the original speaker from my own Reformed tradition) irately insisted that never the twain could meet since Christianity is a metanarrative and postmodernism is defined as incredulity toward metanarratives. Jamie Smith, a contributor to this volume, but a graduate student at the time, gave a succinct and accurate account of what Lyotard actually says about metanarratives and then suggested that Christians have reason to share his skittishness about them. The objector acknowledged the latter point, explaining that he had never read Lyotard and had no idea who Lyotard's targets were, how he defined *metanarrative*, and what his objections to it were.

Even more recently I heard another senior Christian scholar, once again of considerable repute and once again from my own Reformed tradition, taking the metanarrative issue as the nonnegotiable point of irreconcilable opposition between Christian faith and postmodern philosophy. Christianity is a metanarrative, she insisted. "We know how the story ends." I immediately found myself singing (silently), "I know not what the future holds, but I know who holds the future—it's a secret known only to Him," and saying to myself, "Yes, in a certain sense we know how the story ends. But in an equally important sense we do not. And it's important to keep clear about what we know and what we don't."

So what does Lyotard mean by *metanarrative?* In the first place, a philosophy of history, a big story in which we place the little stories of our lives as individuals and communities. In this sense Christianity is undeniably a metanarrative, a *Heilsgeschichte* that runs from creation and the fall through the life, death, and resurrection of Jesus to the second coming, the resurrection of the dead, and the life everlasting. Amen.

But in philosophical discourse, "meta" signifies a difference of level and not primarily of size. A metanarrative is a metadiscourse in the sense of being a second-level discourse designed to legitimize one or more first-order discourses. It is this question of legitimation which is absolutely central for Lyotard and which makes such a tight link between modernity and metanarrative in his mind. Having overthrown various ancient regimes both of knowledge and of social practice, modernity finds itself needing to legitimize its "new authorities," and it resorts to narrative to do so.

There is an irony in this. Modernity has hitched its wagon to science, a form of discourse that challenges and undermines traditional narratives. But in order to legitimize itself, science needs a story of progress from opinion and superstition to scientific truth and on to universal peace and happiness. The Enlightenment project is inseparable from its legitimizing metanarratives.

Modernity's "new authorities" are sociopolitical as well as intellectual, and modernity's big stories concern themselves not only with legitimizing the truth of its knowledge but also the justice of its practices. Lyotard takes the production of self-legitimizing metanarratives *by philosophy* to be the quintessence of modernity. The Enlightenment of the seventeenth and eighteenth centuries told a variety of such stories, and he mentions, for example, the story of the emancipation of the rational subject (Descartes, Locke) and the story of the creation of wealth (Adam Smith). But he focuses analysis on two nineteenth-century versions, Hegel's and Marx's.

Lyotard calls Hegel's story the speculative narrative, the one concerned with the "dialectics of Spirit" and the "realization of the Idea." It primarily concerns itself with the truth of our knowledge and seeks to legitimize modern, Western humanity as the absolute subject whose knowledge of itself as such is absolute knowing. (As a kind of fringe benefit, we might observe, the Hegelian story also seeks to legitimize the modern, capitalist state.) Marx's story is the emancipation narrative. It concerns itself with the justice of our practices and seeks to legitimize the proletarian revolution that will abolish private property and usher in the classless society.

At the descriptive level, Lyotard merely observes a widespread skepticism toward these stories and the self-legitimizing project that gives rise to them, defining the postmodern condition in terms of this incredulity. At the critical level, he sides with the unbelievers who remain outside the temples of Spirit and the Revolution, and not just by describing them as the shrines of unkept promises. The Enlightenment project has not just been unsuccessful; as a totalizing project it is inherently illegitimate.

"Totalizing" is another po-mo shibboleth often bandied about as an undefined hi-tech zapper with which to deep-six anything that is not PC this week. Aim. Click. Vaporize. But here it has a rather precise and plausible meaning. In its quest for universal peace and happiness, modernity has conceived its goal as an essentially homogenized humanity. As science it has sought to suppress conceptual difference; and as either capitalism or communism, it has sought to suppress social difference. Wittgenstein, Lyotard's clear hero, was closer to the truth in recognizing the plurality of language games humanity plays and in refusing to award hegemony to any one of them (or even to the class of language games to which science belongs, those that concern themselves with correctly describing the world).

We saw that Christianity is an onto-theology if all that is needed is the affirmation of a highest being that is the key to the meaning of the whole of being. But we also saw that Heidegger defines onto-theology much more specifically, and that Christian thought is deeply anti-onto-theological (and thus, to that degree, "postmodern"), though it needs to be ever vigilant against its own onto-theological tendencies. Now we can see that Christianity is a metanarrative if all that is needed is to be a grand narrative. But we have also seen that Lyotard defines metanarrative much more specifically. What we now need to see is how Christian thought is not a metanarrative in his sense (and thus, to that degree, "postmodern").

In the first place, the big Christian story that begins with "Let there be light" and ends with the "Hallelujah Chorus" under the baton of the angel Gabriel is not a *meta*narrative. The recital of the *Heilsgeschichte* belongs to first-order Christian discourse. It is kerygma, not apologetics. So far from legitimizing the knowledge of any epoch of human history, it appeals to faith in every epoch.

Second, it has its origin in revelation, not in philosophy, and most especially not in modern philosophy, grounded in the autonomy of the human subject, whether that be the individual as knower (Descartes' *ego cogito*), the individual as bearer of inalienable rights (Locke, Jefferson), or modern humanity collectively as the fulfillment of history (Hegel, Marx, popular American self-consciousness as the city set on a hill). Modernity, not just willing to justify itself but eager to do so, is Plato's dialogue of the soul with itself given outward, world-historical form. Modern, Western humanity talks (as philosophy) with itself (as science, technology, and the state), telling itself the stories that will enable it to sleep soundly (and conquer without qualm) in the serene assurance of being the ultimate embodiment of both truth and justice. Christianity has at least as good grounds as Lyotard to be skeptical and suspicious.

Thirdly, a point implicit in both of the previous points. Originating in biblical revelation rather than in modern philosophy and belonging to kerygma rather than to apologetics, the Christian story legitimizes only one kingdom, the kingdom of God. In the process it delegitimizes every human kingdom, including democratic capitalism and the Christian church, just to the degree that they are not the full embodiment of God's kingdom. Modernity's metanarratives legitimize "us"; the Christian narrative places "us" under judgment as well. In knowing how the story ends we do *not* know which aspects of our work will be burned as wood, hay, and stubble; and we may be more than a little surprised.

Christianity is not Lyotard's target. Nor is it inherently the kind of story he criticizes. But once again it does not follow that we are immune from his critique. On the contrary, just to the degree that he echoes the prophetic stand of biblical revelation, he becomes good Lenten reading for us. He reminds us that we are in danger, by our own criteria, whenever we become too eager to justify ourselves, either by turning to a philosophical apologetics to prove that we are the bearers of the truth or by telling the Christian story in such a way as to privilege our practices with a divine sanction that renders them immune to sober(ing) criticism. We need to remember that what we do know about how the story ends provides no guarantees that our theories and our practices will not need to be significantly overthrown in order to prepare a highway for our God.

Lyotard's critique also warns us against what we might call Christian totalizing. This can happen when we wed ourselves too tightly to Western modernity and its totalizing tendencies in the era of its global hegemony. But even if we do not identify the kingdom with science and technology, democracy and capitalism, it happens whenever we assume, however unconsciously, that when the roll is called up yonder, those who come from every tribe and nation will first have to be homogenized so as to be more or less indistinguishable from ourselves.

◆◆◆

Finally, and all too briefly, a third theme. Postmodernism is widely seen as antithetical to Christianity because of a relativism that undermines theology by abandoning the difference between true and false and undermines morality by abandoning the difference between right and wrong. In spite of the fact that they often describe their political commitments in terms of justice and do not treat this as merely subjective preference, postmodernists are awarded the honor, usually reserved for freshmen and sophomores in their first philosophy class, of holding that any view is as good as any other and that everything is a matter of personal taste. This makes them into the safest of all threats, the threat to public decency that can be denounced without any possibility of being put in question by their critique.

It is true, of course, that postmodern philosophers can generally be described, along with many other contemporary philosophers, as perspectivists. There is a common thread running through Nietzsche's perspectivism, Heidegger's hermeneutical circle, Derrida's deconstruction, Foucault's genealogical analysis of knowledge as power, and Rorty's notion that our vocabularies are not dictated by reality but are "optional." As usual, the details are quite technical, but the basic point is, quite simply, that we are not God. We do not occupy an absolute, all-encompassing point of view but see whatever we see, including right and wrong, from a particular standpoint constituted to a significant degree by contingencies of linguistic usage and sociohistorical location. These points of view, by analogy with vision, enable us to see what can be seen from that site only by hiding from us what cannot be seen from there.

Is perspectivism just another name for relativism? Yes and no. If by *relativism* is meant the view that anything goes, that all views are equally "valid," then no. Perspectivism does not entail that conclusion, nor do any postmodernists I know draw that conclusion. Nietzsche, for example, does not think that Christianity is just as good a religion as the Dionysian piety set forth by Zarathustra (though he denies to both the kind of Truth for which Plato pined). And even Rorty is unwilling to tolerate cruelty as an "alternative lifestyle." Rather, he thinks it is the worst thing we do.

But perspectivism is relativism in this sense—it is the dual claim that our insights, whether they be factual or normative, are relative to the standpoint from which they are made, and that the standpoint we occupy (even when making this claim) inevitably betrays that it is not an absolute standpoint, an all-inclusive, "totalizing" point of view that sees everything and is blind to nothing. In short, perspectivism is the relativism that insists that we are not God, that only God is absolute.

To be sure, postmodernists sometimes overstate the case. They talk as if they had shown that there is no Absolute Truth because there is no one to occupy the Absolute Point of View. This is because they assume as a premise the Nietzschean notion that if we are not God, no one else could be. But the analyses that show how *our* judgments are perspectival and relative provide no evidence for this premise or for the conclusion that requires it.

I mention this unwarranted slide from "we are not God, so our truths are not absolute" to "there is no God, so there is no Absolute Truth" in order to highlight what seems to me an equal but opposite non sequitur. Those who perceive (from what standpoint?) postmodernism to be a threat to religion and morality often insist that there is Absolute Truth (especially in metaphysics and morality). If they are theists, they have good grounds for such a claim. But listen closely and grab your wallet, for almost immediately you will hear the further claim that they are the repositories of that Truth. By some magic God's absoluteness has rubbed off on them. They have become the Son of the Nicene Creed, epistemically of the same substance as the Father. They assume (but why?) that we cannot bear witness to an Absolute Being or an Absolute Event if we and our witness are relative.

I am not suggesting that we swallow postmodern philosophy hook, line, and Derrida. I am suggesting that instead of running in terror from perspectival relativism, we look it in the face to see whether it can be read as a commentary on the limitations of our insight due to our finitude and fallenness.

In a recent issue of *Books and Culture* (Nov/Dec 1998), there is an essay entitled, "C. S. Lewis among the Postmodernists." It makes very interesting reading, exploring what we might call the perspectivist dimension of Lewis's thought. "Like Derrida," we read, "Lewis emphasizes that all analysis is situated, that there is no position of utter objectivity from which one may think about thinking itself." Perhaps Lewis's continuing freshness, the essay concludes, "is rooted in [his] characteristic fusion of metaphysical affirmation and epistemological humility."

This closing line suggests a sequel, "Paul among the Postmodernists." Isn't he the one that said that we "suppress the truth" by our wickedness (Rom. 1:18)? Isn't he the one who said, "Although everyone is a liar, let God be proved true" (Rom. 3:4)? Isn't he the one who said that we have "the light of the knowledge of the glory of God in the face of Jesus Christ . . . in clay jars" (2 Cor. 4:6–7)? Isn't he the one who said that in this life we see "in a mirror, dimly" and know "only in part" (1 Cor. 13:12–13)? He views human understanding, even apostolic understanding, as anything but absolute, and, if there are many different glasses in which we see, darkly, there may even be an incipient perspectivism in Paul. This in spite of his unshakable confidence in divine revelation.

Nor does his possibly perspectival epistemic finitism make him bashful when it comes to kerygmatic mission. I often hear it asked in discussions of postmodernism, How can we preach the gospel if we are not possessors and dispensers of Absolute Truth? My answer: think Paul.

This was originally published in Merold Westphal, "Perspectivism, Onto-Theology and the Gospel," *Perspectives* (April 2000): 6–10. Reprinted by permission of the editors of *Perspectives* journal.

Part II

Response Essays

7

Postmodernism and the Quest
for Theological Knowledge

R. Douglas Geivett

What Is Postmodernism?

I have a feeling that many readers who make it to the end of this book will still be wondering, "So, what *is* Postmodernism, anyway?" One social scientist remarks that "the term post-modern is employed so broadly that it seems to apply to everything and nothing all at once."[1] Today we hear of ministers who desire to build a postmodern church, and of theologians who would replace traditional theology with a postmodern surrogate. Postmodernity began to be reflected in architecture when traditional layouts of living space were supplanted by buildings that "look the way people feel."[2] You can buy postmodern art and postmodern fiction. Body art—piercing, tattoos, and the like—ensures a fashionably postmodern look. Some like their politics postmodern. The postmodern has been exploited for its consumer value. Anything and everything that can be advertised as avant-garde and user-friendly has been called "postmodern." As you read these words, there must be someone hawking postmodern cookery on a street corner somewhere.

In my contributions to this volume, I am concerned primarily with postmodernism as a set of assumptions about the nature and possibility of knowledge. In this brief chapter I'll respond to the main conclusions that other contributors have reached about the value of postmodernism for understanding our cognitive ambitions, especially as they pertain to the quest for religious knowledge.

Merold Westphal on Three Postmodern Themes

Merold Westphal says, "I often find myself *philosophically* closer to my postmodern friends who do not share my faith than to the Christian philosophers who do." I wonder if this is as provocative as it's supposed to sound. On the whole, Westphal paints a pretty tame picture of postmodernism.

This picture has three central features. Each feature correlates with an admonition to Christian theologians.

Onto-theology

First, he says that while Christianity "is deeply anti-onto-theological," Christian theology nevertheless has "strong onto-theological tendencies," and this is a bad thing. Onto-theology is bad for three reasons: (1) it sucks all mystery out of the world, (2) it wreaks havoc with piety, and (3) it paves the way for despotic control of the environment and human persons through technology and other devices.

Westphal explains Martin Heidegger's concept of onto-theology in two stages. At the entry level, onto-theology is nothing more than the innocuous idea "that there is a highest being who is the key to the meaning of the whole of being." This much Christianity rightly confesses. At the next stage, however, we learn that there is more to onto-theology than this, something more sinister. "Onto-theology occurs when philosophy allows God to become a theme of its discourse on its terms and in service of its project." In other words, "philosophy's project is to render the whole of being fully intelligible to human understanding, to have the world at its disposal, first conceptually and then practically." The bottom line is, onto-theology "involves an inappropriate human posture toward the Sacred."

Notice, this posture begins with an attitude that is fundamentally epistemological. It presumes to domesticate the Sacred through classification and analysis, resulting in an exhaustive knowledge of reality. Westphal warns against a slide into system building in the onto-theological sense, where all our questions about God and his relation to the world have been answered neatly and to our everlasting satisfaction. This slide may happen in spite of our determination to submit philosophical analysis to the exegesis of an authoritative word from God, the Bible. Furthermore, with God functioning as a means to human ends, the treatment of other human persons in the same way is sure to follow.

This, it seems to me, is a legitimate warning. I doubt that Heidegger is needed to make it seem more compelling than it should be on a straightforward understanding of scripture and Christian history. And repairing to Heidegger is just as likely to confuse the believer about where knowledge of the Sacred leaves off and mystery begins. As Laurence Paul Hemming writes, for Heidegger all theologies "reduce God to the kind of commodity that technology routinely manipulates. Theology thereby becomes diabology."[3] If it is difficult to pin down the precise nature of Heidegger's atheism, it is partly because he is so skeptical about the possibility of any kind of *knowledge* about God. But there is no question that he is radically opposed to all theologies.

The most serious risk in following Heidegger's (and Westphal's) analysis is that it will foster a lassitude in theological reflection that is unbecoming to creatures made in the image of God, capable of a knowledge of God, and who are the objects of God's desire to be known. Why would God bother to reveal himself if God cannot be apprehended by his creatures? And if God can be apprehended at all, then there is a place for theology and we must have an appropriate account of how our knowledge of God is possible and can be developed.

Sure, there's plenty we'll never know. There are questions we'll never resolve. There are many questions we will probably never even think to ask. But Heidegger's particular conception of onto-theology, so essential to Westphal's perspective, is inimical to even the most minimal of knowledge claims about the divine. If Westphal believes that God can be known at all, then it would be helpful to have him explain how Heidegger's critique of theology can be taken seriously by Christian theologians without also becoming disillusioned with the very possibility of theological knowledge.

Metanarrative

Second, Westphal warns that Christian theology has a misguided tendency to regard its perspective as a metanarrative, in the pernicious sense of a "totalizing" project that is inherently illegitimate. In certain respects, Jean-François Lyotard's concept of metanarrative parallels Heidegger's idea of onto-theology. But with the concept of metanarrative comes the idea of a complete and final body of knowledge that can be worked out systematically, grounded in reason, and wielded as an instrument of violence against others. Westphal writes that "Christian thought is not a metanarrative in this sense."

He allows that Christianity *is* a metanarrative in the sense that it embodies "a philosophy of history, a big story in which we place the little stories of our lives as individuals and communities," and encompasses all that "runs from creation and the fall through the life, death, and resurrection of Jesus to the second coming, the resurrection of the dead, and the life everlasting." But this is unilluminating. We're not told what it means to call Christianity "a big story." We're not told whether this story is true, whether God is our story of him. Westphal says nothing about the conditions for knowing this story to be true. He does not even say whether it *can* be known to be true.

Instead, he draws three contrasts between "the big Christian story" and its transformation into a metanarrative in Lyotard's sense: (1) as kerygma it is opposed to apologetics, (2) it originates in biblical revelation, not philosophy, and (3) it "legitimizes only one kingdom, the Kingdom of God" and "delegitimizes every human kingdom," including the kingdoms of Western modernity that seek hegemony in the world and expect the final state of God's kingdom to resemble their own.

Postmodernists have a curious penchant for talking about "story." Notice, this is the category most frequently used by postmodernists (and their close friends) when talking about the enterprise of theology. But what is the point of calling "the faith once for all delivered to the saints" (Jude 3) "a big story"? As I explained in an earlier chapter, stories have propositional structure. But stories may be regarded as in some sense compelling, even if they are not *believed.* But the "Christian story" is presented as kerygma, and thus it is offered as something to be believed.

The goal of biblical kerygma is conviction that certain things are true—the production of a knowledge of the truth—and with that, salvation (see 2 Tim. 2:24–26). Thus, kerygma is not opposed to apologetics, understood as rational persuasion of the truth of Christianity. We have the example of Jesus in the Gospels and of the apostles in the Book of Acts, for whom the preaching of the gospel was repeatedly accompanied by an appeal to reason and evidence to support its claims. As St. Peter remarked, the believer has a reasonable hope that is so attractive that he or she must be prepared to "make a defense to anyone who asks for a reason" for that hope (1 Pet. 3:15 ESV).

Does kerygma "originate in biblical revelation"? Certainly, kerygma is *known* through divine revelation. And this revelation includes the Bible, the historical presence of Jesus Christ in the world, and the whole panoply of creation as God's handiwork, plus whatever can be discerned about God, his character, and his intentions from his providential oversight of the events of human history. All of this and more is data for the theologian to sort into a coherent, unified, and plausible account of reality that is more than just a big story. The kerygma—the gospel that is preached—can thus be preached in such a way that it is seen to be the "Good News" that it is.

What about the threat of hegemony and violence? For Lyotard, a metanarrative is inherently functionally violent, as if the very acceptance of a rationally supported worldview leads ineluctably to the imposition of that same worldview on unwilling victims. There are, to be sure, cases of autocratic ideologues who resort to smug denunciation of, and painful reprisals against, those who disagree. But this is hardly an ineluctable consequence of the systematic organization of religious knowledge grounded in reason and evidence. On the contrary, rationally grounded conviction should act as a deterrent to demagoguery. When theologians accord to reason a prominent place in their efforts to know divine reality, their methods of persuasion should be anything but violent, repressive, or manipulative.

Meekness is an intellectual virtue. But it is a virtue whose exercise depends upon the existence of a well-stocked cellar of rational beliefs. In response to the arbitrary enforcement of politically correct ideas and behavior—in any arena, whether it be politics, or science, or education, or theology—what is needed is intellectual meekness, not limpness of conviction, or groundless belief, or even a level playing field. It is inherently wrong to use a well-grounded system of belief—arrived at through the agonistic process—as a club to beat conviction into others.

Perspectivism

Third, Westphal worries that Christian theologians have a tendency to regard themselves as the privileged repositories of absolute truth. Postmodernism chastens this tendency with its emphasis on "perspectivism." Perspectivism, says Westphal, is a unifying aspect of the postmodernisms of Nietzsche, Heidegger, Derrida, Foucault, and Rorty. In some sense, we are to believe, perspectivism is a good thing. So what is "postmodern perspectivism," and what are its virtues?

The basic point, says Westphal, is that "we are not God. We do not occupy an absolute, all-encompassing point of view but see whatever we see, including right and wrong, from a particular standpoint constituted to a significant degree by contingencies of linguistic use and sociohistorical location." Perspectivism, he allows, is a form of relativism, but only in the sense that "our insights, whether they be factual or normative, are relative to the standpoint from which they are made, and that the standpoint we occupy . . . inevitably betrays that it is not an absolute standpoint, an all-inclusive, 'totalizing' point of view that sees everything and is blind to nothing."

There are problems with the perspectivism sanctioned by Westphal. First, it is puzzling to hear him insist that perspectivism is *not* a form of the relativism that says "anything goes, . . . all views are equally 'valid.'" The evidence he offers is meager. He points out that Nietzsche believed that Dionysian piety had more going for it than Christianity, and that Rorty repudiates cruelty. But all this means is that Nietzsche and Rorty do take stands on substantive issues. It does not mean that they are not relativists regarding the comparative plausibility of alternative standpoints. If their respective commitments are not grounded in a way that underscores their greater plausibility, then are they not relative in the sense that Westphal denies?

Second, Westphal acknowledges that postmodernists sometimes overstate the case. They talk as if they had shown that "there is no Absolute Truth because there is no one to occupy the Absolute Point of View," such that "if we are not God, no one else could be." In other words, these postmodernists are atheists. But perhaps we should ask why they are atheists and how their atheism is related logically to their perspectivism.

Suppose they believe *no one,* including God, *could* occupy such an objective point of view. If the main argument for postmodern perspectivism is an a priori argument for such generalized perspectivism, then the denial of God's existence is essential to postmodern perspectivism. Postmodernists who "overstate the case" seem to accept the following claim:

If perspectivism is true, then God does not exist.

By *modus tollens,* if God does exist, then perspectivism is false. This says something about the nature of postmodern perspectivism and its motivation. So what is left of such postmodern perspectivism to attract the Christian theologian and act as a tonic for the task of Christian theology? Perhaps Westphal could explain how the specifically postmodern argument for perspectivism does not lead to atheism.

Third, what are we to make of the fact that the Christian theologian does not occupy an omniscient standpoint? Even though we do not occupy an omniscient standpoint, there is a God who does, and this God is in the business of revealing truth to his epistemically fallible creatures.

Fourth, what is the basis for Westphal's own assurance that postmodernists go too far when they deny the existence of God? Why, according to Westphal, should one be a theist rather than an atheist? Even the mitigated perspectivism, that says only that we who are not God occupy a socially conditioned standpoint, must be able to transcend that standpoint to some degree in order to judge that atheism is beyond the pale.

You don't have to be a postmodernist, or find anything attractive about postmodernism, to confess that we do not occupy some privileged perspective from which we see everything and are blind to nothing. Postmodernity's peculiar way of making this point is, I think, inimical to the very idea that we do see some things, that knowledge is possible—even when our knowledge is partial. Postmodernists go over the top, not only when they deny that there is *some* Absolute Point of View, but also when they talk about the relativity of our own standpoint, as if it is so radically socially conditioned that we don't actually know anything that is objectively true. Fallibilism is not by any means a uniquely postmodern distinctive. On the contrary, postmodernism cherishes a distinctive form of fallibilism that more closely approximates epistemological nihilism. Postmodernity's critique of epistemological excess is so shrill that we do well to lend it a deaf ear.

Postmodernism falters in its diagnosis of our cognitive limitations. Westphal says, "instead of running in terror from perspectival relativism," we should "look it in the face to see whether it can be read as a commentary on the limitations of our insight *due to our finitude and fallenness.*" I've highlighted the last part of his remark to draw attention to the fact that his counsel assumes Christian knowledge about the human situation that is denied by the postmodernists he regards as useful guides in the quest for theological knowledge. They know nothing of our "fallenness," or even of our "finitude" in the Christian sense of that term. We are God's creatures; our existence is contingent. Thus, we are *finite.* Furthermore, we have twisted wills that find expression even in our attempts to acquire nonaccidentally true beliefs about the things that matter most. This is because we are not only finite but also *fallen.* These conceptions of finitude and fallenness are distinctively biblical. They are not categories to which the postmodernist as such can appeal in counseling restraint. The biblical diagnosis of human cognitive failure is so much richer, not only for the truth that it tells about our limitations, but also for its optimism about the possibility of knowledge.

So I conclude that Westphal's appeal to postmodern frameworks in epistemology is inherently risky and needs to be counterbalanced with an account of theological knowledge that must be repudiated by the postmodern. As I argued in my earlier chapter, an appropriately modest version of foundationalism is much better suited to the goals of Christian theology.

James K. A. Smith on Incredulity toward Metanarratives

Jamie Smith seeks to clear up some misunderstandings about Jean-François Lyotard's conception of a metanarrative and to show that Christianity is not a metanarrative in Lyotard's sense of the term. Whereas Westphal expresses an affinity for much postmodern reflection, Jamie explicitly labels himself a "postmodern." Jamie believes, first, that Lyotard's conception of a metanarrative has been seriously misunderstood, and second, that once it is understood, Christian theologians should be able to see that Christianity is not a metanarrative at all, and that "postmodernity's incredulity toward 'metanarratives'" is "an ally rather than a foe."

Lyotard famously defined the postmodern as "incredulity toward metanarratives," or what the French call *grands récits*. Jamie worries that Lyotard has been seriously misunderstood by many evangelical critics of postmodernism, and that as a result their criticisms have been aimed at a caricature of postmodernism, or at least of Lyotard's version of it.

Jamie asks, "But *is* the biblical story a 'metanarrative'?" For Lyotard, the Hegelian system, Marx's historical materialism, and the narrative of (or the narrative that is) modern science, are all metanarratives. For Lyotard, metanarratives "are stories which not only tell a grand story . . . but also claim to be able to *legitimate* the story and its claims *by appeal to universal Reason.*" The problem with all metanarratives is that they are themselves "grounded in a myth and faith-commitments."

Jamie argues that Christian faith is not a metanarrative, and here's why: "the biblical narrative and Christian faith do not claim to be legitimated by an appeal to a universal, autonomous Reason, but rather by an appeal to *faith* (or, to translate, 'myth' or 'narrative')." This sounds suspiciously like gobbledygook. The statement allows that "the biblical narrative," whatever that is, is legitimated after a fashion. And how is it legitimated? By "an appeal to faith." And what is an appeal to faith? The question goes without an answer.

What does Jamie mean when he says that Christian belief is not legitimated by an appeal to a universal, autonomous Reason? Is there some other kind of reason, that is not "universal" or "autonomous" in the sense that he reproves, that *could* ground Christian belief?

Well, says Jamie, "all knowledge is grounded in" narrative or myth. It would be a whole lot more helpful if Jamie would explain this idea in terms of specific cases of knowledge. Let him give us some examples of knowledge from a broad range of domains. Perhaps he could start with my knowledge that there's an orange tree in my backyard. Or maybe he would prefer to take one step back and consider my knowledge that I have a backyard. How is my knowledge of such things "grounded in narrative"? What is it for something to be knowledge, if it is grounded in this way? Does knowledge grounded in narrative involve belief? Or truth? These are simple matters of exposition of his own view that he did not take the time to provide.

And what does Jamie mean by "grounded"? Does he mean "epistemically justified"? If he does not, then there are two problems. First, he equivocates in his use of the term *grounded,* meaning one thing by this term when speaking of *reason* as a possible ground of knowledge, and something altogether different (but who knows what?) when speaking of *narrative* (or myth) as a ground of "knowledge." Second, he uses the term *knowledge* in an idiosyncratic, antiepistemological sense that obviates the relevance of epistemic grounding. This, too, is equivocation.

If, on the other hand, Jamie does mean that knowledge is *epistemically* grounded, then his claim that knowledge is grounded in narrative (or myth) suggests that narrative (or myth) is somehow *truth-conducive.* But then he owes us an account of how narrative (or myth) *can* be truth-conducive, how a narrative or a myth can make it likely that what is believed is true (assuming that belief is part of the act of having a narrative).[4]

Jamie says that "modern society is at a loss to adjudicate the competing claims" about morality. "There can be no appeal to a higher court." Why not? If he answers that this is because people will always disagree and remain unconvinced of some other position, what does that prove? There is the possibility that the refusal to be persuaded is sometimes irrational, that what one believes is not epistemically grounded, no matter what one happens to think. And even if various narratives embody competing conceptions of rationality or competing conceptions of what grounds a narrative, it doesn't follow that there is no correct conception. So what is Jamie's case for his brand of relativism?

He says that "criteria which determine what constitutes 'evidence' or 'proof' must be *game-relative.*" But why think that? It may be true that criteria of this sort "will function as rules only for those who share the same paradigm or participate in the same language game." But suppose one group gets the rules right? Why shouldn't members of that group pity those who don't get the rules right? Jamie will say that no one gets them right. But what makes him so sure? He seems pretty sure of himself when he's telling us what counts as a language game and why this is all that rational discourse amounts to. Whom is he seeking to convince, and on what basis?

To say, as Jamie does, that "there is a plurality of logics" seems to mean that each narrative satisfies a certain set of logical constraints, even though these logical constraints happen to be internal to the narratives themselves. Why should this count against their legitimation, unless there is something objectively logically wrong with such bootstrapping? But then there would be some *external* logical stricture against bootstrapping. And external logical constraints on narrative are said to be nonexistent. Postmodern incredulity is in no position to object to bootstrapping, since it cannot appeal to some external criterion for delegitimation. Postmodern incredulity is an exercise in "delegitimation." But exercises in delegitimation are no better off than exercises in "legitimation."

Recall that Jamie says explicitly that he will *argue* that Christianity is not a metanarrative. But why bother with argument if Jamie is himself locked within a narrative with no hope of persuading others of its value? And what counts as an argument if it makes no appeal to reason?

With this in mind, we come to Jamie's claim that "Christian scholars ought to ally themselves" with the postmodern critique of metanarratives. His only criterion for ensuring the safety of such an alliance seems to be that it will not require that we jettison the biblical narrative.[5] That is, we can greet *all* metanarratives with incredulity and still embrace the biblical narrative. This says a lot about what Jamie believes the biblical narrative to be, or not to be. One wonders what he has to say about the many elements in scripture concerned with persuading those who do not yet believe, and who therefore must be playing a different and incommensurable language game (if Lyotard is correct). If Christian theologians are to address the world and beckon others to join in their "language game," on what basis will they do so?

Jamie holds that when Christian theologians follow Lyotard's counsel, "the playing field is leveled, and new opportunities to voice a Christian philosophy are created." How so? By leveling the playing field in the suggested manner, Christian thinkers must abandon all hope of ever persuading nonbelievers of the truth of Christianity. What could possibly be the basis for an appeal to abandon one language game in favor of another if reason has no bearing on the decision? No, when Christian theologians show up for the game wearing postmodern uniforms, a black cloud descends upon the playing field, and the game will have to be called on account of darkness.

John Franke on Nonfoundationalist Theology

John Franke understands postmodernism as an attempt to "rethink the nature of rationality" following the demise of foundationalist epistemology. Moreover, he welcomes the "nonfoundationalist turn," thinking that Christian theologians would do well to reconstruct theology along nonfoundationalist lines.

What unifies the different permutations of postmodernism is its critical agenda, namely, "the rejection of the central features of modernity, such as its quest for certain, objective, and universal knowledge, along with its dualism and its assumption of the essential goodness of knowledge." Franke doesn't take the time to explain what he means by "universal knowledge," "dualism," and "the essential goodness of knowledge." (Readers should like to know what these terms refer to before they are asked to agree that what they refer to is bad.) Apparently, as a package they represent a pretentious form of rationality that must be replaced by something more modest.

Franke's Case for a Chastened Rationality

A "chastened rationality" will have the following several features. First, it will abandon a *realist* view of truth and the world in favor of a *constructionist* view of truth and the world. If this is to be the wholesale exchange that Franke seems to suggest, then there is no world other than the world that is "constructed" by human consciousness, and so no world external to consciousness that may differ from human conceptions of the world.[6] This is what it means to trade a realist view for a constructionist view.

Franke, one may be relieved to learn, is not altogether consistent on this point. For he does speak as if there is some objective world that exists independent of human consciousness in contrast to the world as "constructed" within human consciousness (by means of language, for example). Furthermore, there appears to be some sort of relation between the objective world and the constructed world. Perhaps the constructed world is to be regarded as a representation of the objective world; and this representation may be more or less accurate. Franke does suggest that no such representation will be completely accurate, when he says that "no simple, one-to-one relationship exists between language and the world, and thus no single linguistic description can serve to provide an objective conception of the 'real' world."

His use of quotation marks when speaking of the "real" world does make one wonder whether he believes in the existence of a mind- or language-independent world, which would be a form of realism. It would be nice to have an unequivocal declaration of his conviction about such a basic matter. We don't quite know what to make of his idea of a "constructed world" without clarification on this point. Is the constructed world the mind's response to an independently existing world, or is it ultimately the only sort of world there is? If the former, then Franke is more of a realist than he thinks, and there is real significance in the question, "Do we have knowledge?" For the concept of knowledge, I would argue, requires something to be known. If the latter, then Franke's narrative conception of Christianity is nothing more than a mental or social or linguistic construct with no tie to a mind- or language-independent reality.

Second, within a "chastened rationality," the very idea of metanarrative is no longer credible. Here we are brought back to Lyotard's recommended "incredulity toward metanarratives," which I have already addressed in my discussion of Jamie Smith. What I would add for special emphasis here is that Jamie and Franke have very different conceptions of what Lyotard means, and that Franke seems to be about as reliable an interpreter of Lyotard as he is of Descartes and the throng of living, breathing, and very influential contemporary foundationalists.

Third, and above all, "the chastened rationality of postmodernity entails the rejection of epistemological foundationalism and the adoption of a nonfoundationalist and contextual approach to the theological enterprise." Well, I suppose Franke is at least right in saying that postmodernism "entails the rejection of foundationalism." But the required denial of foundationalism is hardly a virtue of postmodernism. It is one of the best reasons to be wary of postmodernism. Thankfully, since foundationalism is as vigorous as ever, there is no need to flee to a nonfoundationalist, contextualist approach in doing theology.

Of course, in characterizing foundationalism, Franke completely misses the boat. Here's what he says:

> At the heart of the foundationalist agenda is the desire to overcome the uncertainty generated by the tendency of fallible human beings to error and the inevitable disagreements and controversies that follow. Foundationalists are convinced that the only way to solve this problem is to find some means of grounding the entire edifice of human knowledge on invincible certainty.

He immediately and unaccountably adds that "this quest for complete epistemological certitude" is "often termed 'strong' or 'classical' foundationalism." Notice, this itself implies a distinction *within* foundationalist thought. Unfortunately, Franke fails to chase down this distinction, and mistakenly assumes that his critique is so generally effectual that the Christian theologian has no alternative but to embrace a nonfoundationalist approach in theology.

Recall that Franke began with the promise of a generalized critique of foundationalism. What he offers instead is a feeble attack on foundationalism of a certain sort, not foundationalism itself. It is disappointing to see this hapless tendency congeal into an irresponsible habit. René Descartes is the favorite whipping boy of all who lack the patience to understand the central elements of, and the richness of perspective within, foundationalism. In an earlier chapter, I developed and defended a version of foundationalism that explains how knowledge is possible. In its main outlines, it is a version of foundationalism that enjoys widespread support among contemporary epistemologists. And yet, foundationalism is said by Franke to be in dramatic retreat. This is what you might expect from its despisers, but saying so won't make it so.[7]

Franke says, "the heart of the postmodern quest for a chastened rationality lies in the rejection of the foundationalist approach to knowledge." But the suggestion that postmodernism is actively seeking a more chastened rationality strikes me as ludicrous. Neither Merold Westphal, nor Jamie Smith, nor John Franke have anything to say in their chapters about how theological knowledge is possible.

There are problems with Franke's critique of foundationalism. The most basic problem is that it is a caricature of foundationalism. It is to be hoped that Franke will not ignore his responsibility to show how his general critique of foundationalism relates to the more widely accepted foundationalism I delineated in my chapter for Part I of this book. And since his initial chapter focuses especially on the critique of foundationalism, while the other contributors take up different issues, it is to be expected that he will correct this omission in his chapter for Part II of this book.

Franke's Nonfoundationalist Approach to Theology

I conclude that Franke's preference for a nonfoundationalist theology is unmotivated, since it rests on a specious critique of foundationalist epistemology. But his nonfoundationalist alternative suffers from independently debilitating problems as well.

What is Franke's nonfoundationalist alternative? He thinks it should have the following features: First, it should not demand that knowledge systems include a class of beliefs that are immune to criticism. Second, it should maintain that reasoning within the system proceeds conversationally in multiple directions. Third, it should emphasize the local, the particular, and the practical, rather than the universal, the general, and the theoretical.

The first thing to notice is that these are desiderata for a satisfactory approach to epistemic justifications within theology. They do not provide an account of epistemic justification or of how knowledge is possible.

Second, the first desideratum is utterly neutral between foundationalism and its alternatives. Foundationalism may be as modest as you like about the scope of knowledge and the strength of justification. The most promising way to discover the virtue of foundationalism as an account of epistemic justification is to consider particular cases of knowledge, especially those cases where one has a direct awareness of what is known. But of course, humans have finite cognitive faculties and will err. Foundationalism can easily accommodate this fact about the knowledge enterprise.

Third, the second desideratum is too vague to be of much use. What does Franke mean by suggesting that "reasoning . . . proceeds conversationally in multiple directions"? It is dangerous to be guessing about the meaning of a basic axiom for theological practice. But Franke has left us with little choice. Perhaps Franke means that one's method in theology, and hence one's approach to epistemic justification, should encourage dialogue with others, a fair-minded and sincerely open discussion of competing knowledge claims and their rational support. Foundationalism is amenable to this, of course. Perhaps Franke means that a system of rationality must recognize an array of sources of belief and justification for belief. Again, foundationalism is accommodating. Sources of belief, justification, and knowledge include sensory perception, rational intuition, logical inference (deductive and inductive), testimony, memory, religious experience, and so on.

But perhaps Franke means something very different. Perhaps his second desideratum refers to the characteristic postmodern idea "that all groups have a right to speak for themselves, in their own voice, *and have that voice accepted as authentic and legitimate.*"[8] Here foundationalism must demur. Pluralism is not an unqualified virtue. Some voices are plausible, while others are not. Legitimacy will depend on the epistemic status of what is voiced. If the alleged grounds for whatever happens to be proposed are not truth-conducive—if they do not tend to make it likely that what is proposed is true—then they have no place in the discussion. Their voice may be wistful, but it will not be worthy of equal time.

Fourth, Franke favors the local, the particular, and the practical over the universal, the general, and the theoretical. This does not look like a desideratum for an adequate theory of epistemic justification. Certainly it is desirable that our conception of the possibility and ground of knowledge permit more than merely theoretical knowledge. We do naturally desire knowledge of many particular truths, and we do require knowledge that is an advantage in our efforts to lead lives free from illusion, knowledge that is "practical." But again, these are aims that fuel foundationalism; they do not conflict with it.

Franke says that his nonfoundationalist method in theology "involves the interplay of three sources: scripture, culture, and tradition." The first thing to notice is that most of what he says about the function of these sources in his so-called nonfoundationalist method is perfectly compatible with a foundationalist epistemology (not that I would agree with everything Franke says about these matters). So, we're left to wonder, what is distinctively nonfoundationalist in the approach he recommends?

Notice, furthermore, that Franke has nothing to say about why we should trust the three sources of theological knowledge—scripture, culture, and tradition. He doesn't tell us what justifies his conviction that these are bona fide sources of knowledge. And his repudiation of foundationalism leaves him with little hope of offering a rational basis for accepting these sources. When these sources are challenged, is the Christian theologian supposed to be free to dismiss or ignore the challenges? Why should he? And why would he want to if there are good reasons to believe what Franke likes to call "the Christian story"?

In the end, Franke has bid foundationalism a premature farewell and has offered in its place something that is entirely too sketchy to be a genuine alternative to foundationalism, and something that in many respects is entirely consistent with the foundationalist account of knowledge, though he seems not to realize it.

Conclusion

I have had space here to consider in some detail only three of the contributions to Part I of this book. I have addressed the issues raised by Merold Westphal, James K. A. Smith, and John Franke, who all, in one way or another, adopt a postmodernist approach to doing theology. It is disappointing to find that these contributors have so little to say about the possibility of knowledge and the conditions for acquiring knowledge, which are essential aims of theology.

Notes

1. Pauline Marie Rosenau, *Post-Modernism and the Social Sciences* (Princeton, NJ: Princeton University Press, 1992), 17.

2. See John Seabrook, "The David Lynch of Architecture," *Vanity Fair*, January 1991, 126, cited in Rosenau, *Post-Modernism and the Social Sciences*, 7.

3. See Laurence Paul Hemming, *Heidegger's Atheism: The Refusal of a Theological Voice* (Notre Dame, IN: University of Notre Dame Press, 2002), 213. Hemming's book explores Heidegger's complex relationship to theology, and to Christian theology in particular.

4. When Jamie says that "all knowledge is rooted in *some* narrative or myth," he offers this as an instance of knowledge. This is an interesting knowledge claim in its own right. Jamie asserts this like it's an instance of knowledge. Because he doesn't say what he means by *knowledge*, we're stuck with assuming that he means at the very least that what he says is true. The question is, how does he know that it's true?

5. See Franke's chapter in Part I of the present book.

6. Franke doesn't speak of consciousness, but he speaks of language and other social conventions as determining one's conception of the world.

7. As it turns out, some whom Franke adopts into the brotherhood are themselves foundationalists who have been quite critical of postmodern epistemology. Alvin Plantinga is a notable example. See his withering critique of postmodernism in *Warranted Christian Belief* (New York: Oxford University Press, 2000). Franke

fails to see (and so, I think, does Vanhoozer) that Plantinga's repudiation of "classical foundationalism" was not a general repudiation of foundationalism. His conception of properly basic belief in God is best understood as a kind of foundationalism regarding the knowledge of God's existence.

8. See David Harvey, *The Condition of Postmodernity* (Oxford: Blackwell, 1990), 48; emphasis added.

8

Postmodernism and the Priority of the Language-World Relation

R. Scott Smith

In this chapter, my primary purpose is to survey strengths and weaknesses of my fellow contributors' essays, and I will show how the issue of the language-world relation continually recurs. It is, I think, the single most important issue in the whole discussion of postmodernism and its relation to Christianity. I also will anticipate some arguments against my other chapter's points. And, I will advance further support for my contention that postmodernists who hold to an internal relation of language and world actually presuppose an epistemic access to an extralinguistic, objective world. I will offer a few examples to help show that we can, and often do, have contact with such a world. Finally, I will make applications of my argument to a few more of Christianity's core doctrines. Christianity is not the kind of thing that can survive a transformation into a linguistic construction.

Franke, Foundationalism, and the Language-World Relation

There are many strengths of Franke's essay and his closely related book, *Beyond Foundationalism,* which he coauthored with Stan Grenz.

To name a few, Franke rightly points out that too often critics of post-modern thought jump to the conclusion that such views automatically are relativistic.[1] Franke also raises quite interesting ideas regarding three sources for doing theology, namely, scripture, tradition, and culture, and the Holy Spirit's role in each. Here, he takes his postmodern approach quite consistently, and he also provides a way to unify the various local Christian communities by the Holy Spirit's in-breaking into their particular languages. That is, he anticipates and attempts to ward off a problem: if all theological reflection is discrete, and languages also are discrete, how can there be any unity to Christian language?

Now, Franke holds to a tight language-world relation, such that we are inside language and cannot know the world as it is in itself. In light of this, it is worthwhile exploring some of his claims. First, Franke notes that it is hard to pin down what *postmodernism* means. Surely he is right, but a major reason why can be explained by appeal to his view of language and world. If languages are particular, and meanings of terms are their use within particular communities, then there is no essence we may know of *postmodernism*. Instead, there is only *postmodernism* as it is used within particular communities.

The same conclusion applies to Franke's assertion that foundationalism should be given up for dead. From what standpoint is he uttering this claim? Charitably, it is one made from within his particular linguistic community, one that has shaped and made its world by how it uses its particular language. But on his own account, there is no way to get an objective vantage point, so Franke cannot hope to give us the objective truth about foundationalism's state. Instead, he must be telling us how his particular community has made its world, and in it foundationalism is dead. But what world is this? Franke does not tell us, but that information makes all the difference, if indeed languages are discrete and tied to use in particular communities. As I argued before, it will not suffice to appeal to a generalized Christian language, as Christians are not some homogeneous community either. In short, if we take his views seriously, then all he is telling us is how his community has constructed its own world. But that seems to violate the spirit with which he has written. Franke does not tell us that all he has written is just how they talk in his form of life. Rather, he tells us throughout several pages (and more in *Beyond Foundationalism*) that foundationalism is dead, and it is indeed time to move on to a better way. But this kind of writing lends credence to my conclusion that his view presupposes an epistemic access to an extralinguistic world, in order to deny that this is possible.

It also is telling that Franke cites only those with whom he agrees. Never does he quote from any philosopher who is a foundationalist, and there are many, as Geivett points out in the quote from Michael DePaul. It seems odd that Franke does not even countenance a counterargument that a foundationalist might offer. It is as though Franke thinks that no argument is needed to dismiss foundationalism. Perhaps he intends to make a Wittgensteinian gesture to dismiss it, because he may think we should not talk in a foundationalist way anymore.

Moreover, it is curious that Franke writes approvingly of Alvin Plantinga as a Reformed epistemologist. Yet, he never addresses the fact that Plantinga is a type of foundationalist. Plantinga surely rejects Cartesian foundationalism, but he does not give up on foundationalism altogether; otherwise, how are we to understand his appeal to properly *basic* beliefs?

I think, then, that he and others reject foundationalism for a key reason *besides* the frequent charges about a misguided search for certainty. Instead, I suggest that it is due mainly to the acceptance of the idea that language and world are internally related. If that is the case, then we cannot have universal truths that serve as foundational, basic beliefs, since these would be formed by having epistemic access to the real world. This same language-world issue will resurface in Jamie Smith's essay, to which I now turn.

Smith, Lyotard, and "Metanarratives," and the Level Playing Field

Jamie's essay provides a careful exposition of Lyotard, showing us that on Lyotard's own understanding of "metanarratives," Christianity should not be so classified. I also appreciate Jamie's care to show that simply making claims that are universal in scope is not sufficient for a view to be a metanarrative. We can see that in Kallenberg's and Hauerwas's work, where both unapologetically make universal claims but also realize that these are claims made from within a particular way of life.

What intrigues me most, though, are Jamie's views about the language-world relation. He gives us many indications, all the while not explicitly addressing that topic. For instance, Jamie claims that the postmodern condition exposes all knowledge as rooted in some narrative. Further, there is "no appeal to a higher court that would transcend a historical context or language game, no neutral observer or 'God's-eye-view' which can legitimate or justify one paradigm or moral language above another." We cannot transcend our particularity, and every language game has its own rules. So for Jamie it seems we cannot get outside our language and know an objective, extralinguistic world.

In light of this, I find some of his claims hard to understand. For instance, what has Jamie actually given us in his exposition of Lyotard? If we press the strong particularity of languages and communities, and if language and world are internally related, then presumably he has reported how his community talks and has made its world, such that in it, Lyotard means what Jamie reports. But, just as there is no essence to language, there can be no essence to Lyotard; there is only Lyotard-as-he-is-used-in-specific-communities.

This line of argument reflects a kind of incredulity I have toward the many claims people make who tell us that language and world are internally related. Consider other cases, where Jamie tells us that Christianity is not a metanarrative, and where he argues that "what is at stake in postmodernism is *the relationship between faith and reason.*" Now these are interesting claims on one level, but they still suffer from the same besetting problem; namely, they are statements of how his community talks and has constructed its world. And if his community is just discrete, as it should be on this kind of view, then he owes us his readers an account of out of which community he speaks. It makes all the difference, for if we do not share the same community, then we will talk different languages and inhabit different worlds.

Jamie also claims that an advantage of postmodernism is to level the playing field, thereby giving unique opportunities for Christian philosophical reflection. But to whom, and from what standpoint, do we speak as Christians? It seems that in Jamie's particular community, they talk such that the playing field is leveled, and that is what makes it level—for them. But other communities will talk differently, and in their worlds the playing field may not be level, or that concept may not even exist! To be consistent, it does not seem that Jamie can mean that the playing field has been leveled in the extralinguistic world. But, on the other hand, he does not seem content to make a claim that this is just how his community happens to talk. If that were the case, why bother to write this essay for a wide audience? So it seems that Jamie does not want to just tell us how his community happens to talk. Instead, he wants to tell us how things really are, namely, in the *real* world. But of course that conclusion undermines core features of his view.

Westphal, Perspectivism, and Apostolic Knowledge

Much like Jamie, I think we are indebted to Westphal for his pointed expositions of Heidegger and Lyotard. Based upon his interpretation of Heidegger's understanding and critique of onto-theology, Westphal seems quite right in his conclusion that Christianity is not onto-theological. The same goes for his discussion of Lyotard's use of the concept of metanarratives, and how Christianity is not his target. In both cases, Westphal does us a service by pointing out the prophetic nature of their critiques, even as it can apply to some Christians' tendencies to treat our faith.

My focus here, however, will be on Westphal's brief section on perspectivism and his application of it to the apostle Paul. He considers two different understandings of perspectivism. Regarding the first, I agree that I have yet to meet a postmodernist who would advocate that all views are equally valid. A second kind of perspectivism is the dual claim that "our insights . . . are relative to the standpoint from which they are made" and "the standpoint we occupy (even when making this claim) inevitably betrays that it is not . . . blind to nothing."

How should we interpret this claim? On one interpretation, this perspectivism is relatively innocuous, in that he could mean that we simply do indeed talk from particular standpoints, and no position allows us to know everything. For example, just as I am writing from southern California, so Westphal is writing (presumably) from New York, and as humans, we are not omniscient. This interpretation does not preclude our knowing objective truths.

But in another sense, perspectivism is the view that facts *themselves* are relative to language. This is the sense that Brad Kallenberg has in mind. A given world is as it is since a community has talked in such a way as to make it that way. Clearly, this is anything but a trivial claim, as it makes all the difference where one stands.

What is difficult for me to discern, at least from this essay, is where Westphal stands on the language-world relation. Just how tight is that relation for him? It does not seem he would want to argue for the innocuous kind of perspectivism I described above, yet it is unclear to me if he would subscribe completely to the latter version, either. While he does admit that even our factual claims are made from certain standpoints, he also warns that we should not "swallow postmodern philosophy hook, line, and Derrida." But what boundary conditions does he have in mind?

When he asserts that there is no absolute, "blind to nothing" standpoint, he might mean that there simply is no God's-eye view available to us, such that we cannot know objective truths. On the other hand, he might mean that we are not God, and as such, even though we can know objective truths, we still have limited perspectives. So we his readers simply need him to clarify his stance. That is, while I can concede some validity to his point that perspectivism can be a commentary on our human "finitude and fallenness," we need him to spell out what he believes about the language-world relation.

If he were to do this, we likely would see one of two things. First, we might see that he does indeed leave some room for epistemic access to reality, all the while admitting that we do have limited knowledge. I can support this view, as I do believe we can and often do have epistemic contact with an extralinguistic world, although we can get things quite wrong. Later in this essay, I will attempt to support this positive contention. But, second, we might see that he does hold to a tight internal language-world relation. In that case, the same kinds of problems for which I argued earlier resurface. Westphal would be giving us just a construction of how his community happens to talk, and, as we have seen in other writers, he does not tell us which specific community that is.

For Westphal, even though we do not have an absolute point of view, it does not follow that we cannot witness to absolute truth. His exemplar seems to be the apostle Paul, who had great confidence in the gospel message, but also wrote that we only know in part and see in a mirror dimly. I have three points by way of reply. First, yes, Paul did make such claims, and it is not that he was trying to say that as an apostle he had an omniscient grasp of all truth. Yet, this same man also made very direct statements indicating his clear understanding and knowledge of revealed, objective theological truths. For example, in Colossians 2:3, Paul knew that in Jesus are hidden all the treasures of wisdom and knowledge. By using "hidden," Paul indicated that there are many things that we (including himself) do not fully grasp, yet he was quite clear that indeed all these treasures are found in Christ. Later, Paul wrote that in him all the fullness of deity dwells in bodily form (Col. 2:9). He also claimed to know objective, historical facts, and a prime example is the resurrection—"Christ *has been raised* from the dead" (1 Cor. 15:20, emphasis mine).[2] He knew that Christ really rose from the dead because Jesus himself appeared to him. As one more example, Paul knew that believers have been justified by faith, and they have peace with God and stand in grace (Rom. 5:1).

So, yes, Paul did exhibit a chastened rationality in some respects, in that he did not fully grasp all the depths of revelation. But he did not have to have a "blind to nothing" vantage point in order to know objective truths, ones that are true whether or not anyone believes them or talks that way. God had revealed them to him. And, contrary to Westphal, Paul did not have to be "epistemically of the same substance as the Father" to know these truths.

As a second point, we do not have to have an omniscient viewpoint to know objective truth. There are many things we simply know, such as murder is wrong; torturing babies is wrong; $2 + 2 = 4$; and more. These do not require a "blind to nothing" standpoint. Sure, it is possible that we are mistaken; that our claims are blinded by a will to power; or that our culture has distorted our understanding; but why should we think we do not have knowledge of objective truths in these (and other) particular cases?

Third, in order to witness to objective truth, Westphal's latter kind of perspectivism cannot be relativistic all the way down. If it does due to an internal language-world relation, then all these particular Christians will be doing is behaving according to the grammar of *their* discrete linguistic community, and the meaningfulness of verbal and nonverbal behaviors will be found within that community.

Westphal seems to have in mind those who write as Christians who also think we can know objective truths, and his intent seems to be to chasten them in their knowledge claims. Yet, it might be a good reminder that Christian postmodernists also can exhibit this same "totalizing" tone in their own claims. For instance, Kallenberg has written *Ethics as Grammar* with a missionary zeal to help others come and see as he does, as though he has found *the* way we *ought* to see the world. Stanley Hauerwas thinks the gospel is the true story. Likewise, Franke believes foundationalism is indeed dead. These are confident claims, and we expect these kinds of claims when we read someone's viewpoint, but they hardly are ones that exhibit a chastened rationality. Rather, they indicate that they think they have found the truth.

But most important, Westphal needs to give us an account of how he conceives of the language-world relation. To me, this is the most important issue facing his essay. Now I will turn to Kevin Vanhoozer's essay and examine how he treats this and other considerations.

Vanhoozer, Bulverism, and Epistemic Contact with the World

Vanhoozer's essay is ambitious in its scope of authors addressed, the breadth of arguments made, and the balance he tries to find by accepting some, yet rejecting other, postmodern ideas. He disputes a bulveristic kind of postmodernism, one which "rebuts a *thought* simply by calling attention to the genealogy or location of its *thinker*," rather than refuting that thought. Bulverism corrodes "conviction and commitment" and "deprives the will of anything in which to believe ultimately."

To his credit, Vanhoozer tries to find the strengths and weaknesses in postmodernism, and he draws key lessons Christians can learn from it, as well as perils that Christians should avoid. All these seem well taken to me, but I wish to qualify one "benefit." The release from captivity to modernity allows the return of certain themes, such as transcendence, but postmodernism allows us to *talk* of transcendence but not actually achieve it. Once again, the issue of the relation of language and world resurfaces.

Vanhoozer is right on target also in his criticisms that postmodernism teaches us nothing that the Bible has not already taught us. There are other good points he raises, but I will focus on a tension between postmodern ideas he accepts and those he rejects, which makes it difficult to make definitive responses to his arguments. Nonetheless, I will surface one such tension, and it involves the language-world relation.

Vanhoozer tells us he is after having contact with reality, and our interpreting it rightly, which he says comes only from a specifically Christian way of thinking. Reality, he claims, does not depend upon our language and thought. Further, no one set of descriptions can adequately "carve up" reality. Yet he also tells us that reality is only partially accessible to any particular theory. More pointedly, his critical realism "acknowledges the necessity of language and theories for making contact with reality." Following Newbigin, he also asserts that we always think within fiduciary frameworks of belief. So there is an evident tension between these beliefs. On the one hand, Vanhoozer seems to think we can escape language and even our particularity and know objective reality. But on the other, he seems to lean toward some degree of being inside language or theories.

After Vanhoozer asserts that we need language and theories for making contact with reality, he then observes that "certain aspects of reality come to light only under particular descriptions." If this is all he means by the need for language and theories to make contact with reality, then he needs to clarify his choice of terms in some of the above-quoted passages. But as it stands, I think he has overstated the case. Offering a description of something is not the same as making epistemic contact with it. Furthermore, through some case studies, I will argue that language is not necessary for making such contact.

First, consider how a very young child learns to identify objects and colors and associate them with terms. My nineteen-month-old daughter Anna has been identifying various objects (and pictures thereof) as different colors, shapes, fruits, etc. One book has two adjacent pages with pictures of several fruits scattered on them. She will point at one picture (say, of an orange) and utter "hmmm." We have figured out that she wants my wife and me to tell her the name of the object pictured there, so we will utter "orange." Then she will point at pictures of other fruits and repeat the same process. Yet often I will come back and ask her, "Where are the other oranges?" Without my helping her by pointing to them, she will point to the pictures of other oranges. Then she will do the same if I ask her where are lemons, apples, etc. Now, how is it that she does this? Somehow, she has to be able to see that the picture is of a certain fruit, and not another. We have worked to help her have many noticings of fruits. Then we have labeled those fruits, as well as other objects, with a word when we point to it. In this way, she develops the concept of the object, and when she sees another object of that same kind, even if it is not in the book, she is able to see it for what it is and then identify it as that kind of thing.

Now this account shows at least two main points. First, we can see things for what they are, and from many noticings we develop the concept of that thing. If this were not the case, how could she open an entirely different book with other pictures of fruits and yet be able to pick them out as such when we ask her where they are? Then, we can learn to label that object with a word. Furthermore, we can check up on our initial belief that what we see is an orange, but upon closer inspection, we see that it actually is a slightly orange-colored, oversized lemon.

Second, it seems impossible for me or anyone else to be able to identify *for her* her experiences of the fruits and shapes. As Dallas Willard puts it, "we do not, for the most part, even know what it would be like to have to identify the child's—or any one else's—experiences *for* them, or *teach them how to do it* if they did not already know."[3] So, just like each of us, she has to be able to see what a thing is in order to be able to pick it out as a certain kind of thing, and then to match it up with a term.

As a second case, consider that we are at the funeral of a loved one. Here we confront a stark reality: the person is dead. We may describe this state of affairs in different ways, depending on our language and culture. For instance, Christians may say that the person has "passed away" or "gone home to be with the Lord." The New Testament authors wrote of the person as having "fallen asleep." Physicalists, though, might say that the body has "ceased functioning." Hispanic friends of mine might say that "*la persona murió*" ("the person died"). Regardless of the language used, this is one of those kinds of events in which we "run into" reality. There is a clear-cut state of affairs that exists independent of how we talk in language—the person is dead. Now, we may describe it in various ways so various facets come to light. For instance, doctors might say that the person died from a myocardial infarction. But that does not change the state of affairs—the person is dead.

Third, imagine that we work together as veterinarians. How do we know how to use the word *dog* properly? We do not use *dog* when someone brings in a hamster or a cat. When I take a blood sample, I write on the lab form "dog" so it will check the sample's properties against typical dog blood levels. Now suppose someone in our veterinarian "community" uses *dog* when someone brings in something we agreed to call *wolf*. How is it we know how to check up on each other's term uses and correct them? What seems necessary before any language user in this game can know how to use *dog* properly is that he or she needs to *see* that the animal is in fact a dog, and not something else, *before* he or she can know that the use of *dog* is correct. This kind of seeing requires access to the thing in question, in order that we may know how to describe it in language.

These are but a few examples, but they help show that, contrary to much of the received epistemic wisdom of the age, we do not need language to make contact with reality. Language and world are not internally related. Yet Vanhoozer's related point still stands: some things come to light only under particular descriptions and theories.

Yet, as his essay now stands, his view is vulnerable to being assimilated into Kallenberg's approach, whose view is not the kind that Vanhoozer explicitly disputes. To help show that, I will draw upon some key similarities between their views. For one, per Vanhoozer, bulverism claims that we cannot believe in determinate meaning and absolute truth, yet Kallenberg need not deny these. For example, he believes the gospel is the true story, but we cannot know that truth from some abstract vantage point.

Furthermore, Vanhoozer is most concerned about a skeptical impulse behind bulverism, yet Kallenberg is anything but skeptical. He is confident that he has found the right way to see the world. Finally, Vanhoozer thinks that bulverism will keep us from focusing on Christ, but Kallenberg thinks his approach is precisely the way to do that.

Even so, there are ways they explicitly differ, but here, too, Kallenberg has tools to rebut Vanhoozer and situate his arguments. When Vanhoozer writes that postmodern attention is riveted on the process of our attending to objects, there is no object left. But Kallenberg could reply in a twofold way. For one, of course there are determinate objects in the world, but they are what they are in virtue of how we talk and make them within our community. Secondly, Kallenberg could rebut Vanhoozer by showing that he writes in a far too general way here. That is, Vanhoozer must assume he can get outside language in order to know that there are no objects left whatsoever. Similarly, consider Vanhoozer's claim that we do have contact with the world. Here, too, Kallenberg can reply that Vanhoozer has adopted a stance that bifurcates world and language, a stance that has caused much mischief.

So the key issue for Vanhoozer is this: though he claims we can and do have epistemic contact with the world (a view with which I agree), his belief that we need theories and language for making contact with the world leaves his overall view susceptible to being another constructionist account. Kallenberg simply could say that Vanhoozer *talks* as though he can make contact with world, but he has not come to realize that he too is within language.

Once again, the crucial issue of the relation of language and world comes to the fore. It will come to light again in Doug Geivett's topic.

Geivett and Modest Foundationalism

I agree with Geivett's proposal for a modest foundationalism, but I do not agree with him because I *presuppose* foundationalism, as I have been asked before. Indeed, I do not; rather, I think it most accurately describes how justification actually works, which I know by paying close attention to my own awarenesses.

I have a few suggestions, however, that relate to the language-world relationship. First, Kallenberg and Hauerwas would disagree with his claim that "individuals are free to sample a repertoire of narratives to fit the exigencies of their lives in a purely ad hoc manner." For them, this is just the modern story with its stress on the autonomous individual. Also, they would disavow his definition of false beliefs, put in terms of the correspondence theory of truth, since we cannot escape language and obtain such a viewpoint.

They also would disagree with him that it would be a serious mistake if they were to take Christian theism as the correct account of the world. But Kallenberg and Hauerwas do write such that they think they have found *the* truth. On their view, they can make these truth claims consistently if that is how they talk within their communities. Further, they would say that Geivett has adopted a stance that bifurcates world and language, as he assumes (wrongly) he can get outside language in order to make his claim.

One last item: Geivett observes that postmodernism does not offer a substitute for any theory of justification. But once again, Kallenberg and Hauerwas would offer a hearty "amen" to that. They are not interested in building theories, which is why Hauerwas avoids writing a systematic theology. Instead, they think *theoria* is a misguided search for essences, something of which Wittgenstein sought to cure us.

In the same context, Geivett goes on and says that "there is little point to being concerned about believing what's true if there's nothing one can do to improve one's stock of beliefs or one's chances of acquiring true beliefs." But again, they have a rejoinder. They are concerned with believing what is true, and they want to grow in such beliefs, I think. But, how that is accomplished is not by matching up one's beliefs with how the world really is. Instead, they would say we grow in our understanding of truth as we grow in linguistic fluency within the Christian community.

Now, all these examples serve to make a more significant point. I do not dispute Geivett's claims; rather, I think it makes a difference when one appeals to them, if one is dialoguing with postmodernists who hold to an internal language-world relationship. These replies appeal to this relationship as the basis for rebutting Geivett's claims. Of course, it depends upon who is in the audience, and this book surely will have readers with a wide range of views on postmodernism. But in dialogue with postmodernists, I think it is best that one first show that either the postmodernists presuppose, yet deny, an epistemic access to an objective realm, or they are just making claims from their discrete communities. Then, after making that argument, other issues may be examined, such as ones Geivett raises. But the order is important with a postmodern audience.

Implications for Christianity

All authors in this book have been writing as Christians, though they differ about postmodernism's prospects or perils for the faith. I already have argued that two key consequences follow for Christianity if we hold to an internal language-world relation, and we as Christians make our world by the use of our language. First, God becomes a construct of our language, and thus we become idolaters, even on the terms of our own grammar, the Bible. Second, even if God can break through our language, we cannot, so we cannot know what he intended when he gave revelation to us. We construct what the Bible means according to the rules of our discrete communities. So the prospects of revelation are quite dim.

Space does not permit me to explore in detail the implications for several other core doctrines, but I have done this elsewhere.[4] I simply will point to a few such issues related to Jesus and our need for him. Orthodoxy has held that Jesus is fully God and fully human. Now on the linguistic constructionist view I have criticized in my other chapter, Jesus qua God need not be inside language, but qua human being, he, like the rest of us, is inside language. Even worse, he knows both conditions at the same time! This suggests that Jesus was radically schizophrenic, but scripture does not portray him in this manner at all. Nor would a schizophrenic Savior compel our worship.

But scripture also tells us that there is salvation in no one else (Acts 4:12). Yet, if each world is internally related to a discrete language, then Christians make their world(s) by how they talk in their communities. In that case, "Jesus is the Savior for all who believe" is true within the Christian communities because that is how they talk. But in other communities (e.g., secularists or Muslims), they talk quite differently, so Jesus would not be the Savior in those worlds. But this conclusion undermines what scripture clearly teaches.

The same conclusion follows for our doctrines of hamartiology and justification. What really is the human condition, and what is its solution? Again, it is due to how Christians talk, because that is what makes their worlds for them. So Christians beg some of the most important questions of all—we set up the problem for "all" people as well its solution, and this by our talking.

Finally, though Paul seems to treat the resurrection as an objective, historical fact, that conclusion seems unwarranted if we are inside language. The resurrection would be just a result of how Christians talk. Yet, rule following and linguistic usage seem impotent to restore life to the dead, just as my funeral example above illustrated. The key, then, is if the person speaking has the authority and power to give life, which God does. Language use *itself* does not restore life to the dead, but the power and life of God can, and these are not the same thing as language use.

Conclusion

I have surveyed these core doctrines to show that though there are key insights we as Christians can and should learn from postmodernism, Christianity is *not* the kind of thing that can survive a transformation into a postmodern, linguistic approach. This conclusion is critical, but my main point has been that there are reasons we should not accept the claim that we are inside language and cannot get out. Negatively, I have offered criticisms of postmodernists that they presuppose an epistemic access to an extralinguistic, objective realm in order to deny it. But positively, I also have indicated by a few examples that we can and often do have such access. Repeatedly, I have tried to show that the idea of the internal relation of language and world is perhaps *the* most significant issue at stake in this entire discussion. If it is incorrect, as I have tried to show, then postmodernism at best merely gives us insights that, as Vanhoozer said, we already should have known from scripture.

Notes

1. I have argued elsewhere that this is a standard approach taken in criticisms of Alasdair MacIntyre. But this should not be asked until more important issues are first addressed. For example, are we inside language, or can we get outside it to know an extralinguistic world? For a discussion of the charge of relativism after having addressed other more significant issues, see chapter 8 of my *Virtue Ethics and Moral Knowledge: Philosophy of Language after MacIntyre and Hauerwas* (London: Ashgate, 2003).

2. All biblical quotations are from the *New American Standard Bible*, copyright © 1977 The Lockman Foundation (Anaheim: J. B. McCabe Co., 1977).

3. Dallas Willard, "How Concepts Relate the Mind to Its Objects: The 'God's Eye View' Vindicated," *Philosophia Christi*, ser. 2, 1, no. 2 (1999): 5–20.

4. See chapter 7 of my *Virtue Ethics and Moral Knowledge*.

9

Disputing about Words?
Of Fallible Foundations
and Modest Metanarratives

Kevin J. Vanhoozer

Opening Cartographical Comment: Why Do the Christians Rage?

Let me begin with some remarks about the essays as a whole. Picking up my preferred metaphor for knowledge—the map—these opening cartographical comments are intended to show how I see the lay of the land (philosophical, theological, epistemological) and locate my five conversation partners and myself on it.

My impression upon reading the five other chapters was in fact a double take: first, "What an interesting and well-written book this will make!" I truly enjoyed and learned from each chapter. But my second thought was, "We still have a very long way to go if we do not want to keep talking past one another." For though we are all physically located in North America, we are not all located in the same intellectual countryside, if my cartographical calculations are correct.

Four of us write as philosophers, two (Franke and myself) as theologians. Of the four philosophers, two are at home in Anglo-American analytic philosophy (and appear not to have traveled much, philosophically speaking, that is), while the other two are clearly Europhiles, equally comfortable with Continental as well as analytic philosophy, Kierkegaard and cappuccinos, Being and baguettes.

Why do the Christians rage—at postmodernity, at each other? Many, but not all, of our disagreements stem from misunderstandings. We come from different countries, intellectually speaking, and speak different languages. We have had different experiences with people and books that call themselves postmodern. We associate "the postmodern" with different ideas and trends and hence we work with different *concepts* of the postmodern.[1] This becomes apparent especially when one examines two key concepts in particular: our uses of *foundation* and *metanarrative* were all over the map.

I will spare the reader my attempt to plot each of our positions according to the longitude and latitude of my own intellectual chart. Suffice it to say that I see myself positioned somewhere between the two pairs of philosophers. One might say that I occupy the position of the golden mean, the voice of moderate theological reason; or perhaps I am simply caught in the middle. Be that as it may, I note that I have certain affinities and disagreements with each of the positions here represented. Some no doubt will criticize me for what I say about metanarratives, others for what I say about foundations. Now that I know how my interlocutors use these terms, I should be in a better position to articulate my own position. But it will take time . . .

My response will be in three parts: (1) to the propostmodern philosophers on the subject of metanarratives, (2) to the antipostmodern philosophers on foundations, and (3) to the nonfoundationalist narrative theologian about doing theology without foundations.

A final preliminary point: in my lead essay, I studiously avoided taking "sides" between modernity and postmodernity. I am unwilling to buy into either framework wholesale, not least because, in my experience, each leads to forms of egregious exegesis. Exegesis is the soul of theology, and one of the criteria by which I evaluate a theory, system, or worldview is by examining how it affects the process of biblical interpretation. It is to be regretted, therefore, that none of the contributors explore the impact of their views for the practice of biblical exegesis.

To Westphal

I can relate to Merold Westphal's experience of often being philosophically closer to his non-Christian philosopher friends than to the Christian philosophers who share his faith. I suspect that reading through the other chapters in this book will only confirm his experience. The same thing happens to me all the time, and not only with philosophy. I often find that my tastes and interests in music, literature, art—and yes, philosophy—have more in common with a certain type of non-Christian than they do with many Christians I know. The reason, I think, has to do with the relation of gospel and culture.

The church always lives, breathes, and thinks between gospel and culture. Sometimes when we think we are disagreeing with Christians over the gospel, we are in fact disagreeing about culture. One need only think about styles of music in worship, for example. I'm not suggesting that we reduce our disagreements about the nature of knowledge to the level of differing musical tastes, as if some enjoy foundationalism because of its classical sound while others find foundationalism too funky. I am suggesting, however, that there is such a thing as intellectual culture, and that we all, academics included, are socialized into certain kinds of language games and intellectual practices rather than others.

I introduce the notion of intellectual culture not as a license for an anything-goes relativism, but as an explanation for the phenomenon that Westphal and I sometimes experience, a phenomenon that is amply displayed in the present work. Some of the disagreements in this book, I believe, are the result of an intellectual culture clash. Indeed, postmodernity is for many a kind of culture shock.

Cultures are systems of beliefs and values. It so happens that I do think cultures—especially intellectual cultures or philosophies—can be compared and evaluated (though not from a standpoint that is entirely outside culture). One way of thinking about theology is in terms of culture-critique: one of the tasks of the theologian is to preserve the integrity of the church's witness through a process of self-examination. The challenge is to discern whether, and to what extent, the church's language and thought ultimately accord not merely with the surrounding culture, but with the gospel as it is normatively specified in scripture.

I am not as sanguine about the trickle-down effect from philosophy to culture as is Westphal. I think there is still something to be said for Francis Schaeffer's notion that developments in intellectual culture gradually seep into the public consciousness. The masses don't have to be able to give a philosophical account of epistemological relativism to be affected by it. As I indicated in my own chapter, contemporary mass opinion inconsistently vacillates between modern pride and postmodern sloth.

With regard to Westphal's main point, however, I wholeheartedly agree that many of the postmodern critiques resemble that of the biblical prophets to the extent that they are directed not at Christian faith per se but at idolatrous "religion." If onto-theology stands for the philosophical project that assimilates "God" into an all-encompassing metaphysical conceptual scheme (*unaided* "reason seeking understanding") then I agree that it is inadequate for the purposes of Christian theology. Onto-

theology is a species of what Luther called the "theology of the glory";
Christian theology must be a "theology of the cross."

Westphal indirectly raises the very appropriate question, Should
theology be "systematic"? He is right, I believe, to caution against
theology becoming an onto-theological system. What is wrong with such
systems, I think, is that they are governed by a conceptual scheme—by
an ism like Platonism, existentialism, or panentheism—that ends up getting imposed upon the text. Hans Frei calls this "extratextual" theology.
The prophetic warning of postmodern thinkers against such conceptual
totalization is well taken.

Westphal's concluding section, in which he distinguishes relativism
from perspectivism, deserves careful consideration, and I can only begin
to do it justice here. I think he is right to remind us that we are not
God and that, consequently, we do not know as God knows. There is an
absolute point of view—God's—but we cannot presume that our point
of view necessarily coincides with it. Westphal invokes the apostle Paul
as one who could well serve as the paradigm Christian thinker who
has confidence in divine revelation yet admits that he knows "only in
part."

Paul is hardly a poster child for postmodernity. His boldness in preaching the gospel, even his preaching itself, would not go over well with
most postmodern philosophers. Moreover, his status as an apostle gives
him an advantage over the rest of us. Still, I think Westphal's instincts
are right. Paul managed to combine boldness in preaching with a certain
humility in a way that I think postmoderns could find appealing. For
he did not speak with words of metanarrative wisdom, but with words
of rhetorical weakness. He took time to reason with people about the
meaning of the scriptures. He was willing to become all things to all
men (there's perspectivism for you!) in order to save some. And most
importantly, he was willing to suffer and endure for his witness to the
truth.

Unlike Paul, however, our interpretations of the Word of God are
neither inspired nor absolute. How, then, can contemporary preachers proclaim the gospel with any kind of boldness? Again, the apostle
provides a clue. Though we do not have an absolute point of view, nor
do we have the objective "view from nowhere," Christians who follow
Paul's example can approximate the "view from everywhere." Instead
of decrying our lack of an absolute point of view, Christian thinkers
ought to be working on developing a *canonic* and *catholic* perspective.
Instead of relying upon our own reason and insights, that is, we should
seek to be formed by the whole counsel of God in scripture and by the
Spirit-guided tradition across centuries and cultures. Paul's thought was
canonic and catholic because it was first and foremost *christocentric*.
Christ is the key both to the unity of the scriptures and to the unity of the

church. As Paul said, everything else is secondary—rubbish—compared to knowing Christ. I trust we are all agreed on that!

To Jamie Smith

I thoroughly enjoyed Jamie Smith's article on misreadings of Lyotard's notion of "metanarratives," not least because it illustrates the kind of authorial-discourse exegesis that I have elsewhere defended! Jamie's chapter helpfully clarifies how Christians have come to receive Lyotard's famous definition of postmodernity as "incredulity toward metanarratives" in a manner other than it was intended. Let me say straight off that I think Jamie is right. Some Christian scholars have not interpreted Lyotard correctly. What about me? What have I said about metanarratives in my chapter?

A quick rereading confirms that I use the term several times, both in the sense of "governing interpretative or exploratory framework" and in the sense of "monological conceptual scheme." The first sense has a positive connotation, the second a negative one. As far as I can tell, nothing essential in my essay hinges on how I use the term. Though I argue that the canonical scriptures should be the governing interpretative framework for Christian thought, I don't identify this with metanarrative because (1) there is more in scripture than narrative, and (2) I want all the forms of biblical discourse to have authority and not one conceptual scheme only.

Is the Bible taken as a whole a metanarrative? Clearly not in Lyotard's sense, for metanarrative is (according to Jamie's exegesis) a distinctly modern phenomenon that seeks to legitimate its grand story by an appeal to universal reason. Jamie and Westphal agree that the postmodern critique of metanarrative is, in the grand geophilopolitical scheme of things, a net gain for twenty-first-century Christian faith. Why? Because he who is against my enemy (viz., the proud pretensions of autonomous reason) is my friend.

Jamie and Westphal see salvation history—the unifying narrative of the Bible—as kerygma, not apologetics, so it does not qualify as a metanarrative either. The scheme of salvation history does not function to legitimate knowledge. The implication is that using scripture as a Lyotardian metanarrative would be incorrect.[2] This leads me to pose two questions to Jamie (and Westphal).

The canon may not legitimate knowledge the way modern metanarratives were wont do to (e.g., with universal reason), but throughout church history Christian thinkers have appealed to the scriptures to legitimate doctrine or, to state it more provocatively, *to legitimate the knowledge of God.* Bruce Marshall has recently argued that Christians must regard doctrines "as epistemically primary across the board, that is, as themselves the primary criteria of truth."[3] Marshall goes on to accord primacy to scripture too: "The narratives which identify Jesus are epistemic trump; if it comes to conflict between these narratives and any other sentences proposed for belief, the narratives win."[4] Hence, my first question: is a biblical narrative that has the force of epistemic trump a metanarrative or not? According to Marshall, since *all things* hold together in Jesus (Colossians 1), then "there will be no regions of belief and practice which can isolate themselves from the epistemic reach of the gospel."[5]

To return to Jamie's little story about metanarratives, I agree that some Christian thinkers have used the term in a sense other than that originally intended by Lyotard. But my second question is simply, *Why not?* Lyotard does not have a monopoly or patent or copyright on the term. Jamie, as a good student of Derrida, knows that coins and concepts alike can be put to various uses when they enter into circulation. While I think that we must be careful not to impute to authors senses that they did not intend, I also think that concepts can be used by different people in different ways. Whether the biblical account of redemption history is a metanarrative, then, depends on whose definition of metanarrative we are using.

If Lyotard's definition of metanarrative is the one we have to use, then the Bible is not a metanarrative. But what if the term *metanarrative* has taken on a life of its own, beyond Lyotard's use? This is, I think, precisely what has happened. When Walsh and Middleton (and others) worry that "incredulity toward metanarratives" leads to skepticism with regard to scripture, it is because they are using *metanarrative* in something like the following sense: a "grand story" that makes universal claims to which we can appeal in debates about the legitimation of the knowledge of God (but by means of an appeals not to universal reason, but to biblical authority).

What is really at issue, apart from a skirmish about semantics, is whether we can appeal to scripture in order to legitimate claims about doctrine and about the knowledge of God. The authors of *The Postmodern Bible* argue that biblical interpretation tells us more about the readers than it does about the text. Postmodernity has the effect of exposing the political nature of biblical interpretation. There is no point of view or intepretatative approach that is outside or above some "field of power."[6] Postmoderns have become incredulous to the metanarrative of *hermeneutics;* postmoderns excel instead in elaborating the *conditions of impossibility* for gaining knowledge of textual meaning. It is not a matter simply of the hermeneutics of suspicion, then, but of the more radical suspicion of hermeneutics itself.

What I want to know is whether exegesis is possible under the conditions of postmodernity and, if so, what it means and how it is done. Specifically, is there a way of reading scripture that gets us beyond the will to power, beyond the interpretative (and political) interests of the community? To the extent that "incredulity toward metanarratives" encompasses our confidence that we can interpret scripture rightly in order to legitimate our knowledge claims about God, then it does seem to follow that many postmoderns (not necessarily Lyotard) could rightly see a connection between metanarratives and biblical authority. What I would like from Jamie is a positive account of how faith and reason could work together for the sake of biblical exegesis and "sound doctrine."

To Scott Smith

Scott Smith presents a crisp and concise version of the *tu quoque* ("you too") argument. Postmoderns have to assume what they purport to deny, namely, that they have epistemic access to extralinguistic reality. There is some poetic justice (and irony) in this charge. Postmodern philosophers have accused foundationalism of supporting itself with something other than foundations. Scott's point against the postmodern tendency to conflate language and the world is similar. Postmoderns, he says, cannot account for their linguisticalism (for lack of a better term) apart from an appeal to something outside language. The foundationalist strikes back!

Scott is right to focus on the question of the language-world relation. That human experience is linguistically mediated is surely one of the signature themes of postmodernity. In my view, that humanity is "in language" is but one aspect of the postmodern insight into human situatedness. So while Scott is right to focus on one of the leading symptoms, the larger issue concerns human situatedness: finitude, historicality, physicality, etc.

Scott is also right to focus on the idea of a linguistic community. Though human beings are all "in language," the fact of the matter is that there is no one universal language, but many local languages. This is true not only in the literal sense (i.e., some people speak English, others Urdu, French, German, Swahili, etc.) but also metaphorically: even those who speak English may belong to different linguistic communities (e.g., southern, Democratic, Republican, Baptist, Presbyterian, academic, etc.).

The main objection Scott lodges in his article is but one incarnation of a familiar problem, namely, how to account for one's ultimate starting points. The rationalist, for example, has to appeal to reason in order to defend the primacy of reason. And postmoderns have to use language in order to talk about language. Postmoderns who accept the linguistic turn thus have to make an exception in this one case: though they are on the inside of language, in this one case they claim to know something beyond language (e.g., a truth about the human condition and our epistemic access to the world). Scott is onto something here, and I look forward to reading Jamie Smith's and Westphal's rebuttals. Are they willing to acknowledge that their insights about the language-ridden nature of reality are only the insights of their own linguistic communities rather than something (universal!) that characterizes the human condition as such?

I share Scott Smith's nagging feeling that many postmoderns do work with a kind of metanarrative or universal account of the workings of language that, strictly speaking, they should not be able to do. This is a complex question, however, and on the postmodern side of the ledger I have to acknowledge that they may not be making a positive claim so much as articulating a negative transcendental condition. In short: the extralinguistic claim such postmoderns make is a claim about the *conditions of impossibility* for knowledge, conditions that are part and parcel of the human condition.

My own view is that language is part of God's design-plan for human beings. Language is a God-ordained gift and institution that enables us to relate in personal and cognitive ways to the world, to others, and to God. With Wittgenstein, I think it is a mistake to think of language solely in terms of representation (I don't know if this is what Scott means by the "essence" of language or not). This is the picture of language that held moderns captive, for the only two options were meaning (as reference) and meaninglessness. Philosophers like the later Wittgenstein and J. L. Austin have rightly reminded us that there are many things that language does besides "referring" or "representing" the world—for example, making promises.

I want to acknowledge the postmodern point that not every language uses the same system of distinctions in order to speak about the world. The language-world relation is neither universal nor nonexistent, but rather *multifarious*. At the same time, I believe that some languages allow us to talk about, and hence to relate to certain aspects of, reality better than others. And certain other language-games, such as astrology, have very little connection to reality. I find it significant that four Gospels were necessary adequately to render the reality of Jesus Christ. Something similar accounts for the necessity of many languages.

I subscribe to the notion that meaning is use, with the proviso that readers have an obligation to do justice to the *author's* use of language. I share Scott Smith's concern that the meaning of scripture not be identified with the way communities today use the biblical text. God, as real, is independent of what the church says and thinks about him. However, though God is unconstructed, I don't think that our knowledge of God is unmediated. On the contrary, God uses a variety of creaturely media, including the human language of scripture, to make himself known. Do we know God as he is? No, we know God as he reveals himself to us, through the many forms of language and literature that together form a reliable testimony to Jesus Christ. And it is precisely through the linguistic testimony to Jesus Christ that we also have epistemic access to the truth about God, the world, and ourselves.

To Geivett

I am happy to receive advice about how better to do theology from anyone, even philosophers! I therefore welcome Geivett's attempt to cleanse the temple of epistemology. At the same time, I am reluctant to let something extratextual—a scheme or system not derived from scripture but from elsewhere—govern the way I approach and use the biblical text.

Geivett's article is to a large extent an argument about the word *foundationalism* in much the same way Jamie Smith focused on the word *metanarrative*. Each accuses the other side of misconstruing or caricaturing a key idea. Geivett offers a number of stipulative definitions of other terms as well (e.g., *account, narrative*). In general, I found that I could speak his language and follow his arguments on their own terms. But I also know there are other things one can do with these same words.

For example, Geivett distinguishes an explanatory *account* that "makes intelligible" some state of affairs from *narratives* that are stories that represent imaginative worlds. In narrative, imagination has "free rein." Paul Ricoeur, by contrast, sees narrative as encompassing both fiction and history and suggests that narratives are *accounts* in their own right, explaining or making intelligible a series of events through configuration or "emplotment." Geivett's use of the term *narrative* prevents him from appreciating some of what postmoderns want to say about narrative.

I found Geivett's account to be admirably clear, yet it left me uneasy. There seems to be no room for "doxology" among Geivett's doxastic attitudes. It seems that our mental states are like light switches, either "on" or "off," depending on whether we affirm or reject a given proposition. But is that all we do with propositions? Truth is indeed a value, but so, I would argue, is goodness, and beauty. I mention this because I do not think that epistemology—assessing the truth of our beliefs—is the be-all and end-all of theology. Even the demons believe, yet tremble. Christians are not simply to assess or even affirm the truth, but to *do* it, to relate personally to the truth, to *rejoice* in the truth. Mind you, there is nothing in what Geivett says that contradicts this; he is simply silent about these other aspects. He is doing epistemology. But there is more in the scripture than can be contained in his epistemology. Not every sentence in the Bible conveys a proposition that requires our beliefs. There are commands that require our obedience, and promises that solicit our trust.

Back to epistemology: I was quite surprised to see myself included in Geivett's story of the effect of postmodernity on theological method, not least because I intended the book he mentions, *Is There a Meaning in This Text?* to be a critique of certain postmodern trends in philosophy, literary theory, and theology (most readers have recognized it as such!). I do not recognize my approach as being governed by the sensibilities of postmodernity. Indeed, my concern is that Geivett's approach to philosophy is governed by the sensibilities of modernity (see above).

Geivett criticizes me for rejecting what I call "foundationalism," because he likes what he calls "foundationalism." The relevant question, of course, is this: are the two of us using the term in the same sense? He thinks we are; I'm not so sure. What I criticize in my book is what Wolterstorff and Plantinga term "classic foundationalism." This is the position that seeks to ground knowledge claims in what is indubitable, either the certain deliverances of reason (Descartes) or the certain deliverances of direct and immediate experience. I object to this picture of knowledge, and to two assumptions in particular: (1) the idea that the foundation has to be certain and (2) the idea that beliefs, in order to be justified, have to be based on the "directly evident."

Am I guilty of caricaturing foundationalism? Well, my *Oxford Companion to Philosophy* defines foundationalism as follows: "The theory that knowledge of the world rests on a foundation of indubitable beliefs from which further propositions can be inferred."[7] Typically, classical foundationalists appeal to self-evident beliefs, empirically evident (or immediate) beliefs ("I am being appeared to bluely" is Roderick Chisholm's starting point)[8], and rationally evident beliefs ("I think therefore I am").

Now Geivett denies that foundationally justified (e.g., noninferential) beliefs have to be certain. I agree. I consider myself a fallibilist or moderate or chastened foundationalist: I acknowledge that I take certain beliefs for granted and reason *from there*. Still, I am not altogether clear what Geivett means by "direct evidence" or "direct acquaintance." Does he mean by these notions what Plantinga means by "basic beliefs"? If so, it's odd that Plantinga feels it necessary to argue against foundationalism (and evidentialism), and Geivett for it. There must be a real, not merely a semantic, disagreement.

For me, the issue concerns what Geivett means by "direct acquaintance." At one point in his chapter, when he lists the things he knows,

Geivett includes beliefs produced by *testimony*. Does what we know by *testimony* fit under the rubric of "direct acquaintance" or "direct evidence"? It is difficult to see how. Testimony seems to be indirect almost by definition. Yet I would want to maintain that we are within our epistemic rights to believe something on the basis of testimony. To be sure, testimony is as fallible a source as any other (including my own sense experience—why else do I need corrective lenses?). But rationality is not a matter of starting points but of being willing to submit one's beliefs to critical testing. I agree with Thomas Reid that we are rational in believing what we are told unless there is good reason to think that the source is untrustworthy. Beliefs are innocent until proven guilty. My impression is that, for the foundationalist, beliefs are considered guilty until proven innocent. W. K. Clifford claimed that we are ethically wrong to believe anything except on the basis—foundation!—of sufficient evidence.[9] It is precisely such skeptical sentiments that have fueled two centuries and more of biblical criticism.

In sum: as my chapter in this volume attests, I do not abandon rationality, though I am suspicious of at least one form of foundationalism: the "classical," or what Richard Bernstein calls "objectivism."[10] If that is not the kind that Geivett advocates, so much the better. But I resist defining rationality in terms of a theory of evidentialism only. There are other models of rationality available that enable us to treat scripture as more than "evidence" for justifying our theological beliefs. Finally, I would be most interested in seeing how Geivett's epistemology works out in the practice of biblical interpretation.

To Franke

Franke offers us a model of what theology looks like when one makes the nonfoundationalist turn. Perhaps I am just being ornery, but now I want to speak up on the side of the chastened or modest foundationalist. What I find interesting is that, where Geivett and Scott Smith suggest that postmodernity is fundamentally antithetical to Christian faith, Franke's starting point is the fundamentally antithetical nature of modernity to Christian faith. The truth, in my view, is somewhere in the middle: both modernity and postmodernity have aspects that are antithetical to Christian faith, aspects that I have termed "pride" and "sloth," respectively.

My overall feeling, however, is that Franke has capitulated to postmodernity too fast. I agree that there are things we can learn from the postmoderns. I value the prophetic nature of the postmodern critique of modern attempts to "make themselves like God," knowing absolute knowledge. But I resist Franke's too hasty embrace of the postmodern alternative. Is it really the case, for example, that chastened rationality "is marked by the transition from a realist to a constructionist view of truth and the world"? I think this is to confuse an epistemological problem with an ontological one. My own preference would be for a middle position, such as that of Frank Farrell, who argues that some of our languages, vocabularies, and conceptual schemes let certain aspects of reality through better than others.[11] Instead of subscribing to "constructionism all the way down," I prefer to subscribe to "critical realism." The implications of Franke's constructionism for the project of biblical interpretation, if pursued consistently, are in my view devastating to biblical authority.

My general worry about Franke's proposal is that it is simply an upgrade of the modern liberal method of correlation, only now the philosophy with which theology correlates is nonfoundationalism rather than existentialism and ontology, as it was for Bultmann and Tillich. Franke is explicit in his criticism of modern thinkers, yet criticisms of postmodern thinkers are thin on the ground. I was struck by the phrase that refers to nonfoundationalist as "both postmodern and faithful to the Christian tradition." That "both-and" perfectly describes the method of correlation, but in my view that "both-and" is unjustifiably optimistic. The tendency of correlationist approaches is to adopt a framework that is acceptable in the current cultural-intellectual context and then to interpret the Bible in light of that framework. Correlationism is tempting because it lets you have your culture and gospel too—or at least it appears to do so. It's just a worry. But it's a worry that should characterize the theologian, who must remain vigilant not to let culture or concept infiltrate, much less swallow up, the gospel.

My specific worry about Franke's proposal, however, has to do not with the method but with the matter of his theology. Specifically, it concerns his "thoroughly pneumatological" theological approach, and its implications for the place of scripture in theology. It's clear that Franke acknowledges the supreme authority of scripture; it is theology's "norming norm," yet it holds this position only because it is an instrument of the Spirit. (Toward the end of his chapter, Franke says that not even scripture is the ultimate authority in the church, but "only the living God"—how does that work?). The Spirit uses the church's reading of scripture to create an eschatological "world." Strangely, Franke is able to discuss the Spirit's work through scripture without even discussing the Bible's meaning.

We are then informed that the Spirit speaks through culture as well. What is the biblical warrant for this notion? Franke says that scripture "appears to suggest a much broader understanding of the Spirit's presence" which is connected to the Spirit's role as life giver. But does it really follow from the Spirit's creative life giving that "the Spirit's voice resounds through many media, including the media of human culture"? I fear this is a non sequitur.

Jesus says that the Spirit "will not speak on his own; he will speak only what he hears" (John 16:13 NIV). The Spirit's role is to "remind you of everything I [Jesus] have said to you" (John 14:26 NIV). In light of these explicit passages, I am inclined to resist any attempt to "deregulate" pneumatology from Christology. The Spirit ministers the Word (who is Truth and Life), nothing else. As such, the Spirit is the executor of the living Word and the word written. To be sure, Franke rightly says that the voice of the Spirit never speaks against the text. But this claim has purchase, and protects, only to the extent that the text has determinate meaning. I am not sure what to make of his claim that the Spirit speaking through scripture and culture constitutes "one unified speaking." Again, I would like to see the biblical warrant for this claim.

The Spirit is also at work in tradition—but which one? Does Franke believe that there is a single Christian tradition? If so, where is it? How do we know which trajectories of tradition are Spirit-guided and which are not? The problem with nonfoundationalism is that the scripture has meaning only when it is read by such-and-such an interpretative community. My question, then, concerns the ability of the text to speak against and correct the interests and the interpretative strategies of a community. My epistemology and ecclesiology alike are fallibilist, for all human beliefs and practices are distorted by the fall, even Christian beliefs and church practices. That is precisely why we need a "norming norm" that is independent of our systems of beliefs and practices. But this is precisely what a nonfoundationalist approach disallows, if I have understood it correctly.

So, what precisely are the principles of this "principled theological pluralism" if not *exegetical* principles? Yet again, I am left wondering about the implications of this position for biblical exegesis.

Notes

1. A concept is a habit of thought that associates certain ideas and experiences.

2. This reminds me of William J. Abraham's claim that the Reformers made a fateful mistake when they reconceived the scriptures as an epistemic *criterion* rather than as a means for nurturing the faith. See Abraham, *Canon and Criterion in Christian Theology: From the Fathers to Feminism* (Oxford: Clarendon, 1998).

3. Bruce D. Marshall, *Trinity and Truth* (Cambridge: Cambridge University Press, 2000), 4.

4. Ibid., 116.

5. Ibid., 118.

6. Elisabeth A. Castelli, Stephen D. Moore, and Regina M. Schwartz, eds., *The Postmodern Bible* (New Haven: Yale University Press, 1995), 3.

7. Ted Honderich, ed. *Oxford Companion to Philosophy,* (Oxford: Oxford University Press, 1995), 288.

8. Roderick Chisholm, *Theory of Knowledge,* 2nd ed. (Englewood Cliffs, NJ: Prentice-Hall, 1977).

9. W. K. Clifford, "The Ethics of Belief," in Clifford, *Lectures and Essays* (London: Macmillan, 1886).

10. Richard Bernstein, *Beyond Objectivism and Relativism* (Philadelphia: University of Pennsylvania Press, 1985).

11. Frank Farrell, *Subjectivity, Realism, and Postmodernism: The Recovery of the World* (Cambridge: Cambridge University Press, 1994).

The Nature of Theology:
Culture, Language, and Truth

John R. Franke

Before offering a response to the essays in the book, I'd like to first thank the other contributors for their work. I've profited from all of them even where I disagree and have been helped in a number of ways through this engagement. I'd also like to thank Myron Penner for his work conceiving this project and seeing it to fruition. His editorial advice has been consistently courteous and helpful. In accordance with our instructions, my response will engage with the other essays and will also attempt to extend the position sketched out in my initial essay. I will focus on issues related to the nature of theology as they emerge in three of the other essays, those of Professors Vanhoozer, Scott Smith, and Geivett, particularly with reference to the questions of culture, language, and truth. I will not address in detail the essays of Professors Westphal and Jamie Smith due to the large measure of agreement I share with them and their perspectives. However, I will simply offer some very brief comments on each.

I have consistently learned a great deal from Professor Westphal's work, particularly his two books on the hermeneutics of suspicion and finitude,[1] and would recommend that all those who want to engage with the questions of postmodernity include these on their reading lists.

His essay offers a succinct summary of several of the most important questions that emerge for Christians in thinking about the challenges raised by postmodernity, and he regularly frames the issues in ways that promote positive interaction and show what Christians can learn from postmodern philosophy. It is a particularly important observation that the metanarratives of modernity serve to legitimize "us," while the Christian narrative places "us" under judgment. Precisely to the degree that Christians have adopted theologies that legitimate themselves over against others, be they adherents of other religions, secularists, or other Christian traditions, such theologies fall prey to the criticisms of post-modern theory.

Jamie Smith's essay does a real service for Christian thinkers in clearing up the precise nature of Lyotard's oft-cited incredulity toward meta-narratives. He demonstrates convincingly that the biblical story is not a metanarrative in Lyotard's sense and helpfully suggests the ways in which biblical faith and postmodern theory can be positively related. I agree with his conclusion that Lyotard's critique of metanarratives can be "enlisted as an ally in the construction of a Christian philosophy" and would add that it can function constructively in theology as well. However, an important point that Jamie does not develop is that while the biblical story may not qualify as a metanarrative, many systematic theologies that purport to be biblical do, and are rightly susceptible to the critique of Lyotard and postmodernity. Hence, those who are committed to traditional notions of systematic theology will still feel threatened. This suggests that a significant challenge for theology in the postmodern context will be the degree to which it can be disentangled from its accommodation to Enlightenment rationality and its intellectual tendencies.

Let us now turn our attention to matters posed by the other three essays, beginning with the question of theology's relationship to culture. All human knowledge is influenced and shaped by the social, cultural, and historical situation in which it emerges. As a human endeavor bound up with the task of interpretation, the discipline of Christian theology, like all other intellectual pursuits, bears the marks of the particular settings in which it is produced. That is to say, quite simply, that theology is a thoroughly contextual discipline. The expression of Christian thought has taken shape and has been revised in the context of numerous social and historical settings. It has also developed in the process of navigating a number of significant cultural transitions: from an initially Hebraic setting to the Hellenistic world; from the thought-forms of Greco-Roman culture to those of Franco-Germanic; from the world of medieval feudalism to the Renaissance; from the Renaissance to the Enlightenment; and from the developed world to the Third World. Currently, theology is grappling with the challenges raised by the transition from a modern to a postmodern cultural milieu. Throughout this ongoing history, Christian theology has been shaped by the thought forms and conceptual tools of numerous cultural settings and has shown itself to be remarkably adaptable in its task of assisting the church in extending and establishing the message of the gospel in a wide variety of contexts. At the same time, theological history also provides examples of the accommodation of Christian faith to various ideologies and cultural norms. This history, while demonstrating the vitality of Christian theology, also warns of the dangers of too closely associating it with any particular form of cultural expression and raises the question of the proper conception of the role of culture in the task of constructing theology.

Professor Vanhoozer's essay seems to be particularly concerned with the danger of accommodating Christian theology to the norms of postmodern theory. He grants the postmodern insight concerning the situatedness of human beings and affirms that Christians can and should learn something from the postmodern deconstruction of the totalizing and oppressive metanarratives of modernity. However, he quickly adds that postmodernity should not set the Christian agenda and critiques those thinkers who attempt to appropriate postmodern thought for Christian purposes. Indeed, he insists that Christian thought should resist all forms of correlation and the imposition of disciplinary rules and forms of discourse foreign to the community of faith. In light of his concern, Vanhoozer states his preference for a disputational mode of discourse with postmodernity rather than a conversational one. While such a stance may appear to be straightforward and will certainly please those who are already suspicious of postmodernity, it is finally an unsatisfactory response that continues to misunderstand the nature of postmodernity and fails to take *seriously enough* the situated and contextual nature of the human condition.

With respect to the nature of postmodernity, Vanhoozer seems to read the situation as follows: while postmodern thinkers rightly identify the situatedness of the human condition, they "are so preoccupied with the situated self that they cannot get beyond it." They are so riveted on the process of attending rather than on the object of attention that in the final analysis the only thing that remains is situated human perception. The external objects of perception are negated along with truth, goodness, and beauty. Hence, Christian theology, which is rightly committed to truth, goodness, and beauty, cannot and should not seek to align itself with such a fundamentally anti-Christian stance. While such a reading may fit some postmodern theorists, it fails to do justice to the actual breadth of postmodern thought. It is an overstatement to assert that for postmoderns "every issue is ultimately about identity politics, about where, what, and who one is." Postmodern thought is better understood, not primarily as a particular philosophical or social agenda, but as a critique and rejection of the central features of modernity and the attempt to engage in constructive discourse in its aftermath. Numerous thinkers who would describe themselves as postmodern have not abandoned the truth project and are not so preoccupied with the situated self that they cannot get beyond it. Rather, they are attempting to rethink the quest for truth in light of the contextual nature of human thought and the plurality of human cultural expression.

The interpretation offered by Vanhoozer enables him to be more dismissive of postmodern thought and its potential benefit to theology than necessary. It also leads him to be overly critical of those Christian thinkers who would seek to appropriate the insights of postmodernity for Christian thought. While I agree with him that Christians should not pursue a strategy of correlation with philosophy or culture, the direction of his essay leads me to conclude that he does not take seriously enough the situated nature of human thought. Note carefully, I do not say that he denies this; he doesn't. In fact, he agrees with it. Rather, the concern is that human situatedness is not taken on board and integrated into his thinking with sufficient thoroughness. This appears in his assertion that no "concerns and frameworks other than Christ and canon set faith's credenda and agenda." While other concerns and agendas must not compete with Christ and canon, theology is a discipline that must be responsive to developments in culture in order to be faithful to its role in the task to make disciples of all nations (and cultures). This concern also manifests itself in his thesis that postmodernity "has not discovered anything that was not already available, at least implicitly, in Christian scripture and tradition." Such a statement is far too reductionistic and potentially leads to the dismissal of the positive contributions of human culture and intellectual pursuit in our knowledge of truth. It sounds tantamount to saying that culture and philosophy contribute nothing to our understanding of theology and the human condition and can generally be disregarded in the theological task. While the Bible may anticipate many of postmodernity's central claims, as Vanhoozer maintains, many of these themes are only beginning to be explored theologically in light of the postmodern situation. Does this observation not also suggest the role of the Spirit speaking through culture as well as the text of scripture in order to bring neglected biblical and theological concerns into greater relief?

Finally, his preferred motif for engagement, dispute rather than conversation, suggests a form of imperialism that has all too often in the history of the church been detrimental to faithful Christian witness. At its best, the motif of conversation indicates a disposition of conviction coupled with an appropriate humility and a commitment to careful and attentive listening. It also implies a willingness to pursue truth wherever it may be found with awareness that in the wisdom of God it is often discovered in strange and unexpected places. The motif of conversation need not denigrate the seriousness of the encounter between Christian faith and postmodern thought, nor does it exclude places where dispute is appropriate. Some manifestations of postmodern thought are incompatible with the gospel and should be called into question and rejected by Christian thinkers. It does not follow, however, that because some forms are problematic from the perspective of Christian faith, all must be similarly tainted.

Vanhoozer's approach serves to denigrate not only the particular contributions of postmodern thought for theology, but also those of culture in general. And while I do not see his work headed in this direction, the thrust of his essay can be viewed as potentially leading to the assumption of a suprahistorical theology somehow removed from the vicissitudes of time. Taking on board the postmodern awareness of human situatedness in theology demands taking culture more seriously, not less. We need an explicit awareness of the significance and function of culture in the task of theology. Colin Gunton states the point succinctly: "we must acknowledge the fact that all theologies belong in a particular context, and so are, to a degree, limited by the constraints of that context. To that extent, the context is one of the authorities to which the theologian must listen."[2] Many theologians, and particularly evangelicals, have been suspicious of such claims about the role of culture in theology, fearing that they, at least implicitly, dilute the authority of scripture and give rise to a cultural relativity in theology that they believe to be inappropriate for the discipline. Having raised the question of the role of culture in theology in the context of a critique, it seems appropriate to briefly address it from the perspective of the nonfoundationalist approach to theology sketched in my initial essay. In order to do this it will be helpful to gain some clarity concerning our understanding of culture itself.

In recent years the notion of culture as traditionally conceived has come under such strident and thoroughgoing criticism that some thinkers came to believe that the term was so compromised that it should be discarded. While a few favored this radical surgery, most anthropologists agree with James Clifford's grudging acknowledgment that culture "is a deeply compromised idea I cannot yet do without."[3] Thus, rather than eliminating the concept entirely, the criticisms of the term have led to an understanding of culture that takes the historical contingencies of human life and society more seriously.

Contemporary anthropologists have largely discarded the older assumption that culture is a preexisting social-ordering force that is transmitted externally to members of a cultural group who in turn passively internalize it. They maintain that this view is mistaken in that it isolates culture from the ongoing social processes that produce and continually alter it.[4] Culture is not an entity standing above or beyond human products and learned mental structures. In short, culture is not a "thing."[5] The older understanding also focused on the idea of culture as that which integrates the various institutional expressions of social life and binds the individual to society. This focus on the integrative role of culture is now facing serious challenges. According to Anthony Cohen, it has become one of the casualties of the demise of "modernistic grand theories and the advent of 'the interpretive turn' in its various guises."[6] Rather than viewing cultures as monolithic entities, postmodern anthropologists tend to view cultures as being internally fissured.[7] The elevation of difference that typifies postmodern thinking has triggered a heightened awareness of the role of persons in culture formation. Rather than exercising determinative power over people, culture is conceived as the outcome and product of social interaction. Consequently, rather than being viewed as passive receivers, human beings are seen as the active creators of culture.[8]

Clifford Geertz provided the impetus for this direction through his description of cultures as comprising "webs of significance" that people spin and in which they are then suspended.[9] Geertz defines culture as "an historically transmitted pattern of meanings embodied in symbols, a system of inherited conceptions expressed in symbolic forms by means of which people communicate, perpetuate, and develop their knowledge about and attitudes toward life."[10] According to Cohen, Geertz was responsible for "shifting the anthropological view of culture from its supposedly objective manifestations in social structures, towards its subjective realisation by members who compose those structures."[11] Culture resides in a set of meaningful forms and symbols that, from the point of view of any particular individual, appear as largely given.[12] Yet these forms are meaningful only because human minds have the ability to interpret them.[13] This has led contemporary anthropologists to look at the interplay of cultural artifacts and human interpretation in the formation of meaning. They suggest that, contrary to the belief that meaning lies in signs or in the relations between them, meanings are bestowed by the users of signs.[14] However, this does not mean that individuals simply discover or make up cultural meanings on their own. Even the mental structures by which they interpret the world are developed through explicit teaching and implicit observation of others. Consequently, cultural meanings are both psychological states and social constructions.[15]

The thrust of contemporary cultural anthropology leads to the conclusion that its primary concern lies in understanding the creation of cultural meaning as connected to world construction and identity formation. This approach leads to an understanding of culture as socially constructed. The thesis of social constructionists such as Peter Berger is that rather than inhabiting a prefabricated, given world, we live in a social-cultural world of our own creation.[16] At the heart of the process whereby we construct our world is the imposition of some semblance of a meaningful order upon our variegated experiences. For the interpretive framework we employ in this task, we are dependent on the society in which we participate.[17] In this manner, society mediates to us the cultural tools necessary for constructing our world. Although this constructed world gives the semblance of being a given, universal, and objective reality, it is actually, in the words of David Morgan, "an unstable edifice that generations constantly labor to build, raze, rebuild, and redesign."[18] We inhabit socially constructed worlds to which our personal identities are intricately bound. The construction of these worlds, as well as the formation of personal identity, is an ongoing, dynamic, and fluid process, in which the forming and reforming of shared cultural meanings play a crucial role. Culture includes the symbols that provide the shared meanings by means of which we understand ourselves, pinpoint our deepest aspirations and longings, and construct the worlds we inhabit. And through the symbols of our culture we express and communicate these central aspects of life to each other, while struggling together to determine the meaning of the very symbols we employ in this process.

To be human is to be embedded in culture and to participate in the process of interpretation and the creation of meaning as we reflect on and internalize the cultural symbols that we share with others in numerous conversations that shape our ever-shifting contexts. The question of the relationship between culture and theology has been implicit throughout the history of Christian theology. However, in the twentieth century the issue has moved to the forefront of theological concerns as the challenges of globalization and pluralism have infused the question with a new sense of urgency. Two approaches that have gained widespread attention are correlation and contextualization. The chief difficulty with both of these methods is their indebtedness to foundationalism. Rather than acknowledging the particularity of every human culture, correlationists are prone to prioritize culture through the identification of some universal experience and fit theology into a set of generalized assumptions. Contextualists, in contrast, often overlook the particularity of every understanding of the Christian message and too readily assume a Christian universal that then functions as the foundation for the construction of the theology, even though that will need to be articulated in the language of a particular culture. This is especially evident in models of contextualization that are based on a distinction between the transcultural gospel and its expression through neutral cultural forms. Yet with few exceptions, most approaches to contextual theology move in the direction of some form of foundationalism that assumes the existence of a pure, transcendent gospel.

Despite debilitating difficulties these approaches share as a result of their foundationalist assumptions, taken together correlation and contextualization point the way forward. The two models suggest that an appropriate theological method must employ an interactive process that is both correlative and contextual while resisting the tendencies of foundationalism. Theology emerges through an ongoing conversation involving both gospel and culture. While such an interactive model draws from both methods, it stands apart from both in one crucial way. Unlike correlation or contextualization, an interactionist model presupposes neither gospel nor culture as given, preexisting realities that subsequently enter into conversation. Rather, in the interactive process both the gospel and culture are viewed as particularized, dynamic realities that inform and are informed by the conversation itself. Understanding gospel and culture in this way allows us to realize that both our understanding of the gospel and the meaning structures through which people in our society make sense of their lives are dynamic. In such a model, the conversation between gospel and culture should be one of mutual enrichment in which the exchange benefits the church in its ability to address its context as well as the process of theological critique and construction.

For some, such an approach to theology raises the question of truth. If all forms of thought are contextual, on what basis can we be confident of the truthfulness of our convictions? This is the question of epistemic justification. Does the postmodern commitment to contextuality and situatedness close off the possibility of making universal truth claims that can be justified? Two forms of this question prompt the contributions of Professors Scott Smith and Geivett. Scott's essay is concerned with the question of language. He argues that if language constitutes the variety of socially constructed contexts in which human beings participate and cannot escape, all claims to truth become suspect. Indeed, they can be sustained only with the assumption of a neutral, objective, and context-free vantage point from which they can be justified. The serious implication of his view would seem to be that without the sort of extralinguistic epistemic access he assumes, the claims of Christian faith would be unsustainable. The limitations of space do not permit a full-scale critique and response to this position. My chief objection is that this approach makes the veracity of Christian faith rest on a particular *theory* about language.

Scott Smith asserts that either Christians must be able to "get outside of language" to an "extralinguistic realm" or the "prospects for revelation are rather dismal." He then assumes that those who affirm the linguistic turn must finally presuppose that "God has been able to break through" human language to provide access to an "extralinguistic, objective world," thus undermining their methodology. By way of response I would first note that God does not "break through" language. Instead, God *enters into* the linguistic setting and *uses* language in the act of revelation as a means of accommodation to the situation and situatedness of human beings. This position arises out of theological commitments that are Christian and Reformed. The church has long maintained the distinction between finite human knowledge and divine knowledge. Even revelation does not provide human beings with a knowledge that exactly corresponds to that of God. The infinite qualitative distinction between God and human beings suggests the accommodated character of all human knowledge of God. For John Calvin, this means that in revelation God "adjusts" and "descends" to the capacities of human beings in order to reveal the infinite mysteries of divine reality, which by their very nature are beyond capabilities of human creatures to grasp due to the limitations that arise from their finite and fallen character.[19] The inadequacy of human beings to comprehend divine truth of their own accord extends also to the creaturely mediums by which revelation is communicated. In Reformed Christology, the divine and human natures of Christ remain distinct and unimpaired even after their union in Jesus of Nazareth in order to deny the "divinization" of the human nature. The creaturely medium of revelation, in this case the human nature of Christ, is not divinized through union with the divine nature and remains subject to the limitations and contingencies of its creaturely character. In the same way the human words of the prophets and apostles are not divinized in their appropriation by God for revelatory purposes and remain subject to the inherent limitations of human language. Yet in spite of these limitations, God is truly revealed through the appointed creaturely media.

This dynamic is captured in the dialectic of veiling and unveiling that animates the theology of Karl Barth and his notion of "indirect identity" with respect to the doctrine of revelation. This means that in God's self-revelation God chooses to become indirectly identical with the creaturely medium of that revelation. Such revelation is *indirect* because God's use of the creaturely medium entails no "divinization" of it, and yet at the same time God is *identical,* albeit indirectly, with the creaturely medium in that God is truly *revealed* through it. The consequence of this notion of indirect revelation is that it remains hidden to outward, normal, or "natural" human perception and requires that human beings be given "the eyes and ears of faith" in order to perceive the unveiling of God that remains hidden in the creaturely veil. In this conception revelation has both an objective moment, when God reveals himself through the veil of a creaturely medium, and a subjective moment, when God gives human beings the faith to understand what is hidden in the veil.[20]

In this framework of indirect identity, we are able to affirm God's use of language in the act of revelation (and world construction) without

denying our theological and existential awareness of its inherent limitations and contingencies as a contextually situated creaturely medium. It
should be added that Barth secures the divine primacy in God's epistemic
relations with human beings by maintaining the "actualistc" character
of revelation. In other words, revelation in this conception is not simply
a past event that requires nothing further from God. This would imply
that God had ceased to act and had become directly identical with the
medium of revelation. If this were the case, the epistemic relationship
between God and human beings would be static rather than dynamic
with the result that human beings would be able to move from a position of epistemic dependency to one of epistemic mastery. Instead, God
always remains indirectly identical with the creaturely media of revelation, thus requiring continual divine action in the knowing process
and securing the ongoing epistemic dependency of human beings with
respect to the knowledge of God.

   While Scott's essay raises the justification of truth claims implicitly
through his examination of questions related to the linguistic turn, Professor Geivett's essay directly addresses the "retreat from the project of
epistemic justification in the practice of theology" by those who have
been "lured away from foundationalism by the brandishments of postmodernism." The problem, according to Geivett, is that what postmodern theorists offer is "not an alternative theory of justification, but a
substitute for any theory of justification." As mentioned earlier, it is
mistaken to imply that all postmodern thought has given up on the
question of truth and its justification. However, from Geivett's point of
view this criticism appears to be valid, given the postmodern rejection
of foundationalism and his apparent belief that truth cannot be justified
apart from it. For him, this amounts to the abandonment of the project
of epistemic justification.

   With respect to Geivett's position, an important clarification needs
to be made with respect to the nature of foundationalism. In my essay
I cite several philosophers who speak of the demise of foundationalism
as a philosophical consensus, while Geivett cites others who maintain
that it is still the dominant position. As with the term *postmodern,* it is
clear that different understandings of foundationalism are in play. The
various usages move along a spectrum from the "strong" or "classical"
foundationalism connected with Descartes and the Enlightenment to
a range of options termed "soft" or "modest" foundationalism.[21] My
particular concern is with the intellectual tendencies associated with
classical foundationalism as they have been manifested in the discipline
of theology and with the development of an appropriately *theological*
epistemology.

   The rationale for the challenge I have raised to classical foundationalism and its intellectual tendencies is not a matter of capitulating to

postmodern thought, but rather an attempt to think theologically about epistemology. A properly theological epistemology must be appropriate to the subject of theology. As noted earlier, in the Reformed tradition this entails the affirmation of the primacy of God and the dependency of human beings in all epistemic relations concerning the knowledge of God. One of the concerns I have with Geivett, and Scott as well, is that the critiques and positions they offer are not sufficiently theological in nature. Geivett particularly seems to view philosophy as something of an objective intellectual discipline that performs the function of adjudicating on the validity and acceptability of theological proposals. However, like all human intellectual endeavor, the discipline of philosophy is also situated and interpretive in nature and is not in a privileged position with respect to knowledge. This should not be taken to deny the significance of philosophy and its contributions to the task of theology, but rather as a reminder of its limitations. Here I agree with Vanhoozer that the problem is not with philosophy per se, but rather with the "pretensions of philosophy as a discourse that aspires to metanarrative status." If epistemology must be theological, so must our conception of justification. What might a theological and nonfoundational construal of justification look like that takes seriously the situated nature of human knowledge, the socially constructed nature of reality, the limitations of language, the epistemic primacy of God, and Christian convictions concerning revelation? While space does not permit a detailed response, we can briefly sketch out its main features.

First, it views the task of justification as an ongoing participatory process involving convictional communities rather than something to be accomplished objectively in a once-and-for-all fashion. James McClendon and James M. Smith identify three components that make up an important part of such a process: the language of the process, the loci of the process, and the social matrix of the process.[22] While no brief summary can do adequate justice to their rigorous and thoughtful work, let us note the following. In their conception of the linguistic dimension of justification, they move away from a referential theory of language and set forth a position that, drawing on speech-act theory, affirms the situated and contextual character of language and its role in shaping the narrative worlds of those who participate in particular linguistic communities. The "loci" of the process involve what are usually called "ultimate criteria" in justification, concepts such as truth, justice, and peace. As with language, the particular criteria and their content are contextual and will be communally specific, meaning that no single list or exposition will satisfy all communities of inquiry. For this reason, they prefer to think of these concepts not as criteria but as "possible loci of justification" and note that in spite of their contextual nature, these and other central notions "will appear as main intersections, junction points of reflection, criticism, debate, and correction" to

all those who seek to justify their convictions.[23] Hence, they provide places
of interaction in a pluralist world between competing convictional communities in the process of justification. Finally, they note that the social
matrix of the process means that the language of a particular community
is "never a hermetically sealed system, that it is never even static, but is
in a constant process of adjustment to external as well as internal pres-
sure."[24] This allows for the possibility of reform within communities and
for conversation with other convictional communities as well as with the
broader social contexts in which they are situated.

Through these three components McClendon and Smith provide a
general procedure for the process of justification that is nonfoundational
and contextual without any retreat from a robust commitment to truth.
A specifically Christian account of truth and justification requires that
these concerns be situated in the context of particularly Christian convictions. For instance, Karl Barth works out an account of the Word of God
and the knowledge of God that grows out of the doctrine of the Trinity.[25]
More recently, Bruce Marshall has set forth a proposal that takes the
epistemic primacy of the communal Christian belief in the Trinity as the
starting point for a thoroughly Christian account of truth and justification.[26] While the proposals differ with respect to particular details, they
are agreed on the centrality of the Trinity for Christian construals of
truth and the knowledge of God.[27] Marshall's work is particularly suggestive in his delineation of an approach to truth that arises from the
identification of God as triune and the particular primacy of Jesus as
the one in whom all things "hold together" according to the will of the
Father.[28] The epistemic role of the Spirit comes into view as "the one
who empowers us to recognize the epistemic ultimacy of Jesus Christ"
and as the one who teaches us how "to order all of our beliefs around
the narratives which identify the Father's crucified and risen Son."[29]
Thus, the distinctive epistemic role of the Son is inseparable from those
of the Father and the Spirit. Marshall's work produces an account that
develops distinctively Christian understandings of the coherence and
pragmatic approaches to truth and justification in a trinitarian context
in which truth is viewed as christologically coherent according to the
will of the Father and pneumatologically effective through the ongoing
work of the Spirit.

The ongoing work of the Spirit is manifest in the appropriation of
the biblical narrative in order to speak to the church for the purpose of
creating a socially constructed "world" that finds its coherence in Jesus
Christ in accordance with, and in anticipation of, the "real" world as it is
willed to be by the Father. However, the world as God wills it to be is not
a present reality, but rather lies in the eschatological future. Thus, while
acknowledging that there is indeed a certain "objective" actuality to the
world, it is important to recognize that this "objectivity" is not that of a

static actuality existing outside of, and cotemporally with, our socially and linguistically constructed realities. It is not what some might call "the world as it is." Instead, the biblical narratives set forth the "objectivity" of the world as God wills it. Hence, Jesus taught his disciples to pray, "Your will be done on earth as it is in heaven" (Matt. 6:10 NIV). The "real" world is the future, eschatological world that God will establish in the new creation. Because this future reality is God's determined will for creation, as that which cannot be shaken (Heb. 12:26–28), it is far more real, objective, and actual than the present world, which is even now passing away (1 Cor. 7:31). In this way the biblical narratives point to what might be called "eschatological realism."

In relating eschatological realism to the insights of social constructionism, we note that human beings, as bearers of the divine image, are called to participate in God's work of constructing a world in the present that reflects God's own eschatological will for creation. This call has a strongly linguistic dimension, due to the role of language in the task of world construction. Through the constructive power of language, the Christian community anticipates the divine eschatological world that stands at the climax of the biblical narrative in which all creation finds its connectedness in Jesus Christ (Col. 1:17), who is the Word (John 1:1) and the ordering principle of the cosmos. This eschatological future is anticipated in the present through the work of the Spirit, who leads the church into truth (1 John 2:27). From this perspective the Christian community affirms truth, under the guidance of the Spirit, through the construction of a linguistic world that finds its coherence in Christ in accordance with the will of the Father. This community also participates in the Spirit-guided process of justification that is ultimately realized only in the eschatological completion of the Spirit's epistemic ministry. Such an approach, arising out of particularly Christian theological commitments, affirms the participation and responsibility of the Christian community in a process of justification that is vigorous and robust as well as nonfoundational and contextual, while securing the epistemic primacy of God as the one who establishes truth and works out its justification.

Notes

1. Respectively, Merold Westphal, *Suspicion and Faith: The Religious Uses of Modern Atheism* (New York: Fordham University Press, 1998); *Overcoming Onto-theology: Toward a Postmodern Christian Faith* (New York: Fordham University Press, 2001).

2. Colin Gunton, "Using and Being Used: Scripture and Systematic Theology," *Theology Today* 47, no. 3 (October 1990): 253.

3. James Clifford, *The Predicament of Culture: Twentieth-Century Ethnography, Literature, and Art* (Cambridge: Harvard University Press, 1988), 10.

4. Kathryn Tanner, *Theories of Culture: A New Agenda for Theology* (Minneapolis: Fortress, 1997), 50.

5. Roy G. D'Andrade, *The Development of Cognitive Anthropology* (Cambridge: Cambridge University Press, 1995), 250.

6. Anthony P. Cohen, *Self Consciousness: An Alternative Anthropology of Identity* (London: Routledge, 1994), 118.

7. Tanner, *Theories of Culture*, 56.

8. Cohen, *Self Consciousness*, 118–19.

9. Clifford Geertz, *The Interpretation of Cultures* (New York: Basic Books, 1973), 5.

10. Ibid., 89.

11. Cohen, *Self Consciousness*, 135.

12. Geertz, *Interpretation of Cultures*, 45.

13. Ulf Hannerz, *Cultural Complexity: Studies in the Social Organization of Meaning* (New York: Columbia University Press, 1992), 3–4.

14. Claudia Strauss and Naomi Quinn, *A Cognitive Theory of Cultural Meaning* (Cambridge: Cambridge University Press, 1997), 253.

15. Ibid., 16.

16. Peter L. Berger, *The Sacred Canopy: Elements of a Sociological Theory of Religion*, Anchor Books ed. (Garden City, NY: Doubleday, 1969), 3–13.

17. Ibid., 20. See also Peter L. Berger and Thomas Luckmann, "Sociology of Religion and Sociology of Knowledge," *Sociology and Social Research* 47 (1963): 417–27.

18. David Morgan, *Visual Piety: A History and Theory of Popular Images* (Berkeley: University of California Press, 1998), 9.

19. On Calvin's understanding of the accommodated character of all human knowledge of God, see Edward A. Dowey Jr., *The Knowledge of God in Calvin's Theology*, 3rd ed. (Grand Rapids: Eerdmans, 1994), 3–24.

20. For a detailed analysis of the content and development of Barth's dialectical conception of revelation and its relationship to his theology, see Bruce L. McCormack, *Karl Barth's Critically Realistic Dialectical Theology: Its Genesis and Development, 1909–1936* (Oxford: Clarendon Press, 1995).

21. For basic and helpful discussion of foundationalism, see W. Jay Wood, *Epistemology: Becoming Intellectually Virtuous* (Downers Grove, IL: InterVarsity Press, 1998), 77–104.

22. James Wm. McClendon Jr. and James M. Smith, *Convictions: Defusing Religious Relativism*, rev. ed. (Valley Forge, PA: Trinity, 1994), 149–79.

23. Ibid., 155.

24. Ibid., 108.

25. Karl Barth, *Church Dogmatics*, 1/1 and 1/2 (Edinburgh: T & T Clark, 1975, 1956).

26. Bruce D. Marshall, *Trinity and Truth* (Cambridge: Cambridge University Press, 2000).

27. For a general account of the primacy of the Trinity for theology and Christian thought, see Stanley J. Grenz and John R. Franke, *Beyond Foundationalism: Shaping Theology in a Postmodern Context* (Louisville: Westminster/John Knox, 2001), 169–202.

28. Marshall, *Trinity and Truth*, 108–40.

29. Ibid., 181.

11

Who's Afraid of Postmodernism?
A Response to the "Biola School"

James K. A. Smith

In this brief response, I have chosen to focus on the essays by Scott Smith and Douglas Geivett. This is for a couple of reasons: first, in the work of Merold Westphal, John Franke, and Kevin Vanhoozer, I find little to disagree with. Second, and more importantly, I think Scott and Geivett's essays embody a very common conception and critique of postmodernism—one that I have come to call the "Biola School."[1] More specifically, I want to respond to the Biola School's conception and criticism of postmodernism.[2] I will outline three basic features of the Biola School of postmodernism and offer a criticism of each element.

1. Postmodernism Is Antithetical to Christian Faith

The approach of the Biola School is governed by the assumption that postmodernism and Christian faith are mutually exclusive. As Geivett states it, postmodernism "threatens to subvert the enterprise of theology" per se; this is because "any method governed by the sensibilities of postmodernity will be hostile to the traditional aims of inquiry" (and obviously, I guess, Christians should side with these "traditional aims").

Scott suggests that the linguistic turn "will undermine at least one essential doctrine of the faith." I noted in my own essay that one finds
similar sentiments in the work of Brian Ingraffia (formerly of Biola) when
he argues for the absolute antithesis between "biblical theology" and
"postmodern theory."[3] But such assumptions about the antithesis both
beg the question and tend to govern their reading of postmodernism in
such a way that it produces only self-fulfilling prophecies. In contrast,
I think the patient work of Merold Westphal has consistently shown
that such assertions about the antithesis between postmodernism and
Christian faith stem from both a misunderstanding of postmodernism
and a problematic understanding of Christian faith that is too closely
identified with the hallmarks of a rationalist modernity.[4]

2. Postmodernism Is Equated with Postfoundationalism

A second feature that strikes me about the Biola School's take on
postmodernism is its reduction of postmodernism to an *epistemological*
phenomenon (part of the general epistemological fixation of the Biola
School).[5] Further in this vein, Scott and Geivett take figures such as
Hauerwas, Kallenberg, and Grenz and Franke as representative figures
of postmodernism (Hauerwas would be surprised by this, I think),[6]
equating postmodernism with Anglo-American postfoundationalism.[7]
(Indeed, one of the strange features of the Biola School's version of
postmodernism is the almost complete absence of French or other continental philosophical references. Theirs is a postmodernism without
Derrida and Foucault, a movement sans Nietzsche and Heidegger. Not
even Rorty makes a showing. This kind of takes all of the fun out of
postmodernism!)

This equation of postmodernism with postfoundationalism is coupled
with feature 1 above, generating a critique that simply assumes that
Christian faith is committed to foundationalism. Therefore, if postmodernism is post- or antifoundationalist, then it must not be Christian.
This is most carefully articulated by Geivett, who argues that since
"Christian theism is a system of belief," then "one must affirm at least
some of the propositions of Christian theism in order to be a Christian."
Moreover, "Christian theism has a propositional structure"; therefore, in
order to believe "responsibly," the Christian must provide justification
for his or her beliefs, which, Geivett argues, requires an affirmation of
the foundationalist epistemology he offers. It is particularly important
to recall the first moves that bring us to this point. In his discussion of
doxastic attitudes, he defines a "belief" as a "mental state." Further, a
mental state is described as a kind of "attitude"—in particular a "propositional attitude" that is a belief *about* a state of affairs.[8] Our beliefs are

"true" if they stand "in the right relation to the world"—a description left rather vague. One has *knowledge* only if one's beliefs are true: "One has propositional knowledge only if there is something one believes, what one believes is true, and this true belief that one has is adequately grounded."

The key dispute between foundationalism and the postfoundationalism that Geivett identifies with postmodernism is just what would or could constitute "adequate grounding" or justification. I appreciate Geivett's criticism of caricatures of foundationalism (e.g., Franke's) that assume that foundationalism requires "invincible certainty." Nevertheless, he does assert that we can both articulate the conditions for adequate grounding in some universal sense and that these conditions can be met not just for claims such as "There is an orange tree in my yard" but also that "God exists."[9] When Geivett finally describes how such justification happens—by the "mode of direct acquaintance"—it is hard not to feel that we've been shortchanged. It seems that Geivett's answer to how one is justified in one's beliefs ends up being some version of: "Well, it's obvious. It's just 'clear and distinct.' You have this experience or the 'natural light' of reason shows you something which you can't *not* accept."[10] And, to top it off, this is then to function as the basis for a *demonstration* that my belief is true.

I have two serious problems with this rehabilitation of foundationalism and rejection of postfoundationalist epistemologies (though Geivett doesn't really offer a critique of the latter, only an alternative). First, while Geivett does help foundationalism slip out of from under the charge of requiring "certainty" by recognizing our fallibility and lowering the bar for justification, it seems to me that he skirts questions about "objectivity" and "universality." Foundationalist epistemology—and the evidentialist apologetics that Geivett wants to hitch to it—requires the possibility of universal or objective demonstration. But the appeal to "direct acquaintance" seems to beg the question in this regard—akin to Descartes' "proofs" that demand that one accept the premises dictated by "the natural light." But from whence does this natural light shine? And to whom? It is here that the postfoundationalist critique takes hold, by taking seriously the *particularity* of just what appears as "obvious" or "clear and distinct."

This leads to my second problem with Geivett's claim that Christian theology must be committed to a foundationalist epistemology: it simply doesn't square with the New Testament witness. In fact, the scriptures repeatedly emphasize that because of the noetic effects of sin, the minds—and *hearts*—of unbelievers are "futile" and "darkened" (Rom. 1:18–31).[11] It is clear from the Gospel narratives, for instance, that not everyone sees what the centurion sees when on Golgotha he proclaims, "Truly this was the Son of God" (Matt. 27:54 NASB). Of course, all of the observers at Golgotha see and encounter the same material phenomena—crosses, bodies, and eventually corpses—but these material phenomena are *texts* that need to be interpreted—just *what* they're seeing is not immediately clear. So the very fact that both the centurion and the chief priests are confronted by the same phenomena and yet "see" something very different would seem to demonstrate Derrida's point: the very experience of the things themselves is a matter of interpretation. Even if we are confronted with the physical and historical evidence of the resurrection—even if we witnessed the resurrection *firsthand*—what exactly this *meant* would require interpretation, and this interpretive "seeing" is conditioned by the particularities of my horizon of perception. There is no "neutral seeing" of orange trees or resurrected bodies. Only by means of *interpreting* the resurrection of Jesus do I see that it confirms that he is the Son of God (Rom. 1:4).[12]

Moreover, in the epistles we get the same kind of claim, viz., that not everyone can see what the believer sees. While God's invisible attributes are, on the one hand, "clearly seen" (Rom. 1:20 NIV), Paul goes on to emphasize the way in which this is *not* seen by those whose "foolish hearts [are] darkened" (1:21 NIV), who thus construe or interpret the world as something other than God's creation. That interpreting the world as creation is, I would argue, the *true* interpretation, does not negate its status as an interpretation or "conditioned seeing" (contra "direct acquaintance"). What is required to interpret the world well are the necessary *conditions* of interpretation—the right horizons of expectation and the right presuppositions. But as Paul repeatedly emphasizes, these conditions are themselves a gift; in other words, the presuppositions and horizons that make it possible to properly "read" creation are grace-gifts that attend redemption and regeneration (Rom. 1:18–31, 1 Cor. 1:18–2:15; Eph. 4:17–18). I think this is precisely why we shouldn't be surprised that not everyone we encounter immediately grasps the "rationality" of the gospel. In fact, we should expect that someone will not be able to properly "see" creation or the crucifixion without the grace of redemption. Or, to put it another way, I think that presuppositional apologetics (and the more nonfoundationalist epistemology that undergirds it)—such as that developed by Francis Schaeffer, but also by Cornelius Van Til and, to a degree, Herman Dooyeweerd—rejects classical apologetics because it recognizes the truth of the postfoundationalist claim that everything is interpretation.[13]

3. Postmodernism Is Equated with "Narrative" and/or the "Linguistic Turn"

Both Scott Smith and Geivett focus upon the role of story in confessedly postmodern thought (on their reading, Frei and Lindbeck must be postmoderns). However, their rejections of story and narrative are quite different, so I will first focus on Geivett and then turn to Scott's criticisms.

Geivett begins his essay by distinguishing an "account" from a "story": an account is a kind of "explanation" that makes intelligible a state of affairs and complies with "criteria for rational belief"; a "story," on the other hand, does not present *the* world but rather an imaginative entry into *a* world. As such, it does not require the same "compliance" with rational criteria ("imagination has more or less free reign") and does not "represent" a state of affairs. So in the end, Geivett reduces story and narrative to *fiction*, to "make-believe," which doesn't require any "doxastic commitment." The only way that stories could redeem themselves is if they put themselves "in the service of accounts"; analogously, imagination is redeemed only insofar as it is subject to reason. Since Geivett takes theology to be an *account* of God and God's ways, he concludes that Christians must be fundamentally committed to giving accounts, not telling stories.

My criticism of Geivett is twofold. First, behind his hierarchical distinction between accounts and stories I find a very reductionist anthropology—which is consistent with Geivett's epistemology, which reduces *truth* to the realm of the rational and propositional. More particularly, I think Geivett works with *rationalist* anthropology that echoes the Platonic identification of the essence of the human person with "reason" and thus castigates the imagination as either slave or seducer. In other words, the human person is *reduced* to a (primarily or essentially) rational animal, and truth is reduced to an affair of reason. Within such a framework, the imaginative and affective aspects of the human person are relegated to a secondary position at best—or, as in Plato, suspected as sites of deception and *un*truth. So also the communicative phenomena that attend such aspects of the human person—narratives and stories—are either rejected as fictive and therefore *not* true, or reduced to an instrumental value "in the service of" rational accounts.

But such an anthropology that hovers behind Geivett's "account" should be rejected not only as reductionistic but also as unbiblical. I see no good reason to reduce the core of the human person to the rational (and lots of reasons *not* to), nor do I find any compelling reason to reduce *truth* to the rational and propositional. If there is a "core" of the human person indicated by scripture, it is not the *mind* but rather the *heart*. The "heart" is not primarily rational or cognitive (nor is it *ir*rational or anticognitive); it is a complex seat of human identity that cannot be reduced to any one particular aspects—whether reason or imagination or emotion. Again, here I take up Pascal's criticism of just the kind of (modernist) rationalism that Geivett offers. As Pascal emphasizes, "It is the heart that feels God, not reason: that is what faith is. God felt by the heart, not by reason. The heart has its reasons which reason itself does not know: we know that through countless things."[14] Thus Pascal points to an irreducible heart-knowledge that cannot be reduced to the registers of reason since it is a kind of "knowing" that is *felt* rather than deduced. "We know the truth not only by means of reason," he argues, "but also by means of the heart. It is through the heart that we know the first principles, and reason—which has no part in this knowledge—vainly tries to contest them" (§142). In the same way that Heidegger argues that *Verstehen* founds *Erkenntnis,* so Pascal argues that those "first principles" that we know by heart are the condition of possibility for that which we know by reason, for "it is on this knowledge by means of the heart and instinct that reason has to rely, and must base all its argument."[15] Truth, then, is not only a cognitive commodity communicated to the mind; it is also an affective reality known by the heart.

I think a biblically informed philosophical anthropology must begin by appreciating each of the multiple aspects that constitute person- hood as essential and irreducible.[16] The rational does not trump the affective, just as the biotic does not trump the emotional. Nor should we identify "truth" or "knowledge" with only one of these aspects, viz., reason; rather, there is a mode of truth that is proper to each of these diverse aspects of the person. This is why, for instance, art speaks *truth* even when it is "fiction."[17]

In this respect, I find Geivett's rejection of story (all in the name of propositional truth) to be *puritanical* in the worst sort of way—indeed a puritanical critique that would out-puritan one of the Puritan greats: John Bunyan. Bunyan encountered just the sort of rationalist rejections of story and narrative that Geivett offers here—criticisms that reduce story to fiction and narrative to myth. In light of the charge that his tale was fantastic and imaginative, trafficking in "similitudes," Bunyan responds by emphasizing the kind of multimodal character of truth that corresponds to a nonreductionist anthropology, which revalues each aspect of the human person, including the imagination.[18] So quite un- like the Platonic rationalism that informs much evangelical rejection of the imagination as fictive and thus deceptive (as "feigned," Bunyan's detractors would say), Bunyan responds: "Some men, by feigning words as dark as mine, / Make truth to spangle, and its rays to shine." Indeed, he invites us in almost Lyotardian fashion: "Wouldest thou see a Truth within a Fable?"[19] Bunyan rejects the rationalism that restricts truth and knowledge to the narrow bandwidth of cognitive propositions because he appreciates that the human person is the kind of creature whose core—whose *heart*—is reflected in a diversity of aspects.[20]

In addition to a nonreductionist account of truth, Bunyan also dis- cerns a second problem with rejections of story such as that offered by

Geivett: the rejection of narrative in favor of explanatory "accounts" is in tension with the narrative of the scriptures themselves. "Were not God's Laws, / His Gospel-Laws, in olden time held forth / By Types, Shadows, and Metaphors?" Bunyan asks.[21] Indeed, I find it curious that Geivett defines theology as an "account of God." In this respect, the scriptures are not theological, insofar as they do not offer an account but rather a story. Not even the New Testament epistles offer anything like what Geivett describes as an "account," because they seem almost oblivious to the notion of providing rational "justification" for their claims. In this respect, the scriptures must appear remarkably *non*foundationalist. The New Testament is kerygmatic, not demonstrative; the apostles were preachers and storytellers, not "account-ants."[22] In this respect, God's own revelation of himself in the scriptures is in the mode of *story*, not an explanatory account. As Michael Horton has recently shown, God's self-revelation unfolds with the allusivity of a drama, not the unfurling of premises in an argument.[23] It seems difficult to find a foundationalist epistemology in the New Testament; quite to the contrary, we find that the scriptures comprise a narrative of God's actions, and when the apostles seek to proclaim or "demonstrate" that Jesus is the Messiah, their appeal is to the *story* of God's actions in the world. So Geivett's devaluing of story would seem to be at odds with the biblical witness that, one assumes, would undergird the foundationalist theology he is calling for.

Scott's criticisms of narrative are different, and more confusing.[24] Taking on figures such as Hauerwas, Murphy, and Kallenberg (with McIntyre and Wittgenstein in the background), Scott is suspicious of the linguistic turn that undergirds the turn to narrative. As he articulates it, the "core presupposition" of linguistic/narrative epistemologies is that "something stands between us and a real 'world,' such that we cannot know it in itself as it 'really' is." Suggesting that this commits Hauerwas and Kallenberg to a Kantian framework, Scott argues that post-linguistic-turn philosophers posit language as something that stands *between* us and the world. From this he concludes that such thinkers believe that "language and world are *internally related*." But I'm not exactly sure what it means to speak about the "internal relation of language and the world," or what it means to say that they are "internally related." Internal to what? Related how? The claim is so idiosyncratic I find it difficult to respond. From what I can gather, Scott thinks that the linguistic turn commits one to the notion that we are imprisoned in language—that there is a world "out there," but it is a kind of noumenal realm that we can never reach, because we are confined by the strictures of language that come "between" us and the world. "If we cannot get outside language," he notes, "and know an extralinguistic world *as it really is*, then our only contact with that world is by our language use" (emphases mine). As such, it must be the case the language *"constitutes* reality." He then goes on to offer the favorite criticism of the Biola School: that such claims are self-referentially incoherent.

From what I can make of Scott's criticisms, they are misguided because of a restrictive understanding of language. First, language is a part of the world, as are the *users* of language. As Heidegger emphasized, human beings are those beings who are *In-der-Welt-sein*—we always already inhabit the world, and so it is naive to distinguish language *from* the world, or even to abstract "us," its users, as somehow outside the world. Second, "language" for post-linguistic-turn philosophers is not to be equated or reduced to words on a page or words that we speak. Language is to be broadly understood as a semiotic system that construes the things, events, and people I encounter. So it's not a matter of trying to "hook up" to a world "outside" of language—the world I inhabit is always already *interpreted* within a framework of signs or a semiotic system. It is this point that the linguistic turn emphasizes. So even if we take its most radical form—as in Derrida's claim that "there is nothing outside of the text"—it does not entail the kind of stilted Kantianism that Scott paints. In *Of Grammatology,* the book where Derrida makes this claim, he is engaged in an extended analysis of an essay by early modern thinker Jean-Jacques Rousseau, "The Origin of Language." In answering the question, Rousseau (like Scott) tends to think that language is something of an *obstacle* to the world—that language is something that gets in the way of just experiencing the world itself. Language is a lens through which we see the world, albeit with some distortion, simply because there is this lens *between* the world and us. As soon as there is a lens, there is distortion. We can buff this lens for days, or grind it as thin as possible, but insofar as there is this lens, there is *mediation,* and as soon as there is mediation, for Rousseau, there is distortion. As such, Rousseau suggests that language is something that *befalls* us as a contingent evil, in a way corrupting what was a pure, unmediated experience of the world simply "as it is."

The Rousseauan notion that interpretation is something that "plagues" us is illustrated in the film *Memento,* which recounts the challenges of Leonard, who—without short-term memory—must negotiate his way in the world by means of notes scribbled on paper and texts tattooed on his body. Like Leonard, we have a "condition" (a disease, an illness) that requires us to use language in order to make our way in the world. Rousseau longs for the good old days (what he calls "the state of Nature") when we weren't inflicted with this "condition" and could simply experience the world the way it is *without mediation*—without anything between us and the world. In other words, for Rousseau, as soon as the lens of language is inserted, we have to *interpret* the world. As soon as there is *mediation,* there is *interpretation.* The "state of Nature" is a state of immediacy where we don't have to "interpret" things; we simply "know" what they are. That's a cup. That's my wife. This is a computer. It's clear and simple.[25]

But was there ever a time without interpretation?[26] Will there ever be a time when we don't interpret? Do I ever just simply *see* a cup "as it 'really' is," as Scott contends? Enter Derrida. While Rousseau was offering his theory in the sixteenth century—at the heart of the birth of modernity—Derrida thinks that most of us twenty-first-century inhabitants are Rousseauans at heart. This becomes most clear in our ideas of what it means to *read*. Often when we read—and biblical commentaries tend to be a great "case study" for this—we imagine that the text or the language of the book is something that we have to *get through* in order to recover what the author's "original intention" was. In other words, the text becomes something of a hurdle that we have to jump over—or a curtain that we need to pass through—in order to get to this "thing" that is "behind" the text, such as the author's idea, or the "referent" (the "thing" to which the text points). Now, sometimes we concede that such a process requires that bothersome thing called *interpretation*—like when we're reading a poem or C. S. Lewis's more allegorical works. Then we concede that there is a kind of "code" that needs to be broken in order to understand the text. But most of the time, we don't think we interpret; we simply *read*. In these cases, we assume that the text under consideration is "clear" and therefore doesn't require interpretation. Sure, we might need some background or context, but once those pieces are in place, we don't need to interpret. Instead, the text takes on a kind of transparency so that we can simply *see* what it means. So unlike Leonard in *Memento*, who needs notes and texts to help explain his world, we can move around without such supplements. When I read the newspaper, I don't need to "interpret," I simply need to read. And most of us think that when we read the Bible, the same is true: yes, some passages are difficult, or the poetry of Song of Solomon might throw us for a loop, but if I'm reading Paul's epistle to the Romans, things are pretty clear. I simply need to provide a *commentary* that gives me the background and context. Such a commentary is like a cloth that cleans off the text to grant it the transparency that makes interpretation unnecessary.

Now Derrida recognizes this kind of reading (he calls it "doubling commentary") and even concedes that there is a time and place for this kind of project. However, he is worried that it assumes a kind of Rousseauan naïveté precisely because it assumes that there can be a reading (or even *experience*) that does not involve interpretation. In other words, it assumes that *we* (who are either "normal," "healed," or "redeemed"—not beset by a "condition") are different from Leonard. Leonard's a freak; we're normal. Leonard needs notes and texts; we can simply look at the world and see it "as it is." Even if we are reading a text, we can get past it to what is behind it or the thing it's pointing to.

For Derrida, this is a *naive* assumption, because it fails to recognize that we never really get "behind" or "past" texts—we never get "beyond" the realm of interpretation to some kind of kingdom of pure reading. We are never able to step out of our skins. Texts and language are not something that we get *through* to a world without language or a "state of nature" where interpretation is not necessary. If the text is construed as a kind of Alice-in-Wonderland-like "looking glass," on the other side is not a world without language or interpretations, but simply *more* texts and interpretation. Down the rabbit hole of our experience, it's language all the way down. Thus, just before making his famous claim that there is "nothing outside of the text," Derrida says that a reading

> cannot legitimately transgress the text toward something other than it, toward a referent [. . .] or toward a signified outside the text whose content could take place, could have taken place outside of language, that is to say, in the sense that we give here to that word, outside of writing in general.[27]

In other words, if a line of text says, "The blue cup sat on Pilgrim's table," and I understand what it means (I can picture a blue cup sitting on a table), I have *not* according to Derrida, stepped out of the realm of interpretation. Interpretation is not a series of hoops we jump through in order to eventually reach a realm of unmediated experience where I don't have to interpret anymore. Rather, interpretation is an inescapable part of being human and experiencing the world. So even this blue cup sitting on my table, which I am drinking my coffee from "firsthand," as it were, is *still* a matter of interpretation.

When Derrida says that we can't get "beyond" or "behind" the text to a "referent" (or "signified") that is outside of language, he means this in a *radical* way. There are a couple of less radical ways that we could understand this, which he notes but does not emphasize. First, when he claims that there is nothing outside of the text, this isn't simply because "Jean-Jacques' life, or the existence of Mamma or Thérèse *themselves* is not of prime interest to us."[28] In other words, he doesn't mean that we can just choose to act *as if* Mamma doesn't exist and "play" with the text without caring about what it really refers to. That there is nothing outside of the text is not a kind of "voluntary" condition that we can choose to effect. Second, when he claims that there is nothing outside of the text, this is not simply "because we have access to their so-called 'real' existence only in the text and we have neither any means of altering this, nor any right to neglect this limitation."[29] For instance, one might claim that there is no Socrates outside of the text because the only *access* I have to Socrates now is through the texts of Plato or Aristophanes. In that sense there would be "no Socrates outside of the text." But while both of these would be reasons to proclaim that "there is nothing outside of the text," Derrida says that "there are more radical reasons."[30] He goes on to put it this way: "[I]n what one calls the real life of these existences 'of flesh and bone,' beyond and behind what one believes can be circumscribed as Rousseau's text, there has never been anything but writing."[31] It's not just that writing or texts are the portals through which we must pass in order to get to "things," or the gates that provide access to an uninterpreted "reality"; rather, when Derrida claims that there's nothing outside of the text, he means that there is no reality that is not always already *interpreted* through the mediating lens of language.[32] "Textuality," for Derrida, is linked to interpretation. To claim that there is nothing outside of the text is to say that *everything* is a text—which doesn't mean that everything is a book, or that we live within some giant, all-encompassing book, but rather that everything is interpreted in order to be experienced. So he is *not* a linguistic idealist who denies the material existence of cups and tables; rather, in the line of Martin Heidegger (of *Being and Time*), he is what we might call a *comprehensive hermeneuticist* who claims that all of our experience is always already an interpretation.

Texts that require interpretations are not things inserted *between* me and the world; rather, the world *is* a kind of text requiring interpretation (and so am *I*—even to *myself!*). Even experiencing a cup "in person" or "in the flesh" demands that I interpret the thing *as* a cup, and this interpretation is informed by a number of different things: the context in which I encounter the thing, my own history and background, the set of presuppositions that I bring to the experience, and more.[33] Given all of these conditions, the things I experience are subject to interpretation—and as such, they are subject to *different* interpretations. So we never get past texts and interpretations to things "simply as they are" in any kind of unmediated fashion (as Rousseau supposed); rather, we move from interpretation to interpretation. The entire world is a text. Thus, "there is nothing outside of the text."

I see no reason why such a claim is antithetical to Christian faith. Quite to the contrary, I think it is a perceptive analysis of the conditions of finitude that constitute creaturehood. As I've noted above, even the gospel itself is an interpretation of the events in first-century Palestine. The recognition of the gospel's status as an interpretation does not negate its truth, nor does it concede to a sophomoric relativist claim that nothing is true. It simply concedes that its claims are not "clear" or immediately evident to everyone; rather, as the New Testament emphasizes, the gospel is a "reading" or "construal" of the world that is foolishness to the Greeks, a wisdom that is folly to the modern, foundationalist world (1 Cor. 1:18–31).

Notes

1. I first had inklings of this line when I was on a panel with William Lane Craig where we disagreed rather passionately about perspectivalism in science. The notion of a "Biola School" crystallized for me during a stay at L'Abri in Switzerland, where I presented a series of lectures on postmodernism and church. After repeatedly hearing knee-jerk student reactions that sounded all too familiar, I finally asked—somewhat exasperated—whether this was the "Biola School" of philosophy. When three of the students raising the criticisms indicated that they had indeed graduated from Biola, my suspicions were confirmed. So the notion of a "Biola School" seems an apt heuristic to describe a common set of reactions to postmodern thought. The "Biola School" is broader than Biola faculty, however; I would also include Douglas Groothuis, for instance, and the Evangelical Philosophical Society in general.

2. I think one could speak of a broader "Biola School" of Christian philosophy that is devoted to analytic philosophy, a revised foundationalist epistemology, a classical evidentialist apologetics (indeed, it tends to *reduce* philosophy to apologetics), and a biblicist notion of propositional revelation. One might then suggest a contrasting "Calvin School" of Christian philosophy—which is also found at Yale and Notre Dame—which is less religiously devoted to analytic philosophy, offers a postfoundationalist epistemology that criticizes foundationalism, tends toward a presuppositional apologetics, and adopts a less fundamentalist notion of revelation. However, I will not deal with these broader aspects in this brief piece.

3. Brian Ingraffia, *Postmodern Theory and Biblical Theology: Vanquishing God's Shadow* (Cambridge: Cambridge University Press, 1995), 14, 241.

4. For a demonstrative collection, see Merold Westphal, *Overcoming Ontotheology: Toward a Postmodern Christian Faith* (New York: Fordham University Press, 2001).

5. In this respect the Biola School strikes me as reductionist insofar as it reduces almost all questions to matters of epistemology. Even ethics, for instance, is reduced to a matter of how we can *know* what is moral (whereas I would think that the real question in ethics is how we can we *do* what is moral?).

6. See, for instance, his essay, "The Christian Difference: Or, Surviving Postmodernism," in his book *A Better Hope: Resources for a Church Confronting Capitalism, Democracy, and Postmodernity* (Grand Rapids: Brazos, 2000), 35–46, in which he states, "I confess that I have taken great pleasure watching the postmodernists dismantle the pretensions of modernism, but it is still the case that being an enemy of my enemy does not and should not necessarily make me a friend of postmodernism" (35).

7. Admittedly, Franke and Grenz—following the lead of Nancey Murphy—tend to effect the same equation.

8. In section 3 below I return to this emphasis on "propositional knowledge" when I discuss the reductionist anthropology that characterizes the Biola School.

9. Due to space limitations, I will bracket here my general criticism of the notion of "Christian theism." With Pascal, I'm suspicious that the god of theism is incommensurate with the God of Abraham, Isaac, and Jesus Christ.

10. The quotes here play on Descartes' *Meditations*.

11. Cf. Eph. 4:17–18 which describes the noetic state of unbelievers as "futile" because they are "darkened in their understanding and separated from the life of God because of the ignorance that is in them due to the hardening of their hearts."

12. As the Puritan theologian John Owen puts it in *The Holy Spirit* (Grand Rapids: Kregel, 1954), 155: "that Jesus Christ was crucified, is a proposition that any natural [i.e., unregenerate] man may understand and assent to, and be said to receive: and all the doctrines of the gospel may be taught in propositions and discourses, the sense and meaning of which a natural man may understand; but it is denied that he can receive the things themselves. For there is a wide difference between the mind's receiving doctrines notionally, and receiving the things taught in them really." See Owen's lucid account of "Corruption of the depravity of the mind by sin," III.iii (144–169).

13. Robert Webber provides a helpful account of the way in which postmodernity demands a "new apologetic" in ch. 4 of *The Younger Evangelicals* (Grand Rapids: Baker Academic, 2002).

14. Blaise Pascal, *Pensées*, trans. Honor Levi (New York: Oxford University Press, 1995), § 680 (157–58).

15. Ibid., §142. He goes on to say that the heart *feels* and reason *proves:* "The principles are felt, and the propositions proved, both conclusively, although by different ways, and it is as useless and stupid for the heart to demand of reason a feeling of all the propositions it proves before accepting them."

16. This biblically informed anthropology, which I can only sketch here, is more fully articulated in Herman Dooyeweerd, *In the Twilight of Western Thought*, ed. James K. A. Smith, The Collected Works, B/4 (Lewiston, NY: Edwin Mellen Press, 1999), ch. 8 (119–132) and Calvin Seerveld, "A Christian Tin-can Theory of the Human Creature," in *In the Fields of the Lord: A Calvin Seerveld Reader*, ed. Craig Bartholomew (Carlisle, UK: Piquant, 2000), 102–116. I have elsewhere articulated an account of the "affective" aspect in my "Staging the Incarnation: Revisiting Augustine's Critique of Theatre," *Literature and Theology* 15 (2001): 123–139.

17. For a discussion of "aesthetic truth," see Calvin Seerveld, "Dooyeweerd's Legacy for Aesthetics: Modal Law Theory," in *The Legacy of Herman Dooyeweerd*, ed. C. T. McIntire (Lanham, MD: University Press of America, 1985), 41–80; idem., "The Freedom and Responsibility of the Artist," in *Bearing Fresh Olive Leaves: Alternative Steps in Understanding Art* (Carlisle, UK: Piquant, 2000), 23–40; Lambert Zuidervaart, "Art, Truth, Vocation: Validity and Disclosure in Heidegger's Anti-aesthetics," *Philosophy and Social Criticism* 28 (2002): 153–72. For historical precedent in the philosophical tradition, consider Aristotle's claim that "art, therefore, as has been said, is a *rational quality*, concerned with *making*, that reasons *truly*," *Nicomachean Ethics* IV.iii.6 (see also 2–6); my italics. My thanks to Myron Penner for this latter reference.

18. "How doth the Fowler seek to catch his Game / By divers means, all which one cannot name? / His Gun, his Nets, his Lime-twigs, Light, and Bell; / He creeps, he goes, he stands; yea who can tell / Of all his postures? Yet there's none of these / Will make him master of what Fowls he please. / Yea, he must Pipe and Whistle to catch *this*; / Yet if he does so, *that* Bird he will miss." John

Bunyan, *Pilgrim's Progress*, "The Author's Apology," in *The Harvard Classics* (New York: P. F. Collier & Son, 1937), 7.

19. Ibid., 10.

20. "Come, Truth, although in Swaddling-clouts, I find, / Informs the Judgment, rectifies the Mind, / Pleases the Understanding, makes the Will / Submit; the Memory too it doth fill / With what doth our Imagination please; / Likewise it tends our troubles to appease." Ibid., 8.

21. Ibid., 7. He goes on to note: "The Prophets used much by Metaphors / To set forth Truth; yea, whoso considers / Christ, his Apostles too, shall plainly see, / That Truths to this day in such Mantles be" (8).

22. As John Milbank puts it, Christian theology is not a discourse of *demonstration* but kerygmatic *proclamation* and *persuasion*. See Milbank, *Theology and Social Theory: Beyond Secular Reason* (Oxford: Blackwell, 1990), 1. See also Graham Ward, *Cities of God* (London: Routledge, 2000), 74.

23. See Horton's important book *Covenant and Eschatology: The Divine Drama* (Nashville: Westminster/John Knox Press, 2002). Horton demonstrates not only the nonfoundationalism of the scriptural narrative but also the nonfoundationalist framework of Reformed thought in the "Protestant Scholastic" and Dutch traditions.

24. To try to sort out the plurality of Smiths in this volume, I will hence refer to R. Scott Smith as Scott.

25. I have analyzed the "hermeneutics of immediacy" in much more detail in the first chapter of my *The Fall of Interpretation: Philosophical Foundations for a Creational Hermeneutic* (Downers Grove, IL: InterVarsity Press, 2000).

26. By "interpretation," I mean the (often passive) intentional act that "constitutes" experience, seeing things *as* something—seeing the influx of sensible data coming toward me *as* a cup, or hearing the sound waves rushing toward me *as* a call for dinner.

27. Derrida, *Of Grammatology,* 158.

28. Ibid.

29. Ibid.

30. Ibid.

31. Ibid., 159.

32. In this way, I'll concede that Leonard in *Memento* is not a Derridean all the way down. Leonard still operates with a notion that there are "facts" that are not a matter of interpretation. Lenny thinks "memories are an interpretation" but that facts written on his body are not. But the film itself undermines Leonard's naive distinction, because one of the crucial "facts" that he writes down (the license number on Teddy's picture) is a pure fabrication just to give him someone to hunt down.

33. I have analyzed the process and conditions of interpretation in much more detail in my *The Fall of Interpretation*, especially ch. 5 (ch. 4 is focused on Derrida).

12

Of Stories and Languages

Merold Westphal

Of course we cannot identify God with our story of God any more than we can identify Abraham Lincoln with our story about him. Do we not have many stories, each from a distinctive perspective that opens some things to view while keeping us from seeing others? And might there not be other viewpoints from which a different light is cast on what we *can* see from that initial standpoint? So we are reluctant simply to identify any of our stories with their "object" or subject matter. Could these also be reasons why God has given us two creation stories and four versions of the life, death, and resurrection of Jesus?

We are, I suspect, comfortable perspectivists when it comes to biographies of Lincoln. We assume that some are better than others in a variety of ways, that even those that are less complete, less elegantly written, or less accurate may be illuminating and helpful, and that some are so biased or so inaccurate as to do more harm than good in getting to know who Lincoln was. Moreover, we (or experts to whom we turn) make judgments about the relative merits of these various stories in the full awareness that those judgments are at once fallible and perspectival themselves.

But none of us, I suspect, not even Professor Geivett on a good day, equates this perspectivism, as he does by means of apposition in his second paragraph, with "an anything-goes wave of the hand." So my question is, *Who on earth does?* Surely not those famous freshmen in Philosophy 101, for while they stubbornly maintain their anything-goes philosophy as long as they can, they have never heard of perspectivism. Surely not the postmodern philosophers, who in context are the obvious target of this barb. Such thinkers as Nietzsche, Heidegger, Derrida, Foucault, Lyotard, and Rorty (call them the Gang of Six if you like) are with good reason called postmodernists and perspectivists, holding that human understanding is always limited to a particular and contingent horizon. But none of them draws an anything-goes conclusion any more than we do in our perspectivist understanding of the stories about Lincoln. Nietzsche, for example, does not think Platonism or Christianity is as good as the piety of Zarathustra. Nor does Derrida think that any version of what he calls the metaphysics of presence is as good an interpretation of human understanding as deconstruction.

Not only does Geivett give us no *evidence* that anyone of interest holds that anything goes, he does not even *assert* this by naming anyone who allegedly does. Is this because he knows that such a charge cannot withstand textual scrutiny? That "anything-goes" talk is a straw man?

I have another *who-on-earth-are-you-talking-about?* question for Geivett. Who on earth equates stories or narratives with fiction, where "imagination has more or less free rein" in a "fantastic world of make-believe," whose value is "irrespective of how things actually are?" The Gospel of Mark is a narrative, as is Sandburg's biography of Lincoln. But neither invites us to mere "imaginative participation" without "doxastic commitment." *So who on earth besides Geivett reduces narratives to fictional narratives?* I don't know any postmodern philosopher who does. Or any narrative theologian.[1] Nor, N.B., does Geivett so much as name a single person who allegedly fits his description.

It would be easy enough to find both philosophers and theologians who deny that either narratives or accounts can be "objective" in the sense of not being shaped to a greater or lesser degree by the interests of the author, including the interest in being as free from bias as possible. But that is a very different story from the one Geivett is telling. His story appears to be one in which "narrative imagination has more or less free rein." I fear that the anonymous postmodernism Geivett presents is more a figment of his imagination than a product of responsible scholarship.

One brief comment on foundationalism: Geivett tells us that "for a belief to be justified . . . is for the truth of the belief to be indicated with a satisfactory degree of probability by the evidence that person has." But *A* can be an evidential indicator of *B* for me only if I believe *A*. This means that beliefs can be justified only with reference to other beliefs, which seems to preclude the noninferential, direct justification necessary for Geivett's foundationalism.

◆◆◆

There is much to like in Professor Franke's essay, beginning with his observation that the term *postmodern* has no single, clear meaning. That is why in my own work I prefer to focus on particular arguments or themes of particular authors, deriving my view of "postmodernism" from the bottom up, "straight from the horse's mouth," as it were, and especially not from secondary sources in which denunciation prevails over careful attention to the text.[2] It should be noted that within philosophical academia, the term has a relatively narrow range, primarily signifying Nietzsche, Heidegger, and the French poststructuralists. Many others who make similar critiques of philosophical modernity are not normally called postmodernists. Ricoeur and Gadamer, for example, would be identified instead in terms of philosophical hermeneutics, and those whom Nancey Murphy illuminatingly identifies as Anglo-American postmodernists would not normally be so labeled. But since so many others than my Gang of Six, even expanded to Twelve or Eighteen by adding more French thinkers, have contributed to the paradigm shift to which Franke refers, the more inclusive sense of the term as he uses it is quite justified. It should also be noted that while many engaged in interpreting this paradigm shift appropriately use the term *postmodern* to describe it, almost none of the major perpetrators do.

It is important to reject the notion that we are dealing with the alternative between rationality and irrationality, and the notion of a "chastened rationality" is useful. But not indispensable. Most of those just referred to as the perpetrators (those who think postmodernism is a crime will love this) are more likely to speak of understanding, or interpretation, or language, or even knowledge and truth than they are of rationality. It's almost as if they think modernity has spoiled the term and that it is now more misleading than illuminating to define humanity in terms of rational animality. Given contemporary, "modern" reductive analysis of rationality in terms of effective means-end calculation, it may be just as well (and more biblical).

Although *postmodernism* may have no simple, single definition, Franke rightly notes that there are common themes or family resemblances among those who judge the Enlightenment project to be a failure. Before turning to antifoundationalism, the theme to which he devotes his essay, a word about one of the themes he merely mentions, the shift from a realist to a constructionist view of truth and the world. The realism in question here is a double claim about human knowledge: (1) that the real is and is what it is independent of our knowing of it, and (2) that we can know it as it is in that independence, that our knowledge can correspond to it by perfectly mirroring it without reshaping it, can correspond to it in the traditional sense of *adaequatio intellectus et rei*. There isn't much point in defining realism in terms of the first claim, since Kant, the paradigmatic constructionist, takes it for granted. That's what the (in)famous thing in itself is all about. The debate between the realist and the antirealist is about the second thesis.

In spite of its ugliness, I prefer the term *antirealist* to the term *constructionist,* because the latter misleadingly suggests conscious and deliberate activity, as in constructing a house. But the claim that the world as we see, experience, and believe it is decisively shaped by the a priori elements we bring with us has no such meaning (1) in Kant, or (2) in those "postmodern" versions of Kantianism in which our control beliefs or horizons of expectation are historically particular and contingent rather than universal and necessary, or (3) in those forms of antirealism that see in language itself as such a culturally specific a priori. All forms of Kantian antirealism suggest that the human mind is or has become like a black-and-white TV set. It is a receiving or interpreting apparatus that does two things: it gives us real access to the real and, in doing so, it distorts it so that what it really is cannot be equated with the way we apprehend it. Nor can we get a better view of the real by dismantling the apparatus. It is worth remembering that Kant drew the distinction between appearances and things in themselves as the distinction between the way the world appears to human understanding and the way it appears to God, whose knowledge is the true measure of the real. It can be argued that all theists should be antirealists to guard against the illusory presumption of being able to see the world through God's eyes, to peek, as it were, over God's shoulder.[3]

Unlike Geivett, Franke distinguishes between weak and strong foundationalism and recognizes that the latter is not a caricature but an important element in the Enlightenment project.[4] In giving Nancey Murphey's criteria for foundationalism, he calls attention to the hermeneutical circle one finds in postmodern antirealism. I do not just move from my presuppositions (control beliefs, criteria, horizons of expectation) to interpretations they enable; I also find that such interpretations sometimes lead me in reverse direction to revise or even reject those presuppositions that had previously functioned as my a priori. The strong foundationalist is wrong in assuming that my "basic beliefs or first principles must be universal, objective, and discernable to any rational person apart from the particulars of varied situations, experiences, and contexts."

I like the question whether this ideal is either *possible* or *desirable,* but would put it just a bit differently. The hermeneutics of finitude, which can be read in terms of the doctrine of creation, represents one insight into the impossibility of such knowledge. We are not God. The hermeneutics of suspicion, which can be read in terms of the doctrine of the fall, represents a different but supporting insight into the same impossibility. We are not even ideally human. Thus the ideal in question is not desirable, *because* it is impossible. It conflicts with who we actually are, and pursuing it only leads to delusions of grandeur.

◆◆◆

Scott Smith examines the linguistic version of Kantianism already mentioned, the claim that our thought and knowledge have no extralinguistic access to the world. This is not to say that *the* world and human language are internally related but, more precisely, that *our* world, the world as we experience and think it, is internally related to our language. The language of making and constructing inevitably occurs, but to avoid being misled we should think in terms of language as the black-and-white TV or the funny mirror at the circus, which do not make what we see. While language games are the product of human activity, we do not make or construct them (nor, a fortiori, the worlds they shape) as we make a pie or construct a doghouse. They rather happen to us, and our ability consciously to shape them is quite limited. Like Topsy in *Uncle Tom's Cabin*, language games might tell us "I 'spect I growed. Don't think nobody never made me."

Two preliminary points before looking at Scott's two major objections. First, linguistic Kantianism need not be antitheory. With Wittgenstein one might think that some theoretical projects are so confused they should simply be abandoned. Or with Hauerwas one might think that the primary purpose of God-talk in Christian communities is not good theory but good character formation, "cultivating practical, moral skill" in the lives of those who play that language game. One can find more general forms of this view in Kierkegaard and Levinas. But none of these positions preclude the possibility that there are legitimate theoretical tasks for human thought; they only preclude the Luciferian assumption in theory we can "ascend to heaven" and "make [ourselves] like the Most High" (Isa. 14:13–14 NIV), seeing the world through God's eyes.

Second, linguistic Kantianism is in no way compromised by references to the prehuman past or the eschatological future. Like present reality, both of these were/are/will be what God knows them to be. But they can enter *our* thought and knowledge only under the same conditions as present reality; and if language shapes our understanding of the present (in this life), it does the same with reference to the prehuman past and posthistorical future as well.

Scott's first objection to linguistic Kantianism is often described as the problem of self-reference or performative contradiction. The claim is that if the theory is applied to itself, it undermines itself, for it claims to be true while asserting that all our "knowledge" mirrors reality only as the funny mirror at the circus does, thus failing to correspond to the real. This is said to be a performative contradiction, since the very saying undermines the said. Scott puts this as the following dilemma: either one is making an objective, universal claim, in which case one purports to know the real as it really is, or one is merely reporting the linguistic practice of a particular community and making no cognitive claims on those addressed.

But this is a false dilemma. Thinking of a language game as a perspective on the real, careful linguistic Kantians can explain their epistemic claims something like this, using examples from visual perspective:

> From where I stand, that looks to be a house over there. Doubtless you occupy a different perspective, but I think if you look very carefully, you'll be able to see that it is a house (though it will look different to you). If we can't agree (you may think it only a facade on a movie set), we need to investigate the matter more closely to see whose judgments need adjustment. But there's another way in which we might disagree. We both see a house, but I see it as a property with a market value of $275,000, while you see it as the home in which you grew up, filled with memory. These need not be mutually exclusive, and both of us might well adjust our understanding of the place so as to incorporate the other's understanding into our own.

The perspectival character of human understanding is preserved throughout, while at the same time making clear that we can make claims on those who occupy a different perspective (play a different language game). We can work toward mutual understanding, what Gadamer calls the fusion of horizons, without assuming with the Enlightenment project that we can escape our horizons altogether and inhabit "the view from nowhere." A close look will reveal that the linguistic Kantian can even present linguistic Kantianism that way.

> From where I stand, it looks as if human understanding is embedded in and decisively shaped by human language. Language does not convey prelinguistic meaning but shapes the meaning it conveys.[5] Here's what I see that makes me think this. I think if you look carefully from where you stand, you'll be able to see these factors at work both in the differences among natural languages and in the multiplicity of language games that can be played within a single natural language.

Scott's second objection is that special revelation would be impossible unless we can have extralinguistic access to the real. But I cannot see why he should think so. After all, the mighty acts of God in history were revelatory to ancient Israel and the early church only through the mediation of verbal interpretation by the prophets, the apostles, and Jesus himself. Moreover, the Word of God written in scripture comes to us in Hebrew, Aramaic, and Greek and is immersed in those cultures. But, it is repeatedly claimed, revelation means that God has broken through our language. But does that mean that God has freed us from our dependence on language? Perhaps when Paul was caught up into the third heaven—"whether in the body or out of the body I do not know" (2 Cor. 12:2)—he received a revelation apart from human language. But such mysticism, if that is the name for it, is hardly the biblical paradigm of revelation, including biblical revelation itself.

Athens tells us that the truth is found only outside the cave when we are free from our embeddedness in the body, in history, in culture, in language.[6] Jerusalem tells us that the breakthrough is God coming into the cave to meet us there. Revelation is doubtless a breakthrough—God breaking in, not our breaking out. So, to return to our TV analogy, it is not that God takes us into the studio where we no longer need our receiving apparatus; it is rather that after all the sex and violence and commercialism of most TV and even after the better programming one might occasionally find on commercial or public TV, there suddenly is a channel, not exactly authorized by the FCC, on which one hears that Jesus is the Lamb of God who takes away the sin of the world (John 1:29). I am not freed from language games as such, but invited to participate in a radically new one.

Another homely example. I tell my son not to suck on quarters, and he asks why. He has no access to my language about viruses and bacteria, so I break through into his language with a message he needs: "There are little bugs on coins, so small you can't see them, but they can make you very sick if they get inside you." This account does not correspond to the real as I understand it, but it is the "truth" so far as he is able to receive it, and he ought to believe it and act on it. My teacher, Kenneth Kantzer, was doubtless thinking of Calvin,[7] but he was also a linguistic Kantian when he told us, "The Bible is the divinely revealed misinformation about God."

◆◆◆

I agree with Professor Vanhoozer that Christian thinkers must do better than to deny, defy, demonize, or deify postmodernism. But I don't see the need to choose between discussion and disputation. If, as he says (thesis 2), Christians can and should learn from postmodernists, then it would be appropriate to approach them or, more frequently, their texts, in a conversational mode, assuming that both parties can learn from the conversation. Finding points of agreement, such as that we are far more deeply situated than the Enlightenment has taught us to think about ourselves (thesis 1) need not be a concession to the social determinism that says we are "merely" the product of our community (if one can find a postmodernist who actually holds to such a reductionist view—Vanhoozer wisely names none). Nor need it presuppose a method of correlation that violates "Plantinga's law" (thesis 3). Such discussion becomes more fully dialogical when one disputes various postmodernist claims, explicit or tacit. Thus, against the widespread assumption in "Southern" lands that Heidegger's critique of onto-theology and Lyotard's critique of modernity's metanarratives discredit Christian thought, I try to show that they do nothing of the sort but rather help us to see how authentic Christian thought is deeply different from the Enlightenment project and akin to certain postmodern themes.

The Christian thinker must, of course, dispute the assumption of the secular postmodernism that the proper home for these themes is a world without God. The Christian will contextualize these in biblically theistic and trinitarian ways (theses 3–4, 6, 8–10) and will dispute the claim that postmodern insights preclude this possibility. But finding common ground and disputing differences are what conversation is all about.

Vanhoozer tends to be critical of the negative thrust of postmodern irony, deconstruction archaeology, etc. But (1) in addition to critiquing various "modern" models of how human understanding works, the thinkers he has in mind offer alternative, often very illuminating models; they are not merely negative; (2) still, critique is central, and it is surely true that "man does not live by Ex-Lax alone." Yet it does not follow that the laxatives are not very useful when needed, or that companies that produce them should be discredited because they do not also produce nutritious food, especially if they don't claim to do the latter.

Vanhoozer also holds that Christians can and should learn the criticism of isms from postmodernism, but that the latter has not discovered anything not already at least implicit in Christian scripture and tradition (theses 2 and 5). I remember as a child hearing my father fulminate from the pulpit against "cults and isms." It was always about "them," never about "us." It never dawned on him that fundamental*ism* or dispensational*ism* was an ism. So I'm nervous when Vanhoozer identifies the targets of postmodern critique as isms but hopeful when he defines isms as the "conceptual idolatry" involved in treating "any one vocabulary or conceptual scheme as 'final,'" as a "graven ideology." For that makes it clear, or should, that theism, or Calvinism, or evangelicalism, or realism can be as much in need of ideology critique as other isms, especially when they function primarily to legitimize "us" and to demonize "them."

I have argued that the hermeneutics of suspicion, whether in modernist forms (Marx and Freud) or postmodern form (Nietzsche) is deeply indebted to biblical religion, where this kind of critique has its origin; and I've extended that argument to postmodernists of more recent vintage (such as Heidegger and Lyotard, in this volume).[8] I agree with Vanhoozer on this point but hasten to add that many who profess to think biblically deeply resist these forms of critique or see them only as having force against "them." They are like the Sunday school teacher who concluded a lesson on the Pharisee and publican who went up to the temple to pray: "Now children, let us close our eyes, and bow our heads, and fold our hands, and thank God that we are not like that Pharisee." (Lord, I thank Thee that I am not like that Sunday school teacher!) We may need the postmodernists more than we know to help us to see what we are reluctant to see in the Bible.

Finally, I find Vanhoozer's discussion of realism confusing. He defines realism as the view that "our words refer to reality," and "get beyond *self*-description," and that "what there is . . . does not depend on *my* language." But these formulas are far too weak. The Kantian antirealist agrees to all this, while denying both that our words are a transparent medium or perfect mirror of the real to which they refer and that they are *merely* self-description. Derrida, for instance, emphatically insists that language refers beyond itself to its other.[9]

Like Scott, Vanhoozer fears that if interpretation goes "all the way down" this "makes mincemeat of the scriptures." But what is scripture if not a collection of interpretations of the real, normative for Christians? Are these not, moreover, deeply embedded in and shaped by the languages, cultures, and societies in which they were written? And what is our understanding of the scriptures if not one of many different interpretations (just as there are many translations) that have arisen in the history of the church? Is not the very idea that we can escape interpretation and confront the naked facts itself an interpretation of our situation, one that has more Athens in it than Jerusalem? Following Hütter, Vanhoozer speaks of scripture as "*God's* language." Would it not be less misleading to say that it is God's Word, in which God speaks to us, not in the third heaven, but here on earth in human languages written by human authors? Both scripture and the Incarnation tell us that God is not allergic to finitude, and we need not be either.

Vanhoozer "acknowledges the necessity of language and theories for making contact with reality" (presumably cognitive contact) and that the world is "*indescribable apart from human constructions*." But these claims can have two very different senses. The weak sense is that truth and knowledge take the form of judgments, which in turn presuppose language (and even theories as systems of mutually supporting judgments). So, unless humans were language users there would be no human knowledge or truth. But this is fully compatible with an anti-Kantian realism according to which language does not decisively shape (we need to remember that the language of construction is dangerously misleading) the judgments formed in it but is a transparent medium that is capable of perfectly mirroring the real. The strong sense, obviously, is that we have no cognitive access to the real except through languages that give us access but only by compelling the real to adapt to their horizons, particular and contingent as they are, in order to appear. I can't tell what Vanhoozer thinks on this matter. His definitions of realism are so weak as to be compatible with the stronger view, and he regularly affirms our situatedness. But he regularly *disputes* the linguistic Kantianism of postmodernism. Will the real Vanhoozer please stand up?

In a very important way, Vanhoozer need not be a realist. Unlike Geivett, he is more a pragmatist than a rationalist. I'm not just referring to his view that Christian faith is grounded in and expressed as "a story rather than a system," not as propositions but as *"myth become redemptive history."* I mean that he does not think the primary task of theology is to give us the justified true beliefs that are the epistemologist's dream, but rather to help us "negotiate the real world with the aid of biblical maps," or "to navigate our way through the world," or again, "to participate rightly in reality." This is not Rorty's pragmatism that *replaces* the question, "Which language gets reality right?" with the question, "Which language best suits our present purpose?" but a Christian pragmatism that *subordinates* the first question to the question, "Which language best expresses God's purpose?"

Two observations at this point. First, no doubt negotiating, navigating, and participating involve belief as well as behavior; but Vanhoozer's language displaces the static, King Midas spectator interested in filling his treasury with true propositions. It's about the journey, about where we are going and how we travel. Second, realist correspondence is not necessary for this journey. Following C. S. Lewis, whom he uses so effectively, Vanhoozer presents theology as a map. But maps are not photographs and need not even be drawn to scale. Their *adequacy* is pragmatic—the question is not "Do they perfectly mirror the real?" but "Do they effectively guide the journey?"[10] The fatherly revealed (mis)information about invisible bugs on coins is quite sufficient (for the present) to tell my son what he should believe and how he should behave. It could save his life.

◆◆◆

In response to a paper by a Christian scholar based on solid knowledge of Derrida's texts and expressing sympathy for certain themes in them, another Christian scholar, on the verge of apoplexy, got up and said, *"Lyotard* says that postmodernity is incredulity toward metanarratives, but Christianity is a metanarrative. Postmodernism and Christianity are completely incompatible." Professor Smith, Jamie this time, then a graduate student, got up and briefly but accurately described the ways in which Christian faith does *not* have the form of a metanarrative in Lyotard's sense. The objector replied, "Oh, I didn't know that's what he meant. I've never read Lyotard."

Now Jamie is repeating his argument in considerable textual detail and against those who have read Lyotard, but, as he argues, not carefully enough. I agree with his claims that the Christian story is *not* a metanarrative in Lyotard's sense and that the postmodern critique of the pretensions of universal, unsituated Reason should be welcomed by Christian thinkers as a realization that all human thought occurs within some hermeneutical circle or other as some faith or other seeking understanding.

But perhaps a quibble or two may be permitted. Jamie focuses on the question of legitimation. On the one hand, there is the question of how modernity's metanarratives themselves are legitimated, and he joins Lyotard in incredulity toward modernity's claim to accomplish this by universal, disinterested, purely objective Reason. On the other hand, he notes that the metanarratives in question are themselves "discourses of legitimation," that their function is to legitimate modernity's other language games, understood with Wittgenstein as forms of life, so that discursive practices are inextricably intertwined with behavioral practices. So it is the task of metanarrative to legitimate not only the sciences of modernity but also its technologies and its politics. These two dimensions of legitimation correspond to my second and third ways of distinguishing the Christian story from modernity's metanarratives. The biblical story comes from prophets and apostles on the basis of revelation, while the metanarratives come from philosophers on the basis of reason; and the function of the latter is to legitimate "our" discursive and nondiscursive practices.

But Jamie moves back and forth between these two legitimation issues so quickly that the difference between them tends to get lost, along with the distinctiveness of the third difference, namely, that the Christian story is more a delegitimation narrative than a legitimation narrative. This latter motif points back to the first difference I suggest, which remains only implicit in Jamie's account, namely, that the Christian story is a first order discourse, kerygma rather than apologetics. This brings me back to where I started, with a question for Geivett. His theologian, willing to justify himself (Luke 10:29), takes the primary task to be apologetics, showing that Christian beliefs are justified. Is the primary task of the theologian not rather to serve the church's kerygma, to articulate the biblical story in such a way as to provide a biblically derived stimulus and standard for the church's first order God-talk in liturgy, in music, in prayer, in preaching, in catechesis, and in evangelism?

Notes

1. Such as the contributors to *Why Narrative? Readings in Narrative Theology*, ed. Stanley Hauerwas and L. Gregory Jones (Grand Rapids: Eerdmans, 1989).

2. Given the venue in which it first appeared, my essay in this volume is without notes. For a more detailed analysis of Heidegger on onto-theology with reference to key texts, see the title essay of my *Overcoming Onto-Theology* (New York: Fordham

University Press, 2001). To check out my account of Lyotard on metanarrative, see his *The Postmodern Condition: A Report on Knowledge*, trans. Geoff Bennington and Brian Massumi (Minneapolis: University of Minnesota Press, 1984).

3. See my "Christian Philosophers and the Copernican Revolution," in *Overcoming Onto-Theology*, and "In Defense of the Thing," *Kant-Studien* 59, no. 1 (1968): 118–41. The latter gives the textual evidence in Kant.

4. On this point see Alvin Plantinga, "Reason and Belief in God," in *Faith and Rationality: Reason and Belief in God*, ed. Alvin Plantinga and Nicholas Wolterstorff (Notre Dame, IN: University of Notre Dame Press, 1983), 16–93, and my comments in "Totality and Finitude in Schleiermacher's Hermeneutics," *Overcoming Onto-theology*, 116–17.

5. When philosophers talk about propositions, they often assume without even noticing that language is an external bearer of prelinguistic meanings. For a challenge to the "proposition presupposition," see my "Taking Plantinga Seriously: Advice to Christian Philosophers," *Faith and Philosophy* 16, no. 2 (April 1999): 173–81.

6. Plato's Socrates tells us that "we must get rid of the body and contemplate things by themselves with the soul by itself" (*Phaedo*, 66e).

7. See Ford Lewis Battles, "God Was Accommodating Himself to Human Capacity," in *Readings in Calvin's Theology*, ed. Donald K. McKim (Grand Rapids: Baker, 1984), 21–42.

8. See also the essays on Derrida in *Overcoming Onto-Theology*.

9. See, for example, Jacques Derrida, *Writing and Difference*, trans. Alan Bass (Chicago: University of Chicago Press, 1978), 12, 75–76. In his interview with Richard Kearney, he says, "It is totally false to suggest that deconstruction is a suspension of reference. Deconstruction is always deeply concerned with the 'other' of language. I never cease to be surprised by critics who see my work as a declaration that there is nothing beyond language. . . . Certainly, deconstruction tries to show that the question of reference is much more complex and problematic than traditional theories supposed" (Richard Kearney, *Dialogue with Contemporary Continental Thinkers* [Manchester: Manchester University Press, 1984], 123–24).

10. Lewis shows his pragmatism when he writes about the man who turns his attention from the Atlantic Ocean to a map of it. "The map is admittedly only colored paper, but . . . if you want to go anywhere, the map is absolutely necessary. . . . Now Theology is like the map. . . . Doctrines are not God: they are only a kind of map . . . you will not get to Newfoundland by studying [the map]. . . . Neither will you get anywhere by looking at maps without going to sea. Nor will you be very safe if you go to sea without a map" (C. S. Lewis, *The Joyful Christian* [New York: Macmillan, 1977], 33–34).